THE
CIVIL WAR

The author wishes to thank the University of South Carolina Press
for permission to quote from the following copyrighted material:
Arney Robinson Childs: *The Private Journal of Henry William Ravenel,
1859–1887* (University of South Carolina Press, 1947).

(D)

This edition is published by Bonanza Books,
a division of Crown Publishers, Inc.
by arrangement with Thomas Y. Crowell Company

Typography and layout by John S. Blay

Maps by Kathleen Voute

Library of Congress Catalog Card No. 58-12288

THE CIVIL WAR

A Pictorial Profile

John S. Blay

BONANZA BOOKS · New York

This book is dedicated to

JOANNE PALMER

FOREWORD

This book was inspired by the pictorial weeklies of the Victorian period. Throughout the Civil War, the publishers of *Harper's Weekly, Frank Leslie's Illustrated Newspaper,* and *The Illustrated London News,* to name the most prominent publications, gave their readers visual coverage of the conflict.

Sketch artists in the field made rapid drawings in pencil and wash and forwarded them to their home offices. There they were turned into wood engravings so they could be reproduced on the newsprint of the time. Through such pictures, civilians saw the shock of battle and the multiple details of military life.

The sketch artists were able and honest craftsmen. One of them, Winslow Homer, achieved lasting fame in the art world. But many of the artist-correspondents—William and Alfred Waud, Edwin Forbes, Allen Redwood—achieved only transitory recognition for their graphic reporting.

By blending direct observation and imagination, the field artists pictured armies in action and soldiers at work and play. Such coverage was denied to contemporary photographers who were almost unable to register motion because of the necessity for long exposures with their crude cameras.

This book utilizes the picture coverage of the above-mentioned weeklies as well as engravings collected and published in the numerous anthologies popular in the years immediately following the War Between the States. The pictures have been arranged in chronological order and provided with captions, headlines, and a running text to present the Civil War Story as it developed from year to year. Set into the chronology are ten interludes, short text-and-picture features, each describing one phase of the war in some detail.

My thanks are due to the departed editors of the major weeklies, who made this book possible. Henry Chafetz and S. B. Solomon of the Pageant Book Company provided the pictures for this volume as well as much of the research material, and were of immense assistance to me. Frederick Petzoldt, of Compo Stat Service, gave full cooperation in helping process the pictures for reproduction. At the Thomas Y. Crowell Company, John Meyer was a constant source of aid and encouragement from the inception of the book to its completion.

J. S. B.

July 14, 1958

CONTENTS

BACKGROUND

BACKGROUND

PRELUDE TO WAR

"A STORM is rising," wrote Senator William H. Seward of New York in 1854, "and such a one as our country has never yet seen."

The turbulent currents buffeting the nation were caused by slavery. Cornerstone of the Southern economy, a cause of intense moral indignation in the North, this ancient institution had dominated the political scene for decades.

Slavery was commonplace when the United States was born, but the Founding Fathers expressed hope it would die out gradually. The slave trade with Africa was abolished by 1808, and the institution itself soon withered in the country north of Mason and Dixon's line.

In the South, slavery continued to flourish. The plantation economy of cotton, tobacco, rice, and sugar cane was built on the cheap labor of the Negro slave in the fields. When Northerners criticized, the planter answered that he was assuring himself an economical labor supply, Christianizing the

heathen, and protecting him in adversity.

The Northern reply was the formation of abolitionist groups in Massachusetts, Ohio, New York, and elsewhere, calling for complete and immediate emancipation. The abolitionist voice was loud, but did not represent a majority in the North. For the most part, people in that area were content to see slavery remain in the South, but were adamant in declaring it should not spread into new lands opening up in the West.

This clash of feeling over the new territories led to thirty years of argument and adjustment. From the Missouri Compromise of 1820 to that of Henry Clay in 1850, concessions were made to both sides, and slavery was contained within certain geographical limits.

The era of compromise ended abruptly on May 30, 1854, when the Kansas-Nebraska Bill became law. Submitted by Senator Stephen A. Douglas of Illinois, it established the principle of "squatter sovereignty" in the territories mentioned. This meant the question of whether or not slavery would exist in the new lands would be decided by popular vote among their settlers. The new law ended the geographical limitation of slavery and theoretically permitted it anywhere.

Because of the Kansas-Nebraska Bill, the powerful Whig party split into a Northern and Southern wing, and gradually dissolved. Southern Whigs were absorbed by the other major party, the Democrats, and the Democratic "solid South" tradition began.

In the North, antislavery men banded together to form the Republican party at Jackson, Michigan, in July, 1854. Within two years, the Republicans had called a national convention and nominated John C. Frémont of California for president of the United States. Meanwhile, civil war broke out in Kansas over the slavery question.

The wounds of "bleeding Kansas" were stanched in time for the election of 1856, and, with relief, the Democrats saw their candidate, James Buchanan of Pennsylvania, win the presidency. The Republicans had fought hard, and their efforts showed in the electoral vote count, which was 174 for Buchanan and 114 for Frémont. Watching the election, the South called the new party the "Black Republicans" because of their sympathy for the Negro.

Nevertheless, peace and prosperity were the share of the nation as Buchanan began his term. The temporary calm lasted two days and disappeared with the explosive Dred Scott Decision, which came from the Supreme Court March 6, 1857.

The decision declared the Negro was not a United States citizen, had no rights in court and, as the property of his master, could be taken anywhere in the United States. Complete victory now belonged to the South. The executive and legislative branches of the government had endorsed "squatter sovereignty," and now the judiciary declared the slave to be a chattel of his master in any part of the nation.

Different economic systems in North and South produced different methods of labor supply. The Southern planter purchased slaves (upper left). In the North, much of the labor pool was made up of immigrants, who entered the country through such ports as Hoboken, N.J. (below).

THE CRUCIAL ELECTION

THE doctrine of states' rights versus federal power had never been completely solved by the Constitution. Throughout the period of compromise on slavery, and after the Kansas-Nebraska Act, the South strongly defended the rights of the individual states to go their way, regardless of federal authority. Talk of secession had been used as a lever by the South to gain its ends. From 1855 to 1860, in view of the hard stand of the new Republican party on slavery, secession threats grew louder than ever.

In the North, the year 1858 saw Abraham Lincoln of Illinois engaged in a series of debates with Douglas of that state for a Senate seat. Slavery was the subject. Lincoln lost the election, but not until he forced Douglas to admit that, under "squatter sovereignty," the people themselves could elect to exclude slavery from new territories, despite the Dred Scott Decision and all it implied. This pronouncement lost Douglas, an aspiring presidential candidate in 1860,

the support of the Southern Democrats.

Flying high on the recently favorable legislation, the South brought new demands to Congress in the person of Senator Jefferson Davis of Mississippi. Repudiating the doctrine of popular sovereignty, Southerners demanded that Congress protect slavery throughout the United States and called for strict observance of the Fugitive Slave Law in the North.

The Democratic National Convention was held at Charleston, South Carolina, in April. As the supporters of Douglas took the lead, delegates from the Cotton States walked out of the meeting. The Democratic party, now split, met again in Baltimore in two sections. The "old party" members nominated Douglas; members who had left the Charleston convention put up Vice-President John C. Breckinridge of Kentucky.

In Chicago, the Republicans elected Abraham Lincoln of Illinois as their candidate, on the third ballot. The Republican platform

4

repudiated the Dred Scott Decision and called for suppression of the African slave trade, admission of Kansas as a free state, a protective tariff, and a homestead act to open land for new settlers in the West.

John Bell of Tennessee, a fourth candidate with some support in the border states, ran on a simple, neutralist platform silent on the subject of slavery.

The South now called openly for secession in the event of a "Black Republican" victory. The die was cast November 6 when Lincoln won the election with 180 electoral votes against 72 for Breckinridge, 39 for Bell, and only 12 for Douglas. The latter polled a large popular vote, but was defeated by the split in the Democratic party.

On December 20, 1860, the South Carolina legislature met in Charleston, pronounced the Union dissolved, and passed a unanimous vote for secession. Within a matter of weeks, the South Carolina lead was followed by Mississippi, Florida, Alabama, Georgia, Louisiana, and Texas.

The North was stunned. Last-minute compromise attempts were failures. President Buchanan floundered, declaring no state had a right to leave the Union but stating the government had no legal means for preventing such action. In a final, futile action, Buchanan sent a ship to supply the federal garrison in the harbor of hostile Charleston, but it was fired on and turned back.

Lincoln, in the past, had stated he would not interfere with slavery in the South, and it was known he favored the Fugitive Slave Law. He was about to face an opposition majority in Congress and a Supreme Court dominated by Southerners. But the time for reasoned analysis of these facts had passed in the rebellious states.

Southern leaders later said secession was brought about by the denial of constitutional rights to the South. The major question at stake was whether or not protection for slavery in all United States territories *was* a constitutional right. This was the burning issue the great compromises had failed to solve, the one that had tightened tensions to the breaking point.

When news of Lincoln's victory was announced to an overexcited audience at Charleston (upper left), the machinery for South Carolina's withdrawal from the Union was set in motion. Within weeks, Palmetto State artillery was firing at the Union supply ship *Star of the West* (below).

The Inauguration at Montgomery Presented a New Nation That the South Hoped Would Soon Gain World Recognition

SECESSION, to most people, was not necessarily equated with war. The nation had recovered from the Panic of 1857. North and South were prosperous, and large groups in both areas saw no reason to disturb the status quo.

Firm abolitionists believed in letting the Southern states go. Others in the North felt coercion in holding back the "erring sisters" was unjustified and immoral. Northern bankers and merchants had large commercial interests in the South. In New York, Mayor Fernando Wood suggested the city become independent and maintain mutually advantageous trade relations with the separated states. In Washington, an enormous peace movement began but came to nought.

In the South, the delegates met February 4, 1861, at Montgomery, Alabama, to form the Confederate States of America. Jefferson Davis was chosen president and Alexander H. Stephens of Georgia vice-president.

A constitution was drawn up and submitted to the states for ratification. In form and content, it was similar to the constitution of the United States, with a few important exceptions.

The president and vice-president were elected for six-year terms. Protective duties were forbidden. The introduction and protection of slavery in new territories was guaranteed. There was to be no slave trade with Africa (a concession to world opinion). And in the face of potential trouble, President Davis was authorized to call for a loan of $15 million and the creation of a military force of 100,000.

Upon receiving the highest call the new nation could confer, Davis left for Montgomery and was inaugurated February 18, being sworn in by Howell Cobb of Georgia. The inauguration was the occasion for a dazzling display of military maneuvers by crack units from Confederate states.

The Confederate States of America acquired their leader in February with the inauguration of Davis at Montgomery, Ala. (left). Secessionist government was patterned after that of the United States, as demonstrated above by a meeting of the Confederate Senate in the capitol.

LINCOLN wrote his inaugural speech in Springfield, Illinois, locked in a room with speeches by Henry Clay, Daniel Webster, and Andrew Jackson, and a copy of the Constitution of the United States. When the task was finished, he said good-by to his law partner, looked for the last time at his law office, and departed for Washington.

On March 4, the President-elect rode through moderate crowds to the Capitol, accompanied by President Buchanan. Troops filled the streets and sharpshooters were posted on roofs, for rumors of assassination had filled and disturbed Washington.

As Lincoln rose to speak, Senator Douglas leaned forward to take his new black hat. Placing his black cane against the railing, the nation's new President delivered one of the greatest orations in American history.

Solemnly, clearly, Lincoln spoke of the Union and its perpetual quality. He declared secession unconstitutional. He stated he would maintain the authority of the government and protect its military property. He disclaimed the notion of invading the South, and pleaded with the separated states to return to the fold.

"Physically speaking, we cannot separate," he said. "We cannot remove our respective sections from each other, nor build an impassable wall between them. A husband and wife may be divorced and go out of the presence and beyond the reach of each other, but the different parts of our country cannot do this. They cannot but remain face to face, and intercourse, either amicable or hostile, must continue between them. Is it possible, then, to make that intercourse more advantageous or more satisfactory after separation than before? Can aliens make treaties easier than friends can make laws? Can treaties be more faithfully enforced between aliens than laws can among friends? Suppose you go to war, you cannot fight always; and when, after much loss on both sides, and no gain on either, you cease fighting, the identical old questions as to terms of intercourse are again upon you."

Lincoln called for confidence in the ultimate justice of the people, and for long, patient consideration of the secession issue. He ended in a burst of eloquence:

"In your hands, my dissatisfied fellow countrymen, and not in mine, is the momentous issue of civil war. The government will not assail you. You can have no conflict without being yourselves the aggressors. You have no oath registered in heaven to destroy the government, while I shall have the most solemn one to 'preserve, protect, and defend' it.

"I am loath to close. We are not enemies, but friends. We must not be enemies. Though passion may have strained, it must not break, our bonds of affection. The mystic chords of memory, stretching from every battlefield and patriot grave to every living heart and hearthstone all over this broad land, will yet swell the chorus of the Union when again touched, as surely they will be, by the better angels of our nature."

The inauguration behind him, the new President proceeded to the work at hand. Looming large on the agenda was the question of the border states—Delaware, Maryland, Kentucky, and Missouri. In the event of war, it was an open question as to whether these four would remain with the Union.

Of even greater moment was the question of United States military property in the South. The Confederacy had been in existence for a month at the time of Lincoln's inauguration, and had already seized certain government installations.

The focal point of this problem, throughout the anxious March days, was Charleston harbor, which contained several U.S. bases, the most important being Fort Sumter. There, dependent on rapidly dwindling supplies, was a small garrison under Major Robert Anderson.

The situation in Charleston was potentially explosive. But, face to face with secession, the President acted.

Governor Francis W. Pickens of South Carolina was officially notified that supplies, but no men or ammunition, would be sent to Sumter on April 6. The Confederate government, hearing of the plan, ordered Brigadier General Pierre G. T. Beauregard, in charge of Confederate troops at Charleston, to demand the surrender of Fort Sumter. Beauregard twice made such a demand, and both times Anderson refused.

The Nation's First Republican President Took Office in
One of the Darkest Years in American History

Only a moderate crowd turned out to see Lincoln and Buchanan ride through Washington streets to the inauguration. The military appeared in force, however, in response to wild rumors of potential violence from the Rebels.

OPENING GUN

THE burst of a Confederate shell over Sumter on April 12, 1861, made civil war in the United States a terrible reality.

South Carolina had long been a hotbed of anti-Northern sentiment. As the guns spoke, it became the first battleground on which fiery secessionism met Lincoln's stated resolve to preserve the Union and guard its military property.

Moving by night, Anderson had transferred his tiny garrison to Sumter from Fort Moultrie on December 26, 1860. The new location appeared to be better suited for defense than any of the other installations that dotted the harbor. As Anderson mounted his guns, Confederate troops seized and armed the remaining works.

Southern leaders at Montgomery were in a delicate situation. South Carolinians, who had been independent for more than three months, resented the flag of a "foreign power" flying before their eyes.

Negotiations between Union and Confederate leaders went on for weeks. Demands, propositions, and ultimatums were discussed, then rejected or tabled. There was no easy way out, and mounting tension was finally resolved by gunpowder.

Ringed by enemy fortifications, the still unfinished citadel of Sumter was taken under attack by a multitude of Confederate batteries. The entire action was an artillery engagement. Beauregard, an able engineer, had studied the uses of artillery under Anderson at West Point.

Rebel heavy cannon were accurately laid (right) and poured an iron storm of red-hot solid shot and shrapnel-filled shell into the beleaguered fort. Throughout the battle, a relieving Union fleet lay off Sumter, helpless in the face of formidable Confederate guns.

11

The First Major Engagement of the Civil War Was Hotly Contested, But Neither Side Suffered a Single Serious Casualty from Enemy Fire

RISING from a shoal in the narrows of Charleston harbor, Sumter stood three miles off the Southern port. Its walls were seven feet thick, thirty-eight feet high, and pierced for heavy guns. Still unfinished, the fort was being built to withstand siege.

But the odds were against the garrison commander. Many guns were unmounted. He had 65 men to defend an installation built for 650. His food supply was dwindling and relief ships dared not risk enemy fire. Across the water, the Confederates worked busily on their batteries.

Beauregard was well aware of Sumter's vulnerability and pleaded for immediate surrender to avoid bloodshed. Anderson, a native of Kentucky, stubbornly stood his ground. The talking stage ended as a Confederate signal shell winked in the predawn of a spring morning.

A projectile from a 10-inch mortar burst inside the fort. One by one, Southern batteries joined in regular, accurate bombardment. Sumter held its fire for some time.

After several hours on the receiving end, Anderson gave the signal and Union guns slammed out their answer through embrasures in the walls (below). Union gunners picked three targets, the Morris Island batteries, those on James Island, and the group on Sullivan's Island. Near the latter was an ironclad floating battery that shed 32- and 42-pound shot like water. Failing to score on the battery, the Yankees switched their fire to Fort Moultrie, but there sandbags and cotton bales gave adequate protection.

As the day ended, Anderson ceased firing. Rebel guns kept up all night and stepped up the pace the following morning to bring about a conclusion.

The contest lasted thirty-four hours. More than 2,500 shells fired Sumter's barracks and endangered the powder magazine. There were no more powder bags and rations were exhausted. Seeing no other choice, Anderson surrendered the garrison.

Charleston's population paid close heed to the Anderson-Beauregard negotiations, which were conducted with old-fashioned chivalry. A feeling of high drama was in the air. Following the first shellburst, the city's citizens streamed to vantage points along the battery (above) to watch the firing. People climbed out on roofs to follow the battle. When Sumter surrendered, church bells pealed and there was rejoicing in the streets (below) succeeded by a period of celebration.

AS WAR began, Northern forces were ordered to carry out a scorched earth policy before abandoning bases in Southern territory. Among the most important of these was the Gosport Navy Yard at Portsmouth, across the river from Norfolk, Virginia. Here were machine shops, a dry dock, heavy guns with ammunition, and a host of ships, including *Pennsylvania, Columbus, Delaware, New York,* and *United States*.

Major ships were scuttled when possible. Turpentine, cotton waste, and gunpowder were freely used to fire and destroy other ships and shore installations. Heavy guns were spiked, and small arms were thrown in the river.

Destruction was incomplete. Arriving Rebels saved the dry dock and took many guns intact. They also refloated the sunken steam frigate *Merrimac,* rebuilt her, and christened her *Virginia,* and sent her out to make naval history at Hampton Roads the following year.

Put the Torch to Their Military Installations before Retreating

15

The arsenal at Harper's Ferry, Va. (above), made famous by John Brown's raid, was fired by Federal troops and 20,000 stands of arms were destroyed before Virginia forces arrived. Fort Pulaski, Ga. (below), was typical of the important installations that fell into Confederate hands.

In Mid-April, Abraham Lincoln and Jefferson Davis
Acted to Place Their Respective Nations on a War Footing

THE guns against Sumter meant an end to peace, and two days after the fort surrendered, Lincoln called for 75,000 troops to serve for ninety days.

The President also summoned a special session of Congress to meet July 4. Until that time, the Chief Executive took matters into his own hands and ran the government virtually alone.

On April 19, Lincoln declared a blockade of Southern seaports, although this was largely on paper, as the few ships of the United States Navy were scattered around the world. On May 3, the President called for three-year volunteers to go into the Federal Army.

The task of the new troops, in official words, was to put down "combinations too powerful to be suppressed by the ordinary course of judicial proceedings or by the powers vested in the marshals of the law" and was to be carried out against those states that had seceded. The President also stated the new Army's first missions would be the recovery of U.S. property.

By the spring of 1861, there was a good deal of this property to recover. The Confederacy had been a going concern since February and had already laid hands on equipment and installations in the South.

In Confederate hands were Fort Sumter as well as Castle Pinckney and Fort Moultrie in Charleston Harbor; Fort Pulaski near Savannah, Georgia; Fort Morgan at Mobile Bay, Alabama; Forts Jackson and St. Philip below New Orleans; and the navy yard, along with Forts McRee and Barrancas, at Pensacola, Florida.

There was no lack of Southern action following the crucial days at Fort Sumter. President Davis called for 100,000 volunteers and four more states seceded. Virginia passed the secession ordinance April 17, and the months of May and June saw Arkansas, Tennessee, and North Carolina swell the ranks of the Confederacy.

The secession of Virginia involved a personality of immense importance to the future course of the war. Colonel Robert E. Lee of that state, son of a famous Revolutionary War general, had been offered field command of the United States Army by President Lincoln. After wrestling with his conscience for days, Lee stated he could not draw sword against his native Virginia and resigned his commission in the Federal Army. He was made commander of the Virginia troops, and one of the most able military brains of all time was lost to the North.

The border states still presented problems. Delaware, with few slaveholders, went Union. There was strong secession feeling in Maryland but Governor Thomas H. Hicks was on the side of Lincoln. Prompt military action put down a gathering of rabble in arms and secured the state for the North.

Missouri was the biggest thorn in the side of both governments. Governor Claiborne Jackson was a stanch secessionist, but the people of the area were split in their loyalties. Fortunately for the Union, Lincoln had daring and able military and civil authorities in the state, and, after a long period of political and military maneuver, Missouri was counted among the Northern brethren.

Kentucky's population appeared to be on the side of the North, but Governor Beriah Magoffin had refused to send troops to Lincoln and apparently favored the Southern cause. The state finally took up a position of complete neutrality, respected by both Davis and Lincoln, but eventually cast its lot with the Union.

Although Virginia, the "Old Dominion," was as loyal as any state to the Confederacy, the people in its western counties were extremely antisecession. These were small farmers tilling the mountainous soil, a far cry from the plantation owners of tidewater Virginia. The embittered farmers made a series of strong representations in Congress, established a rump government, and by 1863 were nearing their goal. In June of that year, the land these farmers represented was organized as the new state of West Virginia and admitted to the Union.

THE WAR POTENTIALS

THE Civil War split the nation into two competing factions showing sharp differences in size, economy, and way of life.

The Union contained 23 states with 22 million people, as against 11 states and 9 million people in the Confederacy. Of the latter, 3½ million were slaves.

Three-quarters of the nation's wealth was produced in the North, which also contained 65 per cent of the farm acreage and 85 per cent of the factories. More than 70 per cent of the U.S. railroad mileage lay within Union boundaries, and more than 80 per cent of the bank deposits were in that area.

The economy of the North was diverse. Manufacturing and agriculture were both important; and commerce, internally and externally, was brisk. In 1860, Northern manufactured goods were valued at $1,730 million against $155 million for those of the South. From the farms, Northern wheat and corn produced a revenue of $845 million.

The South had chosen a one-crop economy based on cotton. The yield, which was worth $235 million in 1860, was of enormous importance to the United States and also to nations abroad.

"Cotton is king" was the rallying cry of the South and many Southerners firmly believed European nations, desperate for cotton, would break the Northern blockade or even go to war with the North in their efforts to get the precious fiber. In addition, Southerners felt that lack of a protective tariff would make their country a prime market for European manufactured goods.

Discussing the role of Southern commerce with foreign nations, South Carolina planter Henry Ravenel said: "We furnish what is absolutely essential to their commercial & manufacturing prosperity, & we alone—We offer them a market for their goods on better terms than heretofore. We invite their vessels to do our carrying trade, or at any rate throw open the door of competition to them, which has hitherto been open to only U.S. vessels. On the other hand the United States, now that the Cotton States have seceded, can furnish but little toward supplying their wants with cotton—They have in addition imposed such a tariff, as to cut off trade in a great measure. The U. S. are mainly a manufacturing & commercial nation, & must necessarily come in competition with them. In a word, what the U.S. have lost by our withdrawal from the Union, they have gained."

Ravenel's reasoned arguments were widely accepted by secession leaders. They made good sense, but the economic fates chose to ignore them.

England, which imported 80 per cent of the cotton she needed for her textile industry from the Cotton States in the past, suddenly found herself with an oversupply of this raw material. Until this was used, she saw no reason to attempt breaking the blockade. Once cotton was again in demand, the English turned to Egypt.

Further, the English found themselves with a wheat shortage in the 1860's, one which could be supplied by the United States. In return, the U.S. was glad to receive munitions from Great Britain, which supplied both sides during the war. Generally speaking, the ruling class in England favored the South, while the working people showed some leaning toward the North.

Foreign sympathy for the North was based on a dislike for the institution of slavery, the basis of the cotton economy. Social lines were sharply drawn in the South, which lacked a well-defined middle class. Some 380,000 planters owned the bulk of the slaves. More than 5 million Southerners were white people in low economic brackets, unable to compete with the low cost of slave labor.

The North boasted a thriving middle class, much of it made up of immigrants who went into field and factory. Expanding industries and a growing transportation system to improve marketing made for a prosperous labor group.

The factory (upper left) was the symbol of the Northern economy, even as cotton (below) signalized that of the South. In the end, it was no single industry or crop, but the wide diversification between industry, agriculture, and commerce that gave the North the power to emerge victorious.

THE destiny of the Union lay in the hands of a man who combined the talents necessary to greatness in a remarkable degree. Completely honest, a shrewd politician, Abraham Lincoln gained the love of the great and humble by humility, patience, and iron determination. He believed in the people, trusted them, and, because of this trust, learned to delegate authority and refrain from interference.

Born in Hardin County, Kentucky, in 1809, Lincoln soon learned to work for his keep even as he educated himself. Brought up in Indiana and Illinois, the youth split rails, worked his passage on Mississippi flatboats, and helped run a country store.

He served the nation briefly in the Black Hawk War, against the Sac and Fox Indians, as both private and captain. Upon mustering out, he was made postmaster of New Salem, Illinois, and assistant to the county surveyor. While holding these posts, he continued the study of law and politics.

Lincoln served four terms in the Illinois legislature, and set up a law practice in Springfield. From there he went to Congress to serve one term as a Representative, then returned to take up his law practice. He left the practice to receive the Republican nomination for the presidency in 1860.

LEADING the Confederacy was a dedicated, high-strung intellectual. Jefferson Davis was brilliant and earnest, if somewhat short-tempered and inflexible. A fiery man with strong personal prejudices, Davis showed extreme sensitivity to criticism. Unfortunately, he had to face it in abundance, for by its very nature, the new nation was opposed to strong central control.

Like Lincoln, Davis was born in Kentucky, (in 1808), but his rise, unlike Lincoln's, was meteoric. Graduating from West Point, he served on the frontier until 1835, when he became a Mississippi planter.

Davis left the plantation to become a member of the House of Representatives, leaving to serve in the Mexican War, in which he was severely wounded. Following military service he became a member of the Senate, then Secretary of War under President Franklin Pierce.

When his term as Secretary was over, Davis resumed his Senate seat and was made Chairman of the Committee on Military Affairs. During this latter period in the Senate, he was a forceful proponent of extreme Southern views on slavery and secession. His strong position on these issues made him a natural candidate for the presidency of the Confederate States of America.

TWO RIVAL CAPITALS

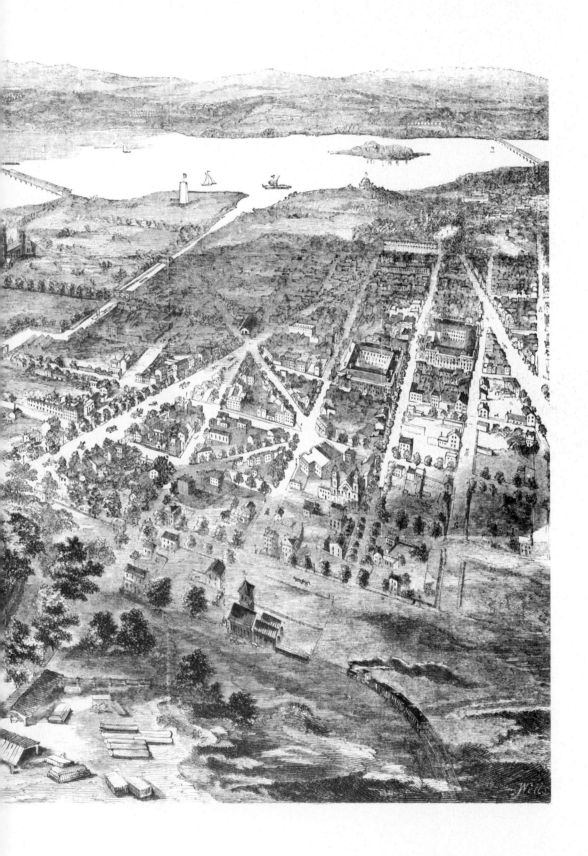

WASHINGTON (preceding page) was the focal point of the Northern war effort. Squeezed between Virginia and Maryland, the wartime capital lay on the east bank of the Potomac River where the Anacostia joined it.

Rising from a small hill was the city's most prominent landmark, the still unfinished Capitol. The cornerstone had been laid in 1793, on a site picked by Pierre Charles L'Enfant, the French engineer who designed the city. When the Civil War began, laborers were still working on a new metal dome to replace the old one made of wood. Work continued throughout the conflict.

With the exception of the Capitol, and the partly completed structure that was to be the Washington Monument, the capital did not dazzle the eye. Capitol Hill itself, according to a contemporary diary, was muddy, dreary, and desolate. The same could be said for a great part of the city.

Washington did have a rough vitality. It was the funnel through which troops poured toward the Virginia fighting front. Freshly equipped regiments from Pennsylvania, New York, New England, and the West made it a soldier's city. Drills and maneuvers brightened parks, squares, and parade grounds.

The cruel side of war was always apparent in the national capital. Many public buildings were made into hospitals. Long ambulance trains became a commonplace sight, and local gentlewomen appeared in abundance to help nurse the wounded.

As secession approached, Washington inhabitants were alarmed, for the city lay between two slaveholding states. The local militia was quickly reorganized by Lieutenant General Winfield Scott and totaled 1,000 by February, 1861. These troops were used as guards at the time of Lincoln's inauguration.

When war was a fact, there was further apprehension as forces from the North were denied passage through Baltimore. The impasse was broken by the 7th New York and 8th Massachusetts, which, in late April, arrived at Annapolis by ship and proceeded to their destination. The capital breathed

easier as troops poured into the city.

There were other threats to the city during the war. Many public buildings, including the Capitol, were barricaded and armed with artillery. The iron plates for the Capitol's new dome were at one time used as armor, and the basement of the building became an army kitchen. But the enemy at no time penetrated the city.

Some hundred miles to the south, the Confederate capital of Richmond sat, like Rome, on seven hills (upper right). A pleasant city on the James River, Richmond had celebrated Virginia's secession with a colorful torchlight parade on April 19. Since Colonial times, the city had been the cultural capital of the tidewater area and was a favorite visiting place for foreign dignitaries.

Richmond had been made the Confederacy's capital, in place of Montgomery, on May 29. It was a vital communications center. One major railroad system started at New Orleans and ran north to Memphis, then east through Tennessee and Virginia to Richmond. Another came from central Georgia to touch at Savannah and Charleston before reaching the Confederate capital. These two great trunk lines leading to Richmond were connected by many spur lines to form the major communications system of the South.

Richmond's position as a railroad terminus was of the utmost importance, for the city functioned as an industrial capital of the Confederacy as well as a political one. Guns, ammunition, and other war necessities moved from Richmond mills to all points in the embattled Confederate states.

At the war's beginning, Richmond was a gay metropolis. Gold braid and polished brass gleamed against the new uniforms of Confederate gray, to the delight of Southern belles. Juleps and tea appeared daily in the stately old homes to salute the departing cavaliers. Balls and cotillions ran into the small hours of the morning.

Within a few years, it was a city of privation. Households were cleaned out of copper, brass, silver, steel, and lead, which all went into the war effort. Gracious living remained but was often threadbare. Belle Isle, in the James River, had become a prison camp for Union men. So had the old Libby warehouse. Short rations and the constant sight of Yankee prisoners brought war to the doorstep of the Southern capital.

THE BATTLEGROUND

THE general features of the Civil War battleground are the same today as in 1860. But at that time there were more wilderness areas, fewer cities, less railroad mileage, and few roads that could be classed as highways.

To the east and south, the area was bounded by water: the Atlantic Ocean and the Gulf of Mexico. In the west, the dominant feature of the terrain was the Mississippi River, which separated the Confederate States. Rolling country formed the northern boundary, split by the great Appalachian Range running from northeast to southwest. In the coastal areas, and near the Mississippi, rivers abounded.

Throughout the war, there was heavy fighting in Virginia. In the coastal section, the tidewater country is made up of low, swampy plains cut by four great rivers (Potomac, Rappahannock, York, James) that create a series of peninsulas reaching out like fingers into Chesapeake Bay.

To the west, piedmont country rises to the 4,000-foot peaks of the Blue Ridge. Between these mountains and the next series of ranges (Shenandoah and Allegheny) lies a series of valleys, the largest being the Shenandoah Valley.

"The Valley" was a prize possession of the Confederacy. It contained some of the richest farm country in America and was a breadbasket for the South. Rebel troops could move northeast through the valley, protected from Union forces by the Blue Ridge, and come out the end either to threaten Washington or to move into the fertile fields of Maryland and Pennsylvania.

Tennessee and Georgia saw heavy fighting. Eastern Tennessee and North Carolina contained steep mountains, which spilled over into northwestern Georgia.

Other major battle areas—Mississippi, South Carolina, and Louisiana—were made up generally of flat, wooded country. There was little action in Texas, Arkansas, Alabama, North Carolina, or Florida. In the North, Missouri, Kentucky, and Pennsylvania saw major engagements.

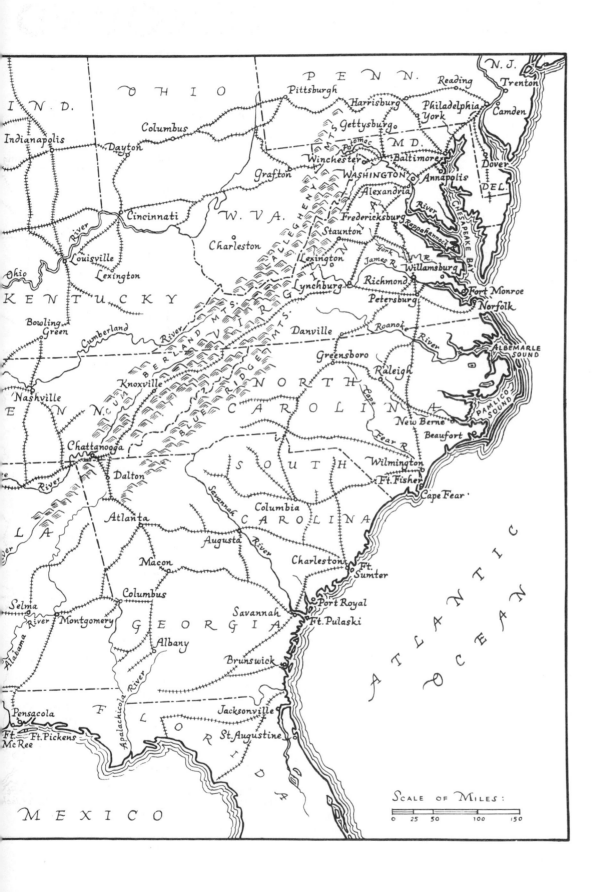

SCALE OF MILES:

0   25   50   100   150

THE Civil War, which had been threatening for years, broke suddenly on the United States. Neither side had a master strategic plan. For a long period, strategy was haphazard.

In the North, the general idea was to blockade the Southern coast, invade the South, and drive on to Richmond. Most of the people, and a good portion of the government, planned on a short war that would end with capture of the enemy's capital.

One Northerner who did not expect a speedy victory was the commander of the United States Army, Lieutenant General Winfield Scott (left). "Old Fuss and Feathers," a popular hero from Mexican War days, was approaching senility. His corpulence kept him from horseback, and he complained often of bodily ills. But he understood the military and knew war. His

OPPOSING STRATEGIES

own prediction was for a long-drawn conflict over a period of years.

Scott prepared a plan. It had two major parts: (1) a firm blockade of the Atlantic and Gulf coasts, and (2) seizure of the Mississippi River with 60,000 troops assisted by gunboats. Once these things were accomplished, said Scott, the Confederacy could be conquered in a matter of time.

Christened "Scott's anaconda" because of its implied constricting power, the plan was widely discussed. It did not meet popular favor. Scott made no announcement of an immediate drive on Richmond, and thus did not meet the public fancy.

In the end, Scott's proposal was followed in its large details. The blockade continued, the Mississippi was taken, and western forces moved east into Confederate territory. Throughout this long process, the Army of the Potomac was kept in Virginia to shield the national capital.

The Northern strategy, as it evolved, was fitted to the Northern war potential. The

anaconda plan called for a great number of men and ships, and great supplies of munitions, to fight over a wide geographical area. The North had the men, the factories, and the money with which to buy blockading ships (below) and guns. The Union was called upon for an enormous effort, and was able to make that effort.

Southern strategy called for standing fast and defending home soil while awaiting possible foreign intervention. The South also expected to be joined by all slaveholding areas, and it was a cruel blow to find the once neutral states going to the Union.

The Confederacy had men, food, textiles for uniforms, and the materials to make gunpowder. Its great lack was steel for the tools of war—guns, ammunition, trains, and ships. Some 95 per cent of American steel producing capacity lay in the North.

The need for steel rails to repair tracks was desperate, and spur lines were torn up to keep main routes in operation. Lacks of such things as needles and horseshoe nails hurt the total war effort. Glass, paper, and drugs, in short supply, were welcomed eagerly when brought through the blockade.

Despite great material needs, the Southerners fought with some advantages. They were operating on interior lines of communication. Also, because they were near their bases, Southern regiments did not at first have the supply problems faced by their brothers in the North.

Secessionists were defending their own soil in a war for freedom, which contributed to morale. And they were better fitted for the military life.

Most Southerners, raised on the land, were familiar with horses and guns from childhood and thought little of living roughly in the open. These advantages showed clearly in the superiority of Southern cavalry in the early years of the war.

Northern officers and men, fresh from banks, factories, stores, and shops, took time to adjust to army life. But when the adjustment was made and the North was battle-hardened, Northern leaders were able to use their fighting force in an over-all strategic plan (created in 1864) that was too much for the hard-pressed South.

THE PREPARATIONS

ONCE the call to arms had sounded, and communications had been re-established between Washington and the North, troops tumbled into the capital at a rapid rate. They were warmly welcomed. The first scare of a Southern invasion had passed; but Virginia, across the Potomac, was known to be full of high-spirited Rebels.

To seal off this sensitive area, Union leaders ordered troops to cross the river and occupy the high ground. Some detachments settled down at Arlington, Robert E. Lee's former home, while others went to take Alexandria.

With Virginia temporarily safe, Washington turned out to watch the flashy, cocky militiamen show off. A contemporary described the sensation in Victorian prose:

"The influx of Northern regiments of troops into Washington during the early days of the war rendered that city every hour in the day a scene of exciting and beautiful military display. The grounds north of the Capitol were used for brilliant dress parades and drills, which attracted throngs of visitors from all parts of the city and surrounding places."

Much the same kind of scene was taking place in Southern communities. In the Confederacy, as in the Union, volunteers joined under the names of their states and were equipped by the states or by wealthy private individuals.

Although volunteers poured in, both North and South eventually turned to the draft. On April 16, 1862, the Confederate States of America announced the drafting of men from eighteen to thirty-five; in 1864 the limits were placed at seventeen and fifty. The draft call for the United States went out March 3, 1863, for men from twenty to forty-five.

The number of men serving on each side has never been accurately ascertained. One reliable estimate (based on three-year service) places Union strength at 1,556,678 as against 1,082,119 for the Confederacy. Many authorities feel this estimate of Southern strength is somewhat high, and that 600,000 to 700,000 would be more realistic.

While some Union troops paraded in Washington (below), others were sent to establish such fortifications as Camp Corcoran (above) at Arlington Heights, Va. In the South, the gentry gathered to appraise such organizations as the Clinch Rifles on parade at Augusta, Ga. (lower left).

ENLISTMENT

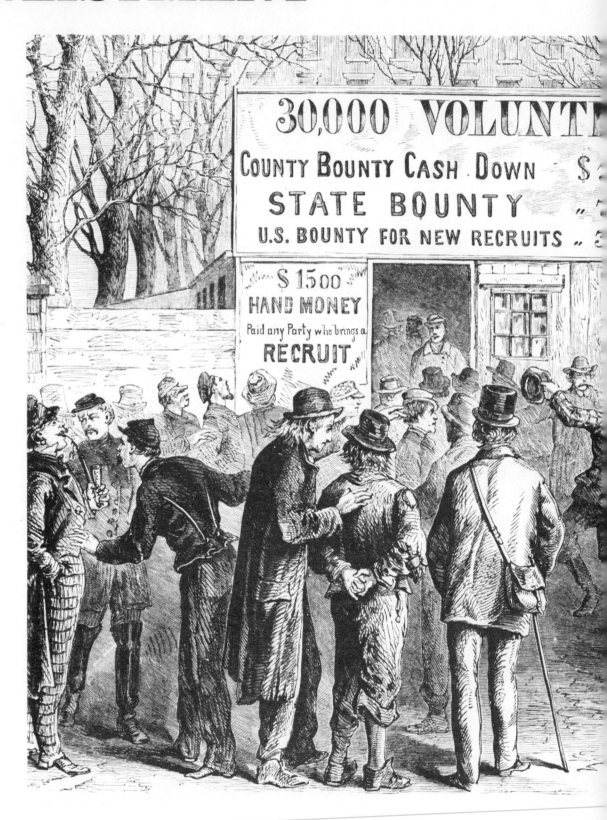

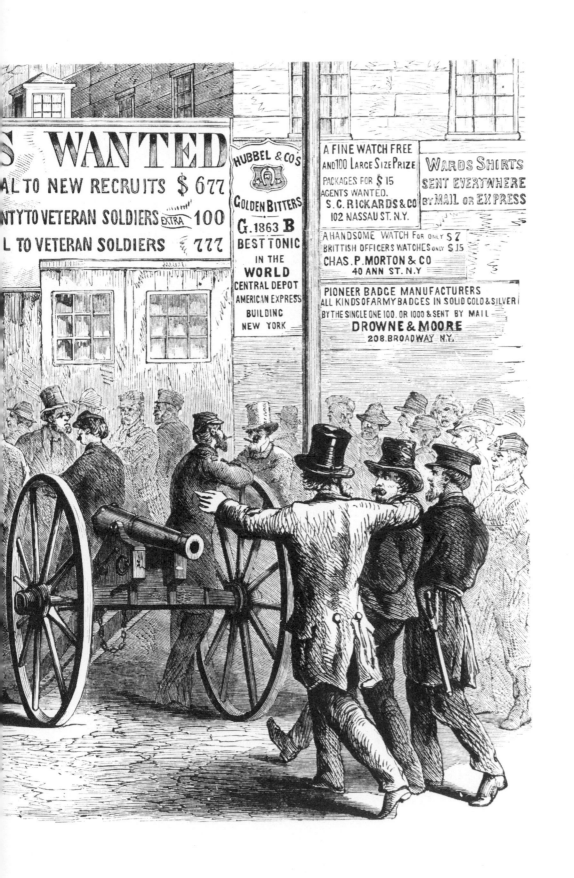

SELDOM in American history have men gone forth to war with enthusiasm such as that manifested in 1861. Patriotism reached a fever peak in the days following Fort Sumter's surrender. Blaring bands, fiery speeches, and the excitement in the air brought citizens streaming into recruiting stations.

To make things easier, bounty systems were established to reward love of country with hard cash. Posters like those in New York's City Hall Park (pages 32-33) offered impressive sums to recruits as the war progressed. But greed was not the prime factor motivating the first soldiers.

A tingling current of patriotism pervaded the North. Flag and country were precious words. The Union must be preserved. Treason had reared its head and would be crushed.

The hurly-burly of recruiting was almost too much to resist. Golden-tongued orators exhorted and pleaded as bugle and drum attacked "The Girl I Left Behind Me" and "Dixie." Old campaigners from the Mexican War inflamed the blood. Lawn-clad maidens vowed eternal devotion to the cause.

On April 15, Lincoln called for 75,000 three-month volunteers. By May 3, after realistic consideration of the nation's needs,

he asked for 500,000 men to serve three-year enlistments. The quota was topped by 200,000.

With a standing army of only 16,000, and lacking machinery for a large-scale military organization, the federal government was almost helpless as war began. Recruiting was done by the states, and troops were technically state militia at the beginning.

Would-be soldiers were brought in at the company level, a company consisting of fifty to a hundred men. Prominent citizens and civic leaders organized companies, hunting recruits and signing them up on their muster lists until the required number were enrolled. As a reward, the organizer became a captain or lieutenant and his company went off to camp, where it was made part of a regiment. State-created regiments eventually came under federal control.

Uniforms and equipment came from states, community subscription, or wealthy citizens. In due time, government issue reached the soldiers, but local officials carried the burden in the beginning.

Some regiments trained in camps near home. Others took train and ship for Washington to protect the capital (upper right). Along the way, patriotic ladies from Baltimore and Philadelphia offered refreshments.

By 1863, Lincoln called for a draft. The law was loose and allowed for paid substitution. Conscription never produced a great volume of men for the North, and it led to the horrible draft riots in New York City, in which unwilling draftees touched off a holocaust. Despite the draft, famed regiments like the Pennsylvania Bucktails continued to rely on enlistment, and sent recruiting parties whirling through city streets to drum up new blood, as pictured at upper left.

EXCITEMENT in the South, when war began, was probably greater than that which ran through the North. Tension over secession had existed for years, and Southern citizens felt a combination of relief and elation that the issue had finally been resolved. There was no shortage of thoughtful men who decried the disruption of union, but their voices were drowned in the popular clamor for action.

Southern patriotism was stirred by the drive for independence. If America had been justified in breaking the bonds laid on her by England, the argument ran, was not the South justified in dissolving unwelcome ties with the North?

Because of desire to flout federal authority, the Southern soldier became a "rebel." Self-determination was not his only spur. The North, he felt, had made war unavoidable and was about to invade his land. Protection of family and fireside were cause enough for enlistments.

The host gathered from far and near. Hat-waving civilians greeted green troops making their way through the James River Canal to western Virginia (upper left). The city of Winchester, in that state, turned out to welcome Tennessee riflemen (left). Missis-sippi volunteers waved their Bowie knives in exultation as they received the salute of General Beauregard, the hero of Fort Sumter (above).

As in the North, the burden of raising and equipping troops fell on the states. They were given help by cities and municipal organizations. These contributed funds to send forth such splendid units as the Washington Artillery of New Orleans and the Georgia Hussars of Savannah, whose outfit cost $25,000.

Most companies were not so fortunate. Lacking funds, they turned to local seam-stresses for uniforms and neighborhood artisans for equipment. Volunteer ladies sewed day and night on clothes. Household stocks supplied bedspreads, quilts, buggy robes, and oilcloth piano covers. These were made into blankets and waterproofs for field use.

Many enlistments were short-term at the beginning, and the government was forced into a bounty and furlough system to bring twelve-month men back into the army when their original terms expired. Despite the patriotism of 1861, volunteer troops proved inadequate in number, and by spring of 1862, Davis adopted conscription.

37

TURNING citizens into soldiers was a back-breaking task. Practically none of the volunteers had any military experience and there were few to teach them. West Point graduates, when available, took over instruction duties. Mexican War veterans lent a hand.

Discipline was crippled at the start because most volunteers elected their own officers at the company level. Having elevated a former acquaintance, the men were ill-disposed to take orders from him. Since he knew no more of the military than the men who elected him, the new lieutenant was forced to tread lightly.

The Civil War soldier resented the "military manner" as something appropriate to European martinets but unthinkable when applied to free Americans. An Alabama cotton planter or Iowa farmer was willing to get on with the war but resented anything that smacked of "playing soldier."

Training camps sprang up across the nation and the "awkward squad" (above) became an everyday sight. Close order drill and the housekeeping tasks of army life were taught at first. Use of weapons (right) and rudimentary maneuvers came later. Federal soldiers guarding the capital often found themselves drilling in the shadow of the Washington Monument (upper right) but most of the western troops went into camp near their points of enlistment.

Volunteers away from home for the first time found camp life fascinating at the start. Sleeping in the open and broiling beef over campfires, away from desk and shop, the recruit felt he had achieved a dream existence. The military rituals of reveille and taps, band music for parades, ceremonies attendant on raising and lowering the flag, were stimulating and impressive.

The glamour faded fast. Guard duty, fatigue details, kitchen police, constant inspections, and fitful weather took their toll of tempers. With the edge of their enthusiasm blunted, the volunteers found ways of avoiding onerous duties and began to complain of things in general. They were becoming soldiers.

39

As company-grade officers imparted basic training, their superiors embarked on the enormous task of creating armies that could be self-sufficient in the field. They had little but theory to work with, for the nation had never conceived of such forces as were coming into being.

Quartermaster organizations to supply food and clothing were basic, as was the ordnance service for weapons and ammunition. Engineers to provide transportation, signalmen to transmit messages, medical personnel to supervise mass sanitation as well as repair wounds—all were mustered into service and assigned to appropriate units.

In this preliminary stage, strong central control was necessary to progress. Such control was exercised by Lincoln and his Cabinet, but denied to Jefferson Davis. "States rights" had led to secession, and the individual states were jealous of their prerogatives.

Davis was authorized to receive arms and munitions from Southern states for the Confederacy, provided the supplies should be volunteered by the "consent of the state." Wearing down local political leaders to the point where they sacrificed minor rights for a major cause taxed the strength of the Confederate president and his associates.

Gradually, the armies of both sides emerged as entities. Tables of organization were similar in terminology, North and South.

The company was the smallest basic unit in the field, where infantry was concerned (its equivalent in the cavalry was a troop; in the artillery, a battery). Several companies, or their equivalents in other services, made up a regiment.

A regiment contained some thousand men in theory. In practice, after losses in battle, regiments had considerably less. A regiment had a number and state designation: the 17th Illinois, the 52nd Tennessee.

Regiments were grouped together in varying numbers to create a brigade; brigades were grouped to make a division; divisions were grouped to make a corps.

Several corps created an army, such as the Army of the Potomac or the Army of Northern Virginia. Southern brigades, divisions, and corps were larger numerically than their Northern counterparts.

As Northern and Southern armies built up, enormous military reviews were held at Richmond and Washington. Lincoln often attended them (above) with interest; Davis did so less frequently.

1861

VIRGINIA SKIRMISHES

BRIGADIER General Irvin McDowell, a conscientious officer with a good record in the Mexican War, acted as field commander of the raw militia that thronged Washington. His job was to set up a staff, insure a supply system, and give his recruits basic military training so he could build up new regiments into units of fighting size. The task sometimes seemed hopeless, especially as volunteers, whose service would be over in ninety days, showed little respect for discipline.

The same problems plagued Southern leaders, who were training recruits in several areas. At Harper's Ferry, the law was laid down by a stern colonel, Thomas J. Jackson, who soon earned his nickname at the first major battle of the war.

Neither side was ready for the test of battle, and war-wise military men on both sides knew it. But the civilian populace cried for the heady news of victory. Horace Greeley, day after day, ran banner headlines screaming "FORWARD TO RICHMOND!" in the *New York Tribune*. The huge head-lines summarized public feeling perfectly.

Isolated incidents in Virginia whetted the nation's appetite for victory. A Lieutenant Charles H. Tompkins, leading some fifty men of Company B, United States Dragoons, ran into a group of Confederate soldiers at Fairfax Court House and slashed his way through the detachment (above). He was a public darling overnight.

Near the little town of Vienna, Southern batteries opened fire on a train carrying Federal soldiers, and wounded several. The North cried for revenge.

Slightly more serious was the affair at Big Bethel, a short distance from Fort Monroe. The latter base, on a peninsula reaching into Chesapeake Bay, was commanded by Major General Benjamin F. Butler.

A detachment from Monroe, on a reconnaissance mission, ran into a considerable Confederate force under Colonel John B. Magruder. Some sharp action took place, and Union troops suffered approximately a hundred casualties.

Major General Robert C. Schenck, with four companies of the 1st Ohio, was approaching Vienna, Va., by railroad in mid-June when the group was fired upon by cleverly hidden Confederate batteries. Several men suffered death or injury and the locomotive was badly crippled.

The battle of Big Bethel took place about six miles northwest of Fort Monroe on June 10. Two Union regiments, part of a reconnaissance force, fired on each other in darkness, alerting the enemy. Some 1,800 C.S.A. troops then fell back to shallow entrenchments. The Federal attempt to reach the enemy was badly planned and resulted in ultimate withdrawal. Among casualties in the four-hour battle were Major Theodore Winthrop, who led the principal assault.

Rugged Mountain Country Formed the Setting for the First Planned Battle between Union and Confederate Soldiers

THE mountain fastnesses of western Virginia held a population intensely loyal to the North, one that had already set machinery in motion to come into the union as a new, separate state. To protect this population, and the Baltimore and Ohio Railroad, Federal troops came into the area. They were Ohio and Indiana men, under recently commissioned Major General George B. McClellan.

As the Yankees entered the state, Brigadier General Joseph E. Johnston, then commanding the Confederates at Harper's Ferry, felt his position threatened and withdrew. But the South determined to save what it could of this Virginia ground and, to that end, sent in a small force under Brigadier General Robert S. Garnett.

Garnett established his base at Beverly, then sent a raiding party under Colonel G. A. Porterfield to operate against the rebellious natives. McClellan heard of the raids, assembled a superior force, and struck Porterfield in a surprise attack at Philippi,

sending his forces fleeing back to Beverly.

With first blood to the Union, Garnett dug in for further battles around the two main passes through the mountains. The bulk of his force was placed at the northern one, Laurel Hill, and he commanded the position in person. A smaller force was at Rich Mountain, to the south, under Lieutenant Colonel John Pegram, on the theory that it was a strong natural defense position and could be held with few men.

McClellan feinted at Laurel Hill, then hit hard at Rich Mountain, sending the Confederates reeling back in retreat. Pegram was pursued by Union forces for a week and finally surrendered his whole command.

Garnett, hearing of McClellan's victory and capture of Beverly, fell back around the mountains in the north. McClellan followed on his heels relentlessly until the Confederate leader turned to fight at Carrick's Ford. The Union general was victorious. Garnett met death and his force broke up. West Virginia was safely in on the side of the North.

Union troops struck the sleeping Confederates at Philippi on June 3 at daybreak. They attacked in two columns of 1,500 men each, one column armed with 6-pounder field guns. Surprised, the Southern force of about 800 fled in what was later described as the "Philippi races."

Southern forces at Rich Mountain, forewarned of surprise attack, poured artillery fire on the Union troops who were in combat for the first time (above). The Yankees worked their way slowly up the mountain, surging forward in a final bayonet charge to win the day (below).

THE first major battle of the Civil War was fought because of political pressure and civilian demand. "On to Richmond" had carried the day. Lincoln ordered McDowell to strike the enemy.

Beauregard, with 22,000 men, was encamped at Manassas Junction, twenty-five miles southwest of Washington. His troops were well entrenched behind a meandering stream called Bull Run. To the west, in the Shenandoah Valley, Confederate General Johnston with 9,000 men faced a greatly superior Union force under Major General Robert Patterson.

Union plans called for Patterson to hold down Johnston. McDowell would advance to Bull Run, cross it, and send the Rebels streaming back to Richmond. Southern leaders knew of Union plans.

The first part of the operation miscarried as Johnston, leaving a few troops to distract Patterson, hurried to Beauregard's assistance. Meanwhile, McDowell, with over 30,000 men, moved toward Manassas.

Finding the enemy at Bull Run, the Union leader planned to move northwest and ford the stream, then strike the Confederate left flank. Beauregard also planned an attack—on McDowell's left flank.

Sunday, July 21, was set for the Union effort. McDowell hit hard that morning, smashing the Confederate line. Continued pressure rolled up the Southern flank as Rebel forces fled before the onslaught, their own offensive canceled. Union soldiers, sure of victory, paused for breath.

During the pause, Confederate resistance began to stiffen. A Southern general, dying of wounds, cried, "Look at Jackson's brigade. It stands there like a stone wall," creating the most famed nickname of the war.

McDowell, strengthened by reinforcements, attacked again and began to gain the advantage (right). But his efforts were nullified by the arrival of a strong group of Johnston's Valley troops and a force under Colonel Jubal A. Early.

Heartened, the Confederates pushed ahead in a desperate offensive. The Federal line broke. Tired, discouraged, and frightened, Union soldiers melted away, leaving the battlefield and the victory to the South.

BULL RUN

McDowell posted two brigades to cover the retreat of his army through Centerville, on the road to Washington (above). In the autumn, the Confederates embarked a group of Federals, wounded at Bull Run, who were picked up at sea by a Union steamer and brought home (below).

The Confident North Was Staggered by the Unexpected
Reversal at Bull Run, and Grimly Settled Down to War

AT BULL Run the Union retreat took various forms. Some men fled in extreme panic. Others sauntered away. There were soldiers who, their thirst for battle having been completely filled, disappeared and were not seen in uniform again. And there were the regulars, and a few uncommitted troops, who did their best to save the wagon trains and carry out an orderly retreat.

There was immense apprehension that the Confederates would follow up their triumph and seize Washington. This was the desire of Richmond. There was little thought of it at the front. "Our army was more disorganized by victory than that of the United States by defeat," said General Johnston.

In Washington, Lincoln (who had heard false news of victory in a wire sent prematurely by McDowell) called a special session of the Cabinet. More troops were ordered to Washington, and McClellan was brought to the capital and given command of the forces

in the immediate area. McDowell found himself in temporary disgrace.

The battle of Bull Run (called Manassas in the South) strengthened the individual Southerner's belief that one Rebel could lick three Yankees any day. It offered the North some lessons in war, taught the hard way.

Officers saw the folly of committing untrained troops to battle. The importance of discipline and prompt obedience to command was clear, for if McDowell's laggard army had moved with more speed it might have engaged Beauregard before Johnston's troops arrived. The value of a clear head in battle was painfully evident (McDowell, under pressure, had sacrificed the power of his army by attacking piecemeal).

Casualty figures, 2,700 Union to 2,000 Confederate, came as a numbing shock to both sides. It was apparent this would be a painful war. Recruiting mounted and North and South dug in for the struggle.

Amateur tactics on the battlefield led to another Union defeat in Virginia, at Ball's Bluff on the Upper Potomac, October 21. Crossing the river, with insufficient support, to seek out the enemy, Yankee troops came up against strong concealed Rebel forces. A withering fire drove them back.

EMBATTLED MISSOURI

THE tug between North and South was probably felt with more intensity in Missouri than in any other state. It was a slave-holding area; Governor Jackson was a strong secessionist. Yet a state convention had overwhelmingly voted to remain in the Union.

Lincoln watched this important border state carefully, for its defection would severely hurt his cause. Because of the state's importance, he gave extraordinary powers to two men resolved to save Missouri for the North.

They were Congressman Francis P. Blair, Jr., who had important ties in Washington and political power in St. Louis, and a regular Army captain, Nathaniel Lyon. Soldier and politician made an effective, audacious team who believed more in action than words and so saved the state.

Adept wire-pulling put Lyon in charge of regular troops in St. Louis and gave him the power to enroll citizens into the service if necessary to defend U.S. property. One of Lyon's first daring strokes was a raid on the St. Louis arsenal, where he and a band of followers, on April 25, removed a sizable supply of muskets, rifles, revolvers, and ammunition and sent them to safety in Illinois via steamboat.

Governor Jackson had been about to move on the arsenal, to help arm the state militia. These troops had been called out by Jackson and were in camp on the edge of St. Louis. They were eventually armed with weapons seized in the arsenal at Baton Rouge, Louisiana.

Lyon investigated the militia camp, disguised as an old lady in sunbonnet and black bombazine. He was assured the militia had been called out merely for their two weeks of annual drill. Apparently he found a hotbed of Confederate sympathizers, for he returned to St. Louis and called for action.

On May 10, Lyon marched his troops to the camp and took the militia prisoners. They were escorted back to St. Louis by Lyon's force of regulars and the recently enrolled citizen's army. Secessionists hooted the troops, words were exchanged, bayonets flashed, and firing broke out. The riot was soon quelled, but blood and death were the portion of St. Louis citizens (left).

In the city, recruiting state militia, was former Governor Sterling Price, soon to become a major general for the Confederacy. Price had established an uneasy truce with Major General William S. Harney, Lyon's superior officer, who had returned from a mission to take over the Union command in St. Louis. Through Blair's machinations, Harney was relieved of his command and Lyon (now promoted to brigadier general) became the army chief.

In a meeting with Jackson and Price, Lyon declared the truce to be at an end and called for complete support of the Union. The meeting broke up, Jackson returning to his capital at Jefferson City while Price continued recruiting activities out in the state.

Leaving St. Louis, Lyon marched on Jefferson City and drove Jackson and the government from the capital. Price, hearing of Lyon's movement, fled southwest to set up training headquarters at Cowskin Prairie and establish contact with Arkansas troops under Brigadier General Ben McCulloch. A Union force sent to intercept him was turned back easily at Carthage. Lyon established his headquarters at Springfield and settled down to training exercises.

By August, Price and McCulloch, the latter commanding, set out to defeat Lyon in battle as a first step toward recovering the state. The Confederate force totaled 11,600; Lyon came out from Springfield to meet them with 5,400 men, but retreated to new positions during the night. The Rebel force pressed on and went into camp at Wilson's Creek, ten miles from Springfield. There on the morning of August 10, Federal troops struck them in a suprise attack, Lyon hitting from the north and Colonel Franz Sigel coming in from the south.

Lyon was killed; and the Union army retreated. Casualties reached about 1,200 for each side, but Wilson's Creek was a definite Confederate victory.

Wilson's Creek was the second major battle of the war. Soldiers, still in the training phase, gave excellent accounts of themselves. Lyon erred tactically in splitting his forces in the face of a superior enemy, and his final charge could not redeem the day, although it let his army escape.

Missouri Was a Maverick State in 1861, but Political Negotiations and Military Victories Brought Her into the Union

During the siege of Lexington (above), troops trapped within the Masonic College made their own ammunition and cast their own shot, but lack of food and water finally led them to display the white flag. Fighting in Missouri was not always confined to formal battles but encompassed a series of guerrilla raids against Union occupying forces in such small towns as Salem (below).

LYON'S superior officer, in command of the Department of the West, was Major General John C. Frémont, explorer, politician, and would-be military leader. It became Frémont's painful duty to watch Price make his attempt to regain Missouri.

After taking Springfield, Price gathered more troops and moved north to Lexington, on the Missouri River. In mid-September he carried out a three-day siege against a small Union force barricaded in a Masonic college. Confederate victory brought rich spoils: 3,500 prisoners, 3,000 rifles and muskets, 750 horses, and some artillery.

Frémont now made his move. Conquering Price was only a part of the grandiose plan he had conceived, which envisioned the capture of Memphis, descent of the Mississippi, and an attack on New Orleans. November saw the end of Frémont's dream. His high-handed methods, dictatorial attitude, and unwise public pronouncements had caused great concern in Washington. He was relieved; and on November 19, Major General Henry W. Halleck took over his post.

Price, in the meantime, had furloughed some of his men and sent representations to Richmond. Missouri had never seceded, and Price's men were fighting as state troops only. An agreement was reached at the Confederate capital and Missouri troops were made part of the Confederate army. Recruiting was begun again, and the end of the year saw Price in winter quarters at Springfield.

Missouri fighting flowed over into early 1862, and crossed the border into Arkansas.

Confederate Major General Earl Van Dorn was given command of the Trans-Mississippi Department January 10, 1862. He arrived with a major plan to retake St. Louis, based on two large forces. He would command one of 18,000; Price one of 15,000. The troops were to be made up of all available in Missouri along with reinforcements from Louisiana, Arkansas, and Texas.

The North moved first. Under Halleck's orders, Major General Samuel R. Curtis attacked Springfield on February 12 and sent Price and his troops into retreat, to end up near Van Buren, Arkansas. McCulloch was in the neighborhood with a force that in-cluded Choctaw, Chickasaw, Cherokee, Creek, and Seminole Indians. Van Dorn arrived for a council of war with Price and McCulloch.

The upshot was a new offensive, against Curtis, encamped at Pea Ridge, Arkansas. Van Dorn moved on March 4, with 14,000 men. Curtis' effectives numbered 11,250 and were well emplaced in a mountainous area.

Van Dorn made Lyon's old mistake and split his force in two in the face of the enemy. McCulloch was to strike from the front; Price, after a long circuit around the Union troops, to come down on their rear. The simultaneous drives came on March 7.

Price's attack, in which Van Dorn participated, was successful. Prisoners and artillery were taken and the Confederates camped for the night, tasting success.

The frontal assault fared differently. McCulloch was killed; so was his second in command; and the force broke and ran from the field, as pictured below. On the following day, Van Dorn and Price went in again; but Curtis, who had been reinforced by Sigel, was much too strong and the beaten Confederates fell back toward Van Buren.

Union losses were 1,400 and Confederate casualties appear to have been about 800, although the report may be incomplete. For the time being, most of Missouri was safely in Union hands.

IN COASTAL WATERS

THE blockade of Southern seaports announced by Lincoln in April was more theory than fact during 1861. Sorely lacking in ships and men, the U.S. Navy found it impossible to function efficiently as a blockading force in the early months of war.

A revolution had overtaken naval warfare in the mid-nineteenth century. Steam power appeared in place of sails. Propellers were replacing the highly vulnerable paddle wheels of early steamers. Armor plate came into use. When the Civil War broke, the U.S. fleet was midway in the conversion from canvas to coal.

Ninety vessels made up the deep-water fleet. Fifty were sailing ships. Of the forty steamers, only thirty-four were available for duty. Nine of these were laid up and seventeen were on foreign service.

Ships in foreign waters were brought home as quickly as possible and those in dry dock prepared for sea. When all possible elements were assembled, they added up to a handful of ships to patrol 3,500 miles of coastline.

Navy Secretary Gideon Welles, an able and conscientious man, had an extremely limited naval background. To overcome this handicap, he made a wise appointment, selecting Captain Gustavus V. Fox to be his assistant. A former Navy officer, Fox conducted operations with zeal.

The team of Welles and Fox purchased 418 ships for the U.S. Navy during the war. Under them, fleet personnel climbed from 9,000 to 59,000. Morale was high, and Northern seamen proved themselves in a series of sharp engagements.

But the beginnings were difficult. Rebel troops seized and controlled Southern harbors along the Atlantic Coast and in the Gulf of Mexico and the tiny blockading squadron was denied bases from which to operate.

At some points, small bands of brave men kept the Stars and Stripes flying in the face of Southern guns. One such place was Fort Pickens, on an island in the harbor of Pensacola, Florida. When Florida troops took the navy yard and mainland forts, Lieutenant Adam J. Slemmer moved a small force of regular U.S. artillery to Pickens and, with eighty-one men, successfully held the position. He was eventually reinforced, and the fort remained in Union hands throughout the war.

The retention of Fort Pickens was a brave, defiant gesture. But it lacked practical value at the time, for Pensacola harbor's major facilities remained in Rebel hands. In the North, military leaders began to put their heads together to create amphibious operations that could capture such important ports as Pensacola for use as U.S. Navy bases.

The first amphibious attack took place against the North Carolina coast, where a long chain of islands separates the water of Albemarle and Pamlico sounds from the Atlantic. Union forces chose as their target Forts Hatteras and Clark, on one of these narrow spits of land. Overlooking Hatteras Inlet, the forts controlled the channel that led into the spacious waters of Pamlico Sound.

Fort Monroe was the departure point for the invading expedition. Two steamers and a tug carried troops of the 9th and 20th New York, 2nd U.S. Artillery, and the Coast Guard, under General Butler. Escorting the transports were seven warships under Flag Officer Silas Stringham.

On August 28, the convoy approached its goal and Stringham's 143 guns took the forts under fire. A few troops were landed, but the engagement was largely an affair of artillery. At night, the Union fleet put to sea, and returned the next morning to continue the bombardment, which resulted in the enemy striking his flag at eleven o'clock.

In the words of a participating officer, "The immediate results of this expedition were the capture of 670 men, 1,000 stand of arms, 35 cannon, and 2 strong forts; the possession of the best sea entrance to the inland waters of North Carolina; and the stoppage of a favorite channel through which many supplies had been carried for the use of the Confederate forces."

Limited rations and the threat of Confederate attack brought the garrison at Fort Pickens to near exhaustion by the time relief arrived (upper left). The same threat faced the men left to hold Forts Hatteras and Clark (below) for a time, but their pleas for help soon brought troops.

When the First Amphibious Operation Proved Successful,
Union Leaders Made Long-term Plans for a Continued Offensive

CAPTURE of Hatteras Inlet gave the Union its first foothold on the Confederate coast. It also destroyed a long-cherished belief of military men around the world: that ships had no chance in battle against land fortifications.

In Washington, the planners were seeking bigger game along the Atlantic. Among them was Samuel F. Du Pont, a career naval officer with a long, distinguished record.

Du Pont, in a series of meetings with Welles, Fox, and others concerning the blockade, called for a truly major base on the coast from which the patrolling ships could be coaled and to which they could run for refitting and repair. Another amphibious operation was planned. The objective was Port Royal, South Carolina, an immense harbor between Charleston and Savannah, Georgia.

Flag Officer Du Pont, chosen to lead the expedition, set about assembling his flotilla. By strenuous effort, the commander put together a fleet of seventy-seven vessels for the attempt on Port Royal. The flagship was *Wabash,* a frigate mounting forty-four guns of 8-, 9-, and 10-inch caliber. The remaining shipping was less impressive and included four new "90-day gunboats," assorted sloops, an ancient ferryboat, and transports to carry 12,000 soldiers under Major General Thomas W. Sherman. Twenty-five schooners went along with coal to bunker the squadron.

On October 29, the flotilla left Hampton Roads, Virginia, under sealed orders, and stood for the South. By the vagaries of war and the deftness of spies, Confederates at Port Royal knew the fleet was on its way to attack them while many officers of the expedition were ignorant of their destination.

By November 4, the Union fleet reached Port Royal and took stations off the harbor entrance. Guarding the channel that led in were Fort Walker, on Hilton Head Island, and Fort Beauregard, just opposite on Phillips Island. There was also a miniature Confederate fleet of three small side-wheel steamers, each carrying two guns, under Flag Officer Josiah Tattnall.

Before making any use of troops, Du Pont planned to place his ships near the forts and submit them to heavy shelling. Ordering the transports to remain outside, he formed his warships into two squadrons, strengthening them with vessels brought in from their blockading positions off Charleston and Savannah.

On the morning of November 7 the two squadrons, in two parallel lines, steamed into the channel. The main squadron, on the left, was to engage Fort Walker. On the right was the flanking squadron. It was to fire on Fort Beauregard and keep an eye on Tattnall's three steamers in case they should attempt to cut out and capture a disabled ship.

At 9:26 the forts opened fire. Du Pont replied and a slugging artillery battle commenced. After the initial salvos, Du Pont concentrated on Fort Walker, making repeated passes at the earthwork but keeping his fleet in constant motion. As his larger ships worked in closer to the fort on their circular course, other vessels took stations above and below it, catching the Confederates in an enfilading fire.

The flanking squadron engaged Tattnall's steamboats; and, unable to face heavy-caliber fire, they retreated up a convenient river where they could not be pursued by the deep-draught Yankee ships. With Tattnall disposed of, elements of the flanking squadron joined in pouring fire on Fort Walker.

Du Pont's naval shelling was hot and heavy, of tremendous destructive power. The Rebels, under Brigadier General Thomas F. Drayton, returned the fire gamely but their guns were pounded to pieces before their eyes. In early afternoon, Drayton abandoned Fort Walker and that evening evacuated Fort Beauregard.

Du Pont moved his ships into the harbor, landed the troops, who occupied the cities of Port Royal and Beaufort, and informed Washington it now possessed a first-class coaling station in Confederate territory.

Du Pont's merciless cannonading smashed the works at Fort Walker, destroyed a good part of the artillery there, and forced the Confederates into full retreat (above). Union troops, pouring ashore (below), had the pleasure of being part of a victory without having had to fight.

IN THE first two years of war, Great Britain and France showed definite sympathy for the Confederate States of America. To help this feeling along, Davis appointed James M. Mason of Virginia as Commissioner to England and John Slidell of Louisiana as Commissioner to France. The diplomats prepared to sail in October.

Leaving Charleston, the Southern representatives successfully ran the blockade and arrived in the Caribbean. On November 7, they sailed from Havana, Cuba, on the British mail packet *Trent*.

The following day, *Trent* was making her way through the Bahama Passage when hailed by the U.S. steamer *San Jacinto,* Captain Charles Wilkes commanding. Wilkes put two shots across the Britisher's bow; she hove to and was boarded by an American party (above).

While chasing a Confederate commerce raider in the Caribbean, Wilkes had heard of Mason and Slidell's journey and determined to capture them at sea. The boarding party demanded the men. Protesting loudly, the British gave in and Mason and Slidell boarded *San Jacinto,* to be taken to prison in Boston harbor as traitors to the U.S.A.

Wilkes's impulsive action laid a major diplomatic crisis in Lincoln's lap. British protests were based on unjustified "search and seizure" at sea of an English vessel. It was a clear violation of international law; the principle involved had led America to war with Great Britain in 1812.

The crisis was eventually solved by the patient diplomacy of Lincoln, Secretary of State Seward, and Charles Francis Adams, the extremely able ambassador to Great Britain. Seward announced the Southerners would be "cheerfully liberated," and stated: "If I decide this case in favor of my own Government, I must disavow its most cherished principles, and reverse and forever abandon its essential policy."

On New Year's Day, 1862, Mason and Slidell boarded a British vessel in Province-town and proceeded to their destination.

THE ILLUSTRATED LONDON NEWS.

No. 1121.—VOL. XXXIX.]   SATURDAY, DECEMBER 14, 1861.   [WITH A SUPPLEMENT, FIVEPENCE

OUR CONTROVERSY WITH AMERICA.

THE attitude and bearing of the people of England under the circumstances which have arisen in connection with the seizure of the Confederate Commissioners on board the Trent have been in all respects worthy of the occasion. This is not the verdict of mere self-complacency, but ample testimony has been borne by the press of France to the mingled dignity, moderation, and firmness of purpose which have been displayed by the whole country, and without exception of class. The bitterest satirists on England and the English have failed to find anything in our conduct on which to base even a sneer; while for an accusation no shadow of a foundation has been discovered. If it were necessary we might quote some of the language of writers in Continental journals in which our national spirit, our unanimity of feeling, and our consciousness of being in the right are held up to admiration in no measured terms; but we only refer to these eulogies for the purpose of illustration, and with no desire to make more of a highly creditable state of things than it deserves. It would certainly have been a melancholy thing if a country like this should on the occurrence of an act of aggression have set about to scold and vapour with all the sound and fury of those, whether persons or nations, who are assured neither of their position nor the rights of the matter in dispute; and therefore, while admitting simply and unostentatiously the justice of any commendation which we have reserved for our conduct in this juncture of our national affairs, we can afford to be almost surprised that any one should have conceived it could have been other than it has been. It is to be observed that, as the time since the intelligence of the Jacinto affair was

CAPTAIN WILKS, OF THE SAN JACINTO.

received has run on, the public mind has taken a calmer view of the situation; but, nevertheless, there has not appeared any abatement of the resolute determination to hold to the honour of England at all hazards which was the first sensation that pervaded the land. If there be any change in the view of this question—and we think there is—it is a growing incredulity with regard to the necessity for a resort to the bloody arbitrement of the sword. Reflection, consideration, examination of the subject in all its bearings, seem to lead to something like a conviction that, if a similar process be applied to the question on the other side of the water, it must result in a peaceable issue. The most recent accounts show that some change has come over the spirit in which most of the Federal so-called organs of public opinions deal with this subject. The tone adopted by these journals is much more serious and practical than that which characterised the delivery of opinions on the first blush of the matter; and something has been done to familiarise the popular mind in America with the surrender of the Confederate Commissioners as a contingency by no means remote. Some of them go so far as to say that the recent event cannot—we suppose because it ought not—be a cause of war; and others have allowed that, if the act of the officers of the Federal navy is not justifiable by the law of nations, it cannot inflict any wound on the national honour to make a suitable apology. The signs of the existence of such a feeling, however feeble they may be, are not without significance, and from them may be drawn auguries of things to come which, we believe, the most sensitive Englishmen would be willing enough to witness. It must be remembered that these indications of a tendency to

MR. MASON.

MR. SLIDELL.

THE CONFEDERATE COMMISSIONERS TO ENGLAND AND FRANCE SEIZED ON BOARD THE TRENT.—SEE NEXT PAGE.

59

WAR AT SEA

IN TWO proclamations made during April, 1861, Lincoln declared the entire Southern coastline blockaded. The Confederate States could not live without imports to sustain the economy and maintain its fighting forces. Northern blockading vessels, by cutting off imports, would help strangle the rebellious states.

In the beginning, the blockade was a paper one. The United States Navy had 90 ships but only about half this number were available for active services. They were a heterogeneous lot, some powered by steam, some by sail. The fleet gathered at the Brooklyn Navy Yard (above) in June, 1861, was a tiny force to patrol the 3,500-mile Confederate coast.

Vessels available were split into two groups, the Atlantic Blockading Squadron, 22 ships carrying 296 guns; the Gulf Blockading Squadron, 21 vessels with 282 guns. Shortly after blockading began, the squadrons were split again, into North Atlantic, South Atlantic, East Gulf, and West Gulf. Navy Secretary Gideon Welles and his

assistant, Gustavus Fox went to work to meet the crying need for ships and men. By purchase, they quickly acquired 79 steamers and 58 sailing vessels of various classes. In government navy yards, 24 ships were laid down. By the end of 1861, private contractors were working on 14 screw sloops, 23 screw gunboats, 12 sidewheelers, and three experimental ironclads. As new hulls were brought to completion in the Northern shipyards (right), the blockade acquired teeth.

By the end of the war, the Navy had 600 vessels to seal off Southern ports and hard recruiting and training had manned them with efficient crews. Aiding the blockading squadrons were amphibious attacks, mounted by Army and Navy in concert, on the major coastal cities. Each time a seaport such as New Orleans, Savannah, or Mobile fell into Federal hands, the task of the blockaders was lightened.

The blockade was ineffective during the first years of war. But by 1864, its constricting pressure was hurting the South.

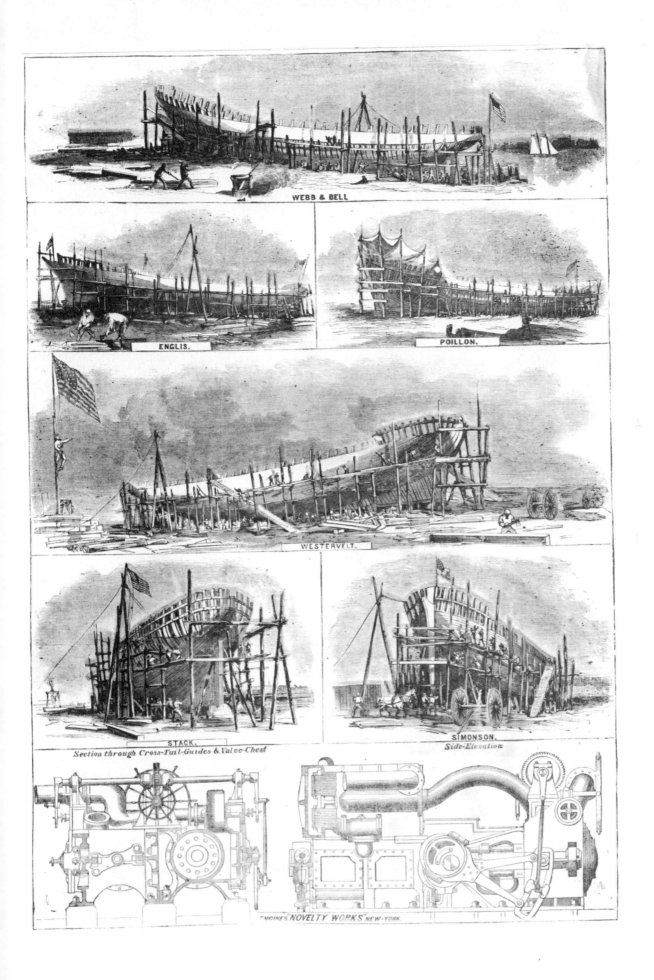

WEBB & BELL

ENGLIS.

POILLON.

WESTERVELT.

STACK.

SIMONSON.
Side-Elevation

Section through Cross-Tail-Guides & Valve-Chest

ENGINES 'NOVELTY WORKS' NEW-YORK.

A SMALL group of tiny vessels made up the Confederate Navy when war began, and occasional capture of a Yankee ship helped swell the total. The little craft packed a sting. About twenty of them were fitted out for battle and given letters of marque, permitting them to prey on Northern shipping.

Rebels vessels sometimes flew the American flag (above) when the Union steam gunboats appeared, but the trick seldom succeeded. More often, the outclassed ships tore into their larger opponents, only to be blown out of the water, as happened to the privateer *Petrel* under the guns of the United States frigate *St. Lawrence* (pages 60-61). But courage and audacity paid off from time to time, and the miniature fleet took or destroyed some sixty Union ships.

Of more immediate value to the Confederate States were the blockade runners. These wrote a chapter into Civil War history. In their holds, the Southern government sent cotton, tobacco, leather, and turpentine, for export via the Caribbean, to be exchanged for gold or munitions.

Ships engaged in this precarious trade sailed from cities such as Charleston, Wilmington, Savannah, Mobile, Galveston, and Corpus Christi, as well as minor ports. Loaded with Southern freight, they slipped through blockading steamers when luck was with them, and made for Bermuda, the Bahamas, Cuba, Mexico, and Brazil. At those places, cargoes were transshipped for other destinations.

On their return trips, blockade runners brought in food, drugs, arms, clothing, and ammunition. They also brought luxuries: brandy, cigars, and lace, to be purchased and distributed by Southern speculators.

Blockade running soon became big business. The Confederate government owned several ships engaged in the trade, as did the individual state governments. Most vessels, however, were the property of private individuals or syndicates, many of them abroad.

Risking their lives, blockade-running captains piled up fantastic profits for their owners and reaped rich salaries for themselves. One trip could net a captain $5,000; two trips paid for the ship.

Blockade running produced specialized vessels like *Lady Davis, Robert E. Lee,* and *Anglia,* shown (top to bottom) at right. Long, low, sleek, powerful, these ocean greyhounds were made to confound Federal warships guarding the coast. The finest blockade runners were British-built, coming from the great shipyards of the Clyde. Painted gray for camouflage, they burned smokeless coal, and many could telescope their smokestacks when pursuing vessels hove in sight, making them all but invisible on the horizon.

No one knows how many blockade runners operated from 1861 to 1865, but United States vessels took a terrible toll, capturing or destroying more than 1,500 of the fleet craft. Despite this attrition, the runners made some 8,000 trips, bringing Jefferson Davis 600,000 small arms, along with medicines, tools, shoes, chemicals, coffee, meat, and metals.

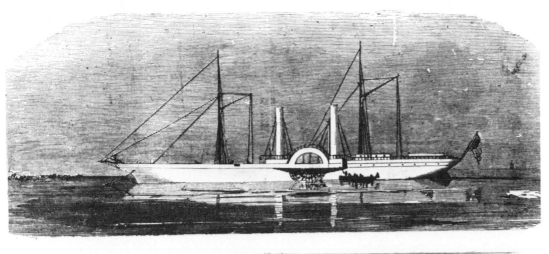

THE Confederate Navy's most romantic ships were the commerce raiders, built to ravage Federal merchant shipping. Queen of them all was the cruiser *Alabama,* under Captain Raphael Semmes (upper right). In twenty-two months, the rakish vessel created a Southern odyssey.

Alabama was built by John Laird of Birkenhead, England, as the dispatch vessel "290," to circumvent British law against arming belligerent powers. Upon launching, she proceeded to the Azores, where another ship met her, carrying guns and ammunition. She was armed, and a crew procured from among the men who brought her out. Semmes and a group of Southern officers boarded the vessel, commissioned a cruiser in the Confederate Navy on August 24, 1862.

Alabama was a seaman's dream: about 1,000 tons, 230 feet long, making 10 knots normally and over 13 under pressure. Two engines drove her 15-foot propeller and she was bunkered with an 18-day coal supply. The ship carried a full set of sails and was barkentine rigged.

Eight guns, six in broadside and one each fore and aft, armed the raider. Her mission was to rove the seas, preying on Yankee shipping, and she did the job to perfection. In her brief lifetime, *Alabama* traveled 70,000 miles, capturing or destroying more than 60 enemy ships (above).

From the Azores, Semmes cruised the North Atlantic shipping lanes off Newfoundland, then went south to the West Indies. Daring the Federal blockade, he entered the Gulf of Mexico, approached Galveston, Texas, and lured the cruiser *Hatteras* out to battle, sinking her in thirteen minutes.

Alabama put in at Jamaica and paroled the crew of *Hatteras,* coasted Brazil, and crossed the South Atlantic to Africa's Cape of Good Hope. A long trip into Far Eastern waters followed, through the Indian Ocean and China Sea, then back through Malacca Strait to the Arabian Sea. Rounding Africa once more, Semmes crossed the Atlantic again to Brazil, returned to the Azores, and went on into the French port of Cherbourg to coal and repair on June 11, 1864.

Throughout the long voyage, *Alabama* burned and sank Northern shipping wherever encountered. The crews were taken on board and transferred to neutral ships or landed at foreign ports. Her victims' stores kept the Southern ship supplied with food, fuel, and luxuries.

66

Hearing the scourge of the seas was at Cherbourg, Captain John A. Winslow brought the United States cruiser *Kearsarge* down from Holland and stood off the French port. Semmes challenged him to battle and was accepted. The ships were roughly equal in size and fire power.

On June 19, *Alabama* steamed forth to engage *Kearsarge*. Both ships steamed in a series of circles as their broadsides roared out (below). Superior Union gunnery holed *Alabama*'s hull and uprooted her guns. Semmes drew off and struck his colors, but the graceful vessel was fatally hurt and plunged to the bottom seventy minutes after the first gun was fired. The majority of the officers and men were rescued.

ALABAMA was the most glamorous of the Confederate raiders, but there were others that made Yankee vessels feel the weight of their metal. Many were acquired through the energetic action of three Confederate naval commissioners: Commodores Matthew F. Maury and Samuel Barron, and Captain James D. Bulloch. Bulloch operated in England as did Maury; Barron was stationed in Paris.

Lacking sufficient shipbuilding capacity, the Confederate government ordered rams and commerce destroyers from overseas. The commissioners were zealous and their efforts, plus those of Southern manufacturers, gave the South eighteen cruisers to injure the Federal merchant marine.

Rebel sea raiding began in 1861 as the Confederate government seized *Habana,* a steamer running between Havana and New Orleans, in the latter port. Christened *Sumter,* she was armed and sent out under Semmes for a series of actions that took seventeen ships.

Treading lightly through legal briar patches, Bulloch had the cruiser *Florida* built in Liverpool, and she was completed in early 1862. Operating in the Atlantic, this ship captured a string of prizes.

In 1863, Maury purchased a new iron steamship on the Clyde River, and after a series of machinations, she was suitably armed and sent to sea as the cruiser *Georgia.* With small coal capacity, her range was limited. After a year's cruise in which only eight vessels were taken, she was sold.

The blockade runner *Atlanta* had a checkered career. After traveling the Bermuda-Wilmington run twice in the summer of 1864, she was turned into a cruiser, rechristened *Tallahassee,* and sent up the Atlantic coast toward Halifax. In three weeks, she captured thirty coasters and fishing vessels. A short time later, her name was again changed and she became *Olustee.* Striking the Atlantic coast once more, she took seven prizes, returned to Wilmington, shed her guns, and became a blockade runner as before, with the apt name of *Chameleon.*

Another Confederate vessel serving both as blockade runner and cruiser was *Nashville.* As a commerce destroyer, she took and burned such vessels as the Yankee merchantman *Harvey Birch* (below).

Alabama and her sisters had sunk much of the Northern merchant fleet by late 1864, and the Confederates struck for the New Bedford whaling fleet in the Bering Strait. The converted merchantman *Sea King,* armed and sent forth as the Rebel cruiser *Shenandoah,* took forty whalers.

1862

KENTUCKY-TENNESSEE

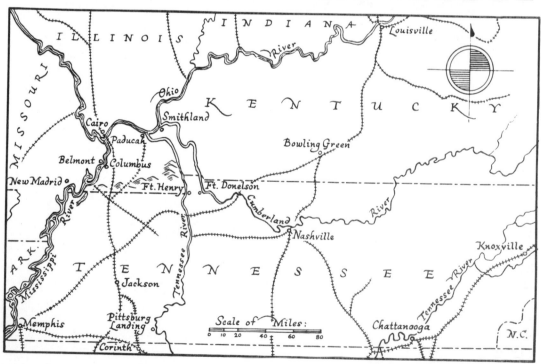

KENTUCKY remained neutral for several months after war was declared. Its governor was a secessionist; its legislature pro-Union. The people's loyalties appeared to be equally divided. Kentuckians were flocking to the colors, enlisting on both sides.

North and South respected the border state's neutrality. Federal recruiting officers worked just over the state line, in Ohio. Their Confederate counterparts were stationed south of Kentucky, in Tennessee.

Confederate Major General Leonidas Polk, onetime Bishop of Louisiana, finally shattered the status quo. In September, 1861, he swept up from Tennessee and took Columbus, on a high bluff overlooking the Mississippi River.

Union troops under Brigadier General Ulysses S. Grant moved immediately from Cairo, Illinois, to seize Paducah. Each side, with a foothold in the state, began to pour in troops. In November, 1861, Grant made a reconnaissance in force (lower right) against Belmont, Missouri, opposite Rebel-held Columbus. Polk's forces went to meet him and repulsed him in a small engagement. There was no further fighting in this area during the first year of the war.

By the opening of 1862, the issue had been joined in this last neutral state. Its strategic importance was obvious to military leaders, and had led them to violations of neutrality.

Eastern Kentucky had no great military value. In the west, the picture was different. There, the state was the key to three great rivers, the Mississippi, Cumberland, and Tennessee. Each led into the South and was a natural invasion path for Northern troops. Further, Kentucky shielded Tennessee from Yankee attack.

To hold the line in Kentucky and protect Tennessee, Jefferson Davis sent one of his finest soldiers, General Albert Sidney Johnston (left). A native Kentuckian and career army man, Johnston was generally considered the best in the Southern military organization. His personal popularity was enormous.

Johnston's defensive line stretched from Mill Springs in the east to Columbus on the Mississippi, running through Bowling Green in the approximate center. That place became the Confederate leader's headquarters, as it had rail connections to Nashville and Memphis. The entire western theater was under Johnston's authority.

On the Union side, command was split as a result of reorganization in Washington. Winfield Scott had retired in the autumn of 1861, and McClellan succeeded him as general-in-chief. To face Johnston, McClellan appointed Brigadier General Don Carlos Buell as commander of the Army of the Ohio, and Major General Henry W. Halleck to lead additional forces in the west. Buell's territory was eastern Kentucky; Halleck was to take care of the western portion of the state.

Buell's command saw action first, on January 19, at Mill Springs. There, Union troops under Major General George H. Thomas struck Confederate units commanded by Major General George B. Crittenden and Brigadier General Felix J. Zollicoffer. The latter was killed as Northern troops won a clean-cut victory.

Crittenden abandoned the field and fell back into Tennessee. Eastern Kentucky was safely in Union hands as 1862 began.

THE three river routes to invasion worried Southern leaders, who decided to place corks in each of these bottlenecks. In the Mississippi, they fortified Island No. 10. On the Tennessee, Fort Henry was constructed; on the Cumberland, Fort Donelson.

The Tennessee flows north through Tennessee and Kentucky to empty into the Ohio River at Paducah. The Cumberland parallels it and reaches the Ohio at Smithland. Forts Henry and Donelson, just below the Kentucky-Tennessee border, were only twelve miles apart. They became part of the Mill Springs—Bowling Green—Columbus defense line Johnston had created to screen the central South.

Grant, operating under Halleck's command, held the two river outlets at Paducah and Smithland. With Halleck, he discussed the possibility of moving up the rivers to crack the forts and open the way to invading troops traveling by boat. Halleck agreed he should make an attempt on Fort Henry.

Enlisting the aid of Flag Officer Andrew H. Foote, whose shipping was operating under army command at this time, Grant planned an amphibious expedition to move south, up the Tennessee, and strike the Confederate fort.

Two divisions of troops in transports were to be covered by seven gunboats: four ironclads and three of wood. The force moved on February 2; and when it reached a position four miles from the fort, the troops were landed. On February 6, Foote's gunboats moved up to shell the work. The four ironclads were abreast, in the lead, with the three wooden ships behind them, firing over their heads.

Strong rains had raised the level of the river and Fort Henry, on low ground, was partially flooded. The situation had led Brigadier General Lloyd Tilghman to send most of his men across the intervening twelve miles to Fort Donelson. He kept a few artillerymen behind, to engage the Yankee gunboats.

Firing was brisk on both sides as the small river boats, defying military tradition, closed in to attack the fort. Confederate shells inflicted some casualties; but Union fire wreaked far more damage, including destruction of a major Rebel gun (above).

Gunboat War Was Brought to the Western Rivers by Grant as He Moved on Forts Henry and Donelson

In two hours, Henry struck its flag. Troops had not been needed. The Tennessee River was open as far as Alabama.

Grant determined to move on Fort Donelson. The ships were sent back down the Tennessee to the Ohio, to come up the Cumberland against the fort. Troops moved overland.

Donelson was a different proposition. Well fortified, on high ground west of the river, it showed a formidable face to the approaching troops. Its garrison numbered 21,000 men against Grant's initial force of 15,000. But the Union leader had floating, mobile artillery in the gunboats.

They moved in, as they had on Henry, and got off their first salvos on February 14. The fort was undergunned but replied gamely and with telling effect. Casualties began to mount in the river vessels and Foote was injured. In the face of superior fire, the flotilla retired.

Grant, in conference with Foote, saw the devastation on board the gunboats and knew the army would have to finish the job alone. The Union leader had three divisions lying in a rough semicircle around the fort, their flanks on water north and south of the work

to seal in the besieged garrison. Major General Charles F. Smith commanded the northernmost division; Major General Lew Wallace was in the center, Major General John A. McClernand to the south.

On the fifteenth, as Grant was returning from his conference, the Rebels attempted to break out, sending 8,000 men against McClernand and rolling up his line. Wallace helped halt the attack. Grant, arriving, ordered Smith to strike on his front and the thrust was effective, taking important Confederate positions. McClernand's men regained their positions (below).

Within the fort, which was unprepared for siege, the game was up and buck-passing began. Two senior brigadier generals, John B. Floyd and Gideon J. Pillow, afraid of the consequences of capture, turned command over to Simon B. Buckner, third ranking brigadier. Floyd and Pillow, along with cavalry commander Colonel Nathan B. Forrest, managed to gather some men and escape.

Buckner asked Grant for terms. Grant said there would be none but "unconditional surrender." On February 16, Donelson fell to the Union.

Capture of the River Forts Gave the North Its First Real Victory, and a New Public Figure as Well

FORTS Henry and Donelson made U. S. Grant a national hero. The obscure, old-time army officer with moments of weakness for the bottle caught the public fancy with "unconditional surrender," which neatly fitted his initials. Admirers sent him cigars. Lincoln sent him a commission as major general.

Halleck, Grant's immediate superior, glowed in reflected glory and demanded complete control of the western theater of war as a reward for Grant's victories. As Washington thought this over, Halleck engaged in a petty feud with Grant, who, the commanding general said, would not keep his paper work up to date. The entire affair was a vague, cloudy one. Halleck finally got his wish, complete command in the west (placing him over Buell), and with his ruffled feathers smoothed by promotion, he forgave Grant.

This first major Northern victory of the war was a blow that left the South gasping for breath. At Donelson, the Confederates lost 2,000 killed or wounded, against 2,600 for the Union. But the "missing" list read 14,600 and most of these were headed for Yankee prisons. Johnston had lost almost one-third of his force.

Of even greater moment was the territorial loss. Two main points of the defense line had been taken, and the system crumbled with their fall. While Donelson was under siege, Johnston had abandoned his Bowling Green headquarters and fallen back down the rail line to Nashville. It soon became apparent defense there was useless, and the Confederate commander chose February 16 to evacuate the Tennessee capital.

Johnston's speedy flight before Buell had forced him to abandon millions of dollars' worth of food, clothing, and ammunition. Incoming Yankee soldiers took what they liked; the government impressed the majority of the munitions.

Nashville (right) remained in Union hands for the rest of the war. As Military Governor of Tennessee, Lincoln appointed former Governor Andrew Johnson.

Defeat at Mill Springs loosened the eastern end of Johnston's defense line. Forts Henry and Donelson, Bowling Green, and Nashville had melted away, removing the central portion of the system. On the Mississippi, there remained Columbus. To inspect its defenses and position, Johnston sent Beauregard, who had recently been sent from the east to act as second in command in the important western theater. Johnston moved his troops to Murfreesboro.

Beauregard decided against holding Columbus, recommending Rebel defenses in the Mississippi area be based on Island No. 10. Johnston was forced to create a new defensive line.

It ran from Memphis, on the Mississippi, to Chattanooga, Tennessee, in the mountains. The central section of the line passed through Corinth, Mississippi, a small town but important for its rail junction, where north-south and east-west railroads crossed. A primary purpose of Johnston's new defensive system was protection of the Memphis and Charleston, an important railroad Lincoln was anxious to seize. It ran through Mississippi, Alabama, and Tennessee to enter Virginia. This road connected the western and eastern portions of the Confederacy. Over it passed Texas cattle and Louisiana rice to feed the east, and it could carry troops great distances in emergencies.

Johnston settled down at Corinth, on this rail line, made the town his headquarters, and began to piece together a new army. Polk, who had evacuated Columbus, brought 13,000 men. From New Orleans came 3,000; from Pensacola, 10,000. Some 15,000 more were due from Arkansas. With the exception of the small garrisons left at Island No. 10, Memphis, and Fort Pillow—all to protect the great river—the Confederacy was stripping its outposts to create a formidable force for its greatest general.

Generals Buell (left) and Halleck (right) were asked by Lincoln to cooperate fully in the territory they were to share. Of similar temperaments, graduates of West Point, and Mexican War veterans, they tangled. The crisis was solved when Halleck was put over Buell. Shortly after occupying Nashville, Buell was made major general, but was relieved of command in October, 1862.

CARNAGE AT SHILOH

CORINTH, with Johnston's headquarters and the important rail junction, was the next Yankee objective in the west. Now in command of the Army of West Tennessee, Grant urged immediate action.

Halleck said no. There was no point in taking the offensive until an overpowering force had been assembled. Accordingly, he ordered Grant to move south along the Tennessee River and go into camp. There he would be joined by Buell from Nashville. When the juncture was made, Halleck would appear to take over field command.

Grant picked Pittsburg Landing, on the western bank of the river, twenty miles above Corinth, and bivouacked. He had 43,000 men in six divisions under McClernand, Lew Wallace, and Brigadier Generals Benjamin M. Prentiss, Stephen A. Hurlbut, William T. Sherman and W. H. L. Wallace.

Five divisions set up tents at the landing; that of Lew Wallace encamped several miles to the north. The troops were green but no enemy action was expected. Entrenched positions were not ordered and the army was deployed in a haphazard fashion. Grant himself was down river, at some distance from his men.

In Corinth, Johnston knew Grant was awaiting Buell before coming to attack him. The situation demanded prompt, decisive action, for the combined forces of Grant and Buell could smash the Confederates without trouble. Johnston, a great and daring commander, decided to play a long shot: a surprise attack on Grant before Buell's troops arrived.

Johnston's carefully gathered force totaled 40,000, in three corps under Polk and Major Generals William J. Hardee and Braxton Bragg. Brigadier General John C.

Breckinridge (Lincoln's old political opponent for the presidency) held an additional corps in reserve. Johnston's men were as green as Grant's.

The Rebel army left Corinth on April 3. The march they made was one of ragged disorder. Young soldiers, strangers to battle, skylarked, shot squirrels, fought mock battles, and thoroughly enjoyed themselves. The noise and confusion convinced Beauregard that Yankees would soon spot the moving troops. He suggested turning back. Johnston pressed on and, on a Saturday, camped two miles from Pittsburg Landing. Federal pickets fired at what they thought were isolated Rebel skirmishers.

On April 6, a balmy Sunday morning, Johnston struck. The Yankees, in bed or yawning their way toward breakfast, were victims of complete surprise. Trying to dress, load rifles, and arouse their comrades, they fell back in panic.

Johnston's initial attack was a juggernaut. Men of Prentiss', McClernand's and Sherman's commands were hurled back toward the river. Confederates streamed past a bare log chapel called Shiloh Church that would give its name to the battle. Everywhere there was Yankee confusion, retreat, and a vain bawling of commands. Partially trained, partially disciplined troops would not rally.

The sound, smell, and chaos of battle were terrific, beyond anything ever experienced by the officers or dreamed of by the men. Confederates fought desperately, to eliminate the stigma of Fort Donelson. They had the advantage of complete surprise and numerical superiority (Lew Wallace's Union division was miles from the battle).

Southern pressure rolled up the Yankee flanks but resistance stiffened in the center. There, blue-clad soldiers had found a sunken road that functioned perfectly as a trench. This area, the "hornet's nest," became the center of Union resistance.

Prentiss, having held back the enemy's initial thrust as best he could, was forced to surrender. Union General W. H. L. Wallace received a fatal wound. And Johnston, leading his men, was killed in the heat of battle.

Rebel troops, storming into camp, took McClernand's headquarters while nearby Union artillery hastened to limber up and escape (upper left). As the day progressed, the cry of "Ambulance!" became more frequent (below). For the first time, the full horror of war was brought home.

GRANT, several miles downstream, heard the sound of heavy firing and leaped aboard a steamboat to reach the battle and take over. Surveying the disorganized field, he made crisp decisions.

The Union chief sped messengers to bring in Lew Wallace's division and urge Buell to hurry his advance. Orders flashed to two wooden gunboats, *Tyler* and *Lexington,* to take stations opposite the landing and open fire. Siege guns were mounted and brought into action. Upon Grant's orders, officers rounded up disorganized men and created rough fighting units.

The Rebel drive lasted from sunrise to sundown. Southern troops were showing their mettle, but by the end of the day Yankee organization was felt and Northern forces were holding their own (right). Nevertheless, as night fell, the South was near victory. Beauregard, commanding after Johnston's death, called a halt to fighting so his men could sleep.

That halt, which was necessary, may have cost the Confederates the battle. Throughout a night of streaming rain, Grant's reinforcements moved in. Lew Wallace, who had become lost the day before, arrived with 7,000 men. Unit after unit of Buell's forces crossed the river. When the sun rose again, Grant had 25,000 fresh men to hurl against the battle-weary Confederates.

Exploiting his new strength, Grant went over to the offensive on the morning of April 7. The night's rest had renewed the Rebel fiber, and they put up a stubborn resistance. Sheer weight, and the morale-smashing fact of Johnston's death, finally beat down the gallant Southern army, which left the field and returned to Corinth.

By the skin of its teeth, the North had snatched a major victory from almost certain defeat. The price was horrible, for Shiloh was one of the bloodiest battles of the war. More than 10,000 Union soldiers had been killed or wounded, and Confederate figures were approximately the same. It was an expensive price tag for a wooden chapel and a steamboat dock.

The Union leader, a people's darling of weeks ago, came under attack; and politicians clamored loudly for his dismissal.

THE MISSISSIPPI

FOLLOWING evacuation of Columbus, on the Mississippi River, Confederate forces retired to Island No. 10, some thirty miles to the south. The fortified island made an effective obstacle in the river, preventing Northern transports from moving downstream. At the time of Shiloh, Union troops under Major General John Pope were attempting to reduce this Rebel stronghold.

Pope's offensive in spring of 1862 began a new kind of warfare, that on the Mississippi and its tributaries. It was a strange, amphibious, half-man–half-alligator operation.

Wind and weather kept the waters moving in unpredictable ways. Land could be dry canebrake one week and flooded marsh the next. Federal troops using river boats to seek passages through the dark bayous had to clear the waters of sunken logs and clinging vegetation (above).

A new Union fleet, sometimes known as the Western Flotilla, was created to operate on the Mississippi, Ohio, Red, Yazoo, and contributing streams. More than a hundred vessels made up this fleet, which was under Army control until October, 1862, when the Navy took over.

The fresh-water flotilla began in May, 1861, with purchase of three river steamboats, which were armored and turned into fighting craft. Then contractor James B. Eads was called in and ordered to produce seven armored gunboats. He did, and Northern newspapers of the time began to carry the names *Cairo, Carondelet, Cincinnati, Louisville, Mound City, Pittsburgh,* and *St. Louis.* Turned out in forty-five days each, they were heavily armored on the bow and some areas amidships, and carried guns up to eight inches in caliber. These "turtles", as they were known to the public, made history under Flag Officer Foote.

"Tin-clads" operating on the Mississippi, so-called because of their light armor, had romantic names: *Forest Rose, Romeo, Juliet.* These were shallow-draught vessels that "could sail in a light dew" and often moved inshore to give troops support.

Also within the Western Flotilla was the Ram Fleet, created by Colonel Charles Ellet, Jr. As steam replaced sail, Ellet called for a return to the ram used by Greek and Roman galleys to puncture enemy shipping.

The War Department bought Ellet's scheme and commissioned him to purchase nine river boats and arm them with rams. He carried out his plan, and the ships, among them the well-known *Queen of the West,* saw action on the inland rivers.

Rams were not limited to these ships alone but incorporated in such large vessels as the 1,000-ton *Lafayette* and *Choctaw,* ironclad steamers among the best in the fleet. Comparative giants such as these were rare but extremely useful when heavy fire had to be delivered against forts or heavily entrenched positions.

The Western Flotilla (below) was widely diverse in content but performed yeoman labor throughout the war, escorting transports, carrying food and munitions, providing courier service, and fighting pitched battles when necessary.

The Confederate side could never equal it. On the Mississippi they had the River Defense Fleet of fourteen steamboats made over into rams, but the force was poorly used and eventually destroyed.

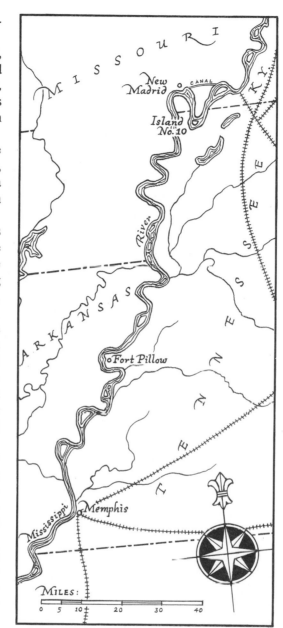

For three weeks a powerful fleet of ironclads and mortar boats laid down blanket shelling on Island No. 10 (below). In the end, the little *Carondelet's* run through the night (above) proved more effective than massed naval gunfire in bringing the garrison to the point of surrender.

IN ITS course, the Mississippi River makes innumerable hairpin curves. Island No. 10 lay in the bottom loop of one of these, a fort with about fifty guns, blockading the river. It was a powerful position, as the island was supported by guns along the river bank in areas still in Confederate hands.

Pope controlled much of the ground in the area and had troops at New Madrid, Missouri, and in other sections west of the river. If he could cross the Mississippi, he could seize the one road used to supply the fort and thus starve out the garrison.

His transports lay upstream, and dared not come down past the fort's guns; his troops, therefore, could not be moved.

The problem was solved by Pope's engineers. They saw that Island No. 10 lay in the lower extremity of a U-shaped curve in the river. They also found that north of the island both arms of the U were roughly connected by a series of bayous. If these could be cleared and deepened, transports might drift through, completely by-passing the enemy position.

The Engineer Regiment of the West, twelve companies of selected workmen, took over. Ingenious underwater saws were used to cut timber blocking the channels. A passageway was opened, the transports went through, and Pope prepared to embark his men and land on the river's east bank.

One important factor still blocked him: enemy batteries on the east bank that would cut his crossing force to ribbons. Union gunboats, because of their deep draught, could not cross through the bayou system.

At a naval conference, Commander Henry Walke volunteered to take an ironclad and attempt a run past the enemy batteries at night, to come to Pope's assistance. The offer was accepted. Walke carefully prepared his ship *Carondelet* for the ordeal. Chains and ropes were wound around the pilot house, a barge filled with coal and hay to stop shellfire was lashed to the port side, and hoses were prepared to douse boarding parties with scalding water.

On the night of April 4, in a spectacular electrical storm, *Carondelet* made her run. Enemy fire went wild and she arrived safely.

Soon after her arrival, the gunboat steamed opposite the Confederate batteries on the river's east bank and, one by one, knocked them out. Pope's troops crossed without incident. As they moved in, the enemy withdrew from the island, now hopelessly cut off, and surrendered at the nearby town of Tiptonville, Tennessee (above).

Pope captured three generals at the surrender, which took place April 8. Another Mississippi bottleneck was eliminated and Union forces prepared to move farther downstream.

WITH Island No. 10 in its pocket, the Union Army and Navy began to move down the Mississippi. Confederate defenses lay in a string of forts along the Tennessee side of the river. Pope was preparing to invest one of these, Fort Pillow, when his force was ordered elsewhere. Left to do the job alone, the Navy anchored several mortar boats across from the fort and hurled 13-inch shells into the work.

In early May, the wounds suffered by Flag Officer Foote at Fort Donelson proved too much for him and he was forced to request transfer (he died a little more than a year later). Flag Officer Charles H. Davis took command of the Western Flotilla, which soon found itself in battle (above).

On May 10, eight vessels of the Rebel River Defense Fleet attacked the mortar boats in the waters off Fort Pillow. *Cincinnati* came to their defense, followed by *Mound City* and *Carondelet.* The first Federal ship felt the power of Confederate rams, but Yankee gunfire soon drove the Rebel

steamers away and they went back downstream after a one-hour battle. Within a month, the Southerners set fire to Fort Pillow and abandoned it, the Federal Navy coming ashore to take over.

Davis now determined to aim at Memphis, the foremost objective on the upper Mississippi. On June 6, he found the city defended by eight vessels drawn up in a double line of battle. The Union commander had two rams—*Queen of the West* and *Monarch*—and five gunboats—*Benton, Cairo, Carondelet, Louisville,* and *St. Louis* —to oppose the enemy.

Colonel Ellet's rams, commanded by him and his younger brother, engaged the enemy first despite the fact they carried no guns and had only their steel beaks as weapons. Upon closing with the enemy, they were followed by the gunboats, laying down a curtain of immensely effective fire.

Lasting one hour and ten minutes, the engagement was a disaster for the South. Of the Confederate vessels, *General Lovell*

Land Forces Carried the War into Confederate-held Mississippi

and *Beauregard* were sunk; *Jeff Thompson* burned to the water's edge; *Sumter* was captured; *General Price, Little Rebel,* and *Bragg* were run ashore and abandoned. Only *Van Dorn* escaped down river.

Crowds thronged the river bank to watch the battle. Their cheers turned to laments as the fleet was crushed and the last large city in Tennessee lay open to the invaders. The Yankees took six large steamers at Memphis, a substantial quantity of cotton, and destroyed *Tennessee,* a large steam ram still on the stocks.

While the gunboats and rams were busy on the river, a ponderous land army was crawling south from Pittsburg Landing, under Halleck, who came down to lead the troops in battle, making Grant second in command.

The new Union field commander was known as "Old Brains" from his textbook knowledge of war and the publications he had written. Nobody's fool, Halleck was no daredevil either. He moved only when the odds were with him, and then with cau-

tion, in the prescribed military manner.

"Old Brains" put together an enormous force, consisting of Buell's army, Grant's, and that of Pope, which had been ordered down from New Madrid and Fort Pillow. Approximately 120,000 men cautiously moved out in April.

The objective of this massive movement was Corinth, to which Beauregard had retreated after the costly battle at Shiloh. Hastily putting together a new army, he called for reinforcements from every place in the South. He had brought back 30,000 men from the battlefield. Additional troops came from Arkansas, Missouri, east Tennessee, South Carolina, Georgia, and the Gulf States. In all, he managed to gather 53,000 men, and was no match for the steam roller inching toward him.

Halleck averaged less than one mile per day as a result of his painstaking methods. As he came within sight of his goal, Beauregard quietly pulled out and fell back south to Tupelo. Union troops entered Corinth on May 30.

Beauregard's evacuation of Corinth was a masterpiece, for it was carried out with complete secrecy almost under the eyes of the enemy. Sick and wounded were carefully removed. Artillery was shipped to Tupelo, 50 miles away, and the troops followed. Incoming Yankees found a completely abandoned town, with bridges and buildings on fire and only a handful of Rebels.

THE CRESCENT CITY

NEW ORLEANS was stagnating because of the blockade. Commerce, which poured men and money into the Crescent City, had ceased; docks were empty and deserted. Warehouses had been padlocked. The small industries the city boasted were turning out materials of war.

Food was scarce and deflated currency was making it ruinously expensive. The young men were not there to care; they had gone north to war. Their fathers and uncles made up a home guard, which drilled in the streets against the inevitable day of invasion.

The city was the largest in the Confederacy and queen of the Gulf. As the South's biggest port, it maintained a brisk trade with nations in the Caribbean until the blockade left ships rusting at their docks. As the major city on the Mississippi, New Orleans would make a rich prize for the North, which was seeking control of the river.

The people of the city knew they were a potential target for Northern forces. For their defense, they had Major General Mansfield Lovell and a group of soldiers reported to number 10,000.

Southern assurance came not so much from local troops as from the forts below the city. The Mississippi, when it leaves New Orleans, flows some hundred miles before it empties into the Gulf. On the river, seventy miles south of New Orleans, were two formidable structures, Fort Jackson on one side and Fort St. Philip on the other.

Jackson was a star-shaped, stone-and-masonry fort with seventy-four guns. St. Philip, across the river, mounted fifty-two cannon and was built of brick and stone. Each fort was well provisioned, had abundant ammunition, and was garrisoned by about 700 men.

The best passage up river ran close to Fort Jackson. There the Confederates constructed a boom made up of half-sunken

taking New Orleans, with Lincoln and Welles and found them enthusiastic. McClellan agreed to supply 20,000 troops under General Butler. The Navy was to create an invasion fleet of seventeen sloops and gunboats and twenty mortar schooners. The latter ships, devised by Porter, each carried a single 13-inch mortar to bombard the fortifications.

Chosen to command the expedition was Flag Officer David G. Farragut (left), the saltiest character of the war. Farragut, who was over sixty when given his command, had entered the U.S. Navy at the age of nine. He fought in the War of 1812, chased pirates, served in Tunis, and left his Norfolk, Virginia, home to go into semiretirement at Hastings-on-Hudson, New York, when the war broke out.

The Yankee expedition rendezvoused at Ship Island, then moved up the passes into the lower Mississippi. Farragut's flagship, Hartford, was a wooden vessel, as were all the others in the fleet. It was another case of wooden ships against stone forts, contrary to all tactical rules for naval warfare.

The flag officer reconnoitered the enemy, then ordered the twenty mortar schooners, commanded by Porter, to take stations near Forts Jackson and St. Philip and open fire. Shooting began on April 18, each mortar firing once every ten minutes. The forts replied with heavy shelling against the little ships, which were camouflaged with tree branches as they lay against the river bank.

For five days, Porter's schooners pounded the forts while the rest of the fleet lay idle. Destruction was heavy inside the works, and Jackson at one point blazed with a serious fire. When the mortars ceased, 16,800 13-inch shells had been hurled at the Confederates, one schooner was sunk, and the men were exhausted.

Despite the intense barrage, neither fort showed signs of surrender. Porter suggested landing the troops and taking the structures under siege. Farragut, impatient, resolved to run his ships past the forts at night and go on up to New Orleans. On April 20, two Yankee vessels succeeded in cutting the boom enough to permit passage of the Northern fleet.

hulks, log rafts, and chains. It stretched across the river, effectively denying passage to enemy ships, but could be opened for friendly ones.

There was also a small flotilla, made up of the partially completed ironclad Louisiana, a small ram called Manassas, six boats of the River Defense Fleet, and a group of other vessels that had been armed and armored. Behind these defenses, New Orleans felt secure.

The Union, since the blockade was proclaimed, had been eyeing the big Southern seaport. Northern forces seized a potential base for operations against the city when they took Ship Island, in the Gulf, off the Mississippi coast. The island was headquarters for the West Gulf Blockading Squadron.

Commander David D. Porter had discussed plans for entering the Mississippi, bombarding and capturing the forts, and

ON APRIL 24, just after 2 A.M., two red lights blinked, and the Union fleet steamed through the barricade and approached the forts. The Confederates, well warned in advance, lighted bonfires on both shores to silhouette the passing vessels.

The fleet was steaming in three columns, *Cayuga* leading one division, *Hartford* the second, and *Scioto* the third. The forts blasted the Northern ships and the small Rebel fleet fell on them with fury.

The Union ship *Varuna,* rammed again and again, dispatched one of her opponents before going to the bottom. *Pensacola* hammered away at Fort St. Philip. Red haze from the hot muzzles of guns and bursting shells lighted the night sky.

Hartford, moving in to slug it out with Fort St. Philip, ran aground just as an enemy tug pushed a blazing fire raft against her. Flames shot halfway up her masts. As the fire control party staggered back from the inferno, Farragut shouted, "Don't flinch from that fire, boys. There's a hotter fire for those who don't do their duty." The flames were quenched.

Itasca, shot through her boiler room, floundered helplessly to shore and sank on the shoals. *Winona* and *Kennebec,* severely punctured, were ordered out of action. *Brooklyn* was hulled badly by enemy shellfire, and rammed by *Manassas,* the cigar-shaped Rebel ship that carried only one gun but wreaked heavy damage with her powerful beak.

The Yankee *Mississippi,* upon Farragut's orders, steamed toward *Manassas* to run her down. The ram's commander put her onshore and the crew fled. *Mississippi* pounded her heavily with shellfire.

Throughout the battle the still unfinished *Louisiana,* to be the pride of the Southern Navy, lay lashed to the shore pouring destructive fire from her heavy guns. To increase Northern firepower, Porter's mortar vessels moved in as close as they dared and laid down a continuous barrage on Fort Jackson.

Suddenly it was over. In seventy minutes, Farragut had smashed his way through the well-guarded passage at the relatively light cost of 210 casualties.

During the passage of the forts (above), a discharge of grape from Fort Jackson struck the deck of the gunboat *Iroquois*, killing eight and wounding seven of the crew of 25 tending a Dahlgren gun (below). Casualties such as these were somewhat reduced by rigging chains to hang down over the hulls of the ships, acting as light armor. Farragut also had his vessels camouflaged.

MOST of the small Confederate fleet sank in the river action. The forts, damaged and cut off from their base, soon surrendered.

Farragut paused after the battle to bury the dead, succor the wounded, and repair the damage to his ships. With his affairs in order, he moved on upstream. The flag officer reached New Orleans April 25. Panic had preceded him.

General Lovell's troops withdrew from the city. Wealthy citizens fled, taking $4 million from the banks as they left. More than 15,000 bales of cotton were burned on the levee. Molasses, sugar, and rice were dumped into the river. River boats, and naval vessels under construction, fired and cast adrift, menaced navigation.

A shouting, gesticulating mob of the city's riffraff met Farragut's officers as they landed on the wharf (above). Women spat at the Yankees and men waved flags and swords. The city refused to surrender. Farragut's men were forced to take over and run up the Stars and Stripes on public buildings.

On May 1, Butler arrived, set up headquarters at the St. Charles Hotel, and established a military government. There are indications that his administration was efficient in many ways and kept the city from disease and famine. But the population would have none of it and showed fiery resistance to occupying forces.

Soldiers were repeatedly insulted in the streets and restaurants. When the crowd was getting completely out of hand, Butler hanged one of its members for destroying an American flag, and issued Order No. 28, which stated that any female showing contempt for officers and soldiers of the United States should "be regarded and held liable to be treated as a woman about town plying her avocation."

The Union leader became "Beast Butler" in the South and was probably most hated of the Northern conquerors. Pressure against him became so great that Lincoln was forced to remove him and reassign the general to military operations.

With the fall of New Orleans, the South lost its wealthiest city and prime seaport. Seizure of the mouths of the Mississippi was of enormous importance to the North. Grand strategy now called for Farragut to move up river and meet with Commander Davis traveling down river from Memphis.

Butler, an able Massachusetts politician, showed less talent as a general, but was prominent in the public eye for victory at Baltimore in 1861.

FARRAGUT started up river, capturing Baton Rouge and Natchez on the way. The former city was retaken by the Confederates but Union forces moved in again during late 1862 (below).

Upon reaching Vicksburg, Farragut bombed the city with mortar boats, then successfully ran his ships past the place to meet with Davis and his squadron. The defenses of Vicksburg were stout and the Union commander reported strong land forces would be needed to capture the place.

While Davis and Farragut were meeting, a David and Goliath story took place under their eyes. The Confederate ram *Arkansas,* mounting ten guns, appeared in the river and took on the combined fleets of the two Yankee leaders. She inflicted some damage and a great deal of confusion before she dropped downstream to be destroyed. After the incident, Farragut returned south.

ARMY LIFE

THE Civil War soldier belonged to an eighty-five-year-old nation with no military tradition. He had never fought in a major war. Discipline went against his grain. Yet he quickly adjusted to his fellow man and learned to endure hardships, win battles when he could, and accept defeat stoically.

He was sustained by a cause. The Southerner fought to be left alone, maintain his people's way of life, prevent race equality, and break the ties with Northern bankers whose high tariff policies would starve the South. In the North, the battle was to preserve the Union, stamp out secessionism, keep slavery from new Western lands, and teach the Rebels a lesson.

Faith in his cause was of great importance to the fighting man, for the physical facts of army life in the 1860's were grim. Neither side was prepared for a war of any length. The lack of preparation showed in bad rations, unsuitable clothing, scarcity of standardized weapons, inadequate training, and a callous disregard for the soldier as an individual.

As the war progressed, some of these evils were partially corrected. Northern soldiers began to get enough food, although its quality remained doubtful. Transportation tie-ups often kept the Rebels on short rations.

Yankee uniforms were in plentiful supply but had been designed for cold-weather operations. In the steaming summers of Georgia and Mississippi, they proved a curse. Confederate clothing was somewhat scanty, but the average Rebel liked to travel light. Unencumbered by heavy equipment, he was an agile foe.

Mass production from big arsenals like Springfield enabled the Union to standardize rifles in a short time, simplifying the ammunition problem. Limited production facilities kept the South from achieving this goal, and it was forced to purchase arms abroad. The Rebels, however, were adept at stripping battlefields and many of them fought with Northern arms.

As troops gained battle wisdom, the need for intensive training disappeared. Units were built around tough veterans who did not coddle recruits. Officers and noncoms taught their men to fight, ignoring recreation and off-time amusements.

Under this treatment, Yank and Rebel flourished. They learned fast, became self-sufficient, proved dependable, and emerged as first-rate fighting men, equal to any the world has ever seen.

Between engagements, soldiers found means of fighting monotony. In large camps, ball games, horse races, foot races, and even snowball fights satisfied the competitive instinct. Chess and checkers whiled away hours. Newspapers and paperback books passed from hand to hand until tattered. Band concerts and amateur shows were arranged regularly.

Vice never ran rampant through either army. Few cities in line of battle were large enough to boast organized red-light districts. Camp followers operated, but Civil War literature carries little mention of prostitution. Drinking was sporadic, as liquor was usually confined to officers' messes. Gambling never ceased, but low pay kept the stakes down.

The soldier of the 1860's, for all his toughness in battle, was both moral and sentimental. Most of the rank and file were away from home and its stern religious background for the first time. The lonesome sentry watching the rising moon (left) thought long and hard of those he left behind and put these memories into oversentimental music.

"Lorena," a sugarplum of a song, was probably most popular of the Civil War ballads. "Weeping Sad and Lonely," "The Vacant Chair," "All Quiet Along the Potomac" mixed tearful sorrow and devotion.

This excess of tearful tribulation may sound strange to modern ears, but it was a sentimental era. There was reason for sorrow. The Civil War had the highest proportionate casualty rate of any war in American history.

Yank and Rebel alike helped create that rate. Through four bitter years they fought bravely with their heads held high. They were good soldiers.

THE comparative luxury of barracks life vanished when troops went into the field. From that time on, shelters were based on government-issued canvas, arranged in ways limited only by the ingenuity of individual units.

At the war's beginning, several tent types existed but two were basic: the Sibley and the wedge. The first was large and bell-shaped, supported by a center pole. It could sleep 12 men but was unwieldy, hard to handle, and bulky to move. More popular was the wedge, an A-shaped structure supported by a ridgepole resting on two small poles driven into the ground. Such a tent accommodated four, five, or six people.

On the luxury level was the hospital or wall tent, with four upright sides. Occupants could stand erect in these, and move about in a small area.

In good weather, semipermanent camps consisted of wedge tents arranged in parallel lines, the ground between these lines becoming company streets. The company street was a common meeting ground (below left) where men met to gossip, clean rifles, take turns at barbering, and pass the time of day.

When winter came, if no move appeared imminent, the wedge-tent villages were transformed. Logs were joined to form low walls and tent canvas was then slung over these to make a roof. Fireplaces of mud and stones were built into one wall, and chimneys of barrels and fence pickets carried off the smoke (left).

More fastidious soldiers constructed California furnaces. These were rough fireboxes within the tents connected to long earthen tunnels that ran several feet beyond the tent walls to culminate in chimneys made of stacked up cans. Such devices carried fumes well beyond the tents.

Inside winterized shelters, occupants often dug well below ground level (to make more head room) and laid rough floors of logs or straw. Bunks and rude furniture were constructed.

When on the move and near actual battle, soldiers sought shelter in pairs. Each man carried a square of canvas, with buttons and buttonholes on its edges, called a shelter half. Two of these, buttoned together and supported by poles, made a tiny tent that would just cover two sleeping men (below). Yanks and Rebels both carried these, and were also equipped with ponchos or rubber blankets. The latter, folded, were laid on the ground inside the pup tents to break the chill from the earth. In times of extreme fatigue, bunkmates dispensed with tents altogether, stretching out on top of their rubber blankets with shelter halves over them.

SOLDIERS' rations were similar in North and South when war began. Theoretically, each man was entitled to about one pound of meat per day; a somewhat larger quantity of bread, flour, hardtack, or corn meal; and a generous allowance of coffee and sugar. These basic foods were to be supplemented by peas, potatoes, rice, molasses, and spices.

Theory never became fact. Crooked contractors, venal supply sergeants, inadequate transportation, and lack of preservation facilities soon killed off good intentions. As early as 1862, the Confederacy reduced the basic ration. Rebel and Yank learned to supplement their food with produce from the countryside.

Beef cattle on the hoof accompanied armies in the field. Whether the yield from these tough and stringy animals was good or bad depended on the quartermaster's luck as he stood in line to draw food for his unit.

Hardtack, a tough, plain flour-and-water biscuit, made up the staple bread ration. When fresh, it was edible and moderately sustaining. After long storage, the biscuits sheltered maggots and weevils.

Coffee made up for hardtack. It was the supreme luxury of the fighting man, and he consumed it in copious quantities. Union soldiers were well supplied with coffee; the Rebels were not so fortunate.

The food available was prepared by a variety of systems. In barracks or permanent camps, the company method predominated. Rations were cooked in quantity in a central building (top). The steaming buckets contained meat, potatoes, and coffee; and troops lined up with tin plates and cups for their share, plus bread and butter if these were available. KP details were rotated unless there was a permanent kitchen staff. Such a staff was often made up of contraband Negroes.

The mess plan of cooking was employed in the field, four to eight men making up each mess. Every soldier took his turn at cooking for his messmates (lower left). This was the usual procedure in semipermanent tent cities.

On the battlefield or on picket duty, it was every man for himself. The soldier made flour-and-water dough when possible. Threading this, along with pieces of meat, on a saber or ramrod (below, left), he toasted his dinner over a campfire. Scouts learned to watch for the twinkle of evening fires, a sure sign an enemy detachment was in the neighborhood.

To break the monotony of government rations, there was the sutler's store (bottom), roughly similar to the modern post exchange. The sutler was a civilian merchant who traveled with the troops by boat or wagon, pitching his tent and hanging up his shingle wherever he could. He sold delicacies: pies, oranges, lemons, fruitcake, liquor, plug tobacco, and cigars.

Charging what the traffic would bear, his prices were sky-high. Occasional semiofficial attempts were made by authorities to control sutler prices, but these were of little avail. Sutlers had few friends among the troops, but were suffered for the goods they handled. These traveling merchants were gold mines of gossip, and many were supposed to have acted as spies.

commanding officers did not. In North and South, minor infractions of rules and regulations were punished in similar ways (below).

Company punishments were planned to produce fatigue and aching muscles. A man might be made to walk a beat, carrying a heavy log along with a ball and chain. Another might stand on a barrel head or ride a sawhorse for hours at a time.

"Bucking" was popular with disciplinary officers. The soldier to be bucked sat on the ground with his knees drawn up. His hands, tied together, were slid well over his knees and a stick was run under his knees and over his arms. Bucked men were often gagged as well, a bayonet or stick being placed in the open mouth and secured by ties around the head.

Miscreants were tied to trees, or strung by their thumbs from tree branches so the toes barely touched the ground. Others were spread-eagled on spare wheels carried by artillery caissons and left in the sun. Flogging, though forbidden, was often described in contemporary letters.

The severity of company punishment was left to the discretion of the commanding officer. Serious offenses such as desertion or cowardice brought court-martial, and such punishments as prison, dishonorable discharge, or death.

SOLDIERS' privileges included the right to vote. Because of this franchise, they were assiduously wooed by politicians. Party workers traveled from camp to camp with electioneering posters. These were attentively read (above).

Some men were furloughed for the specific purpose of voting. Others cast their ballots in the field. The soldier vote was an important factor in the state elections of 1863 and the presidential election of 1864.

Politicians might woo soldiers, but their

THERE was always work to be done. As troops reached the fighting front, drills were forgotten and labor details became more important.

Care of the army mule, who provided transportation for equipment and supplies, was a never-ending job. This patient, obstinate beast was cursed, reviled, and abused, but always carefully shod (right) to keep him fit for duty.

Soldiers not tending animals worked on fortifications and entrenchments. Making gabions (right) was a typical occupation. The trunks of saplings were joined together and wrapped with pliable branches to make rough cylinders that could be filled with sand. Gabions were placed around cannon to serve as bulletproof armor in front of the gunners.

Digging became more important as the war progressed. The individual soldier, who fought over open fields in the beginning, soon began to find safety in the ground. In dangerous territory, commanders threw up defensive earthworks (right) when halts were called. During the great sieges, such as Vicksburg and Petersburg, both sides built complicated defense systems from mud, timber, and sandbags.

For their labors in the field, Yank and Rebel were theoretically paid at regular intervals, but the paymasters seldom appeared as scheduled. On the Union side, signing in for pay was an elaborate ceremony that might involve a roll call and review before the pay books were signed. Once this was done, the signatures were taken to Washington for review. At two-month intervals, a money-carrying major was supposed to appear to pay off the men (bottom).

The sums involved were small. At the war's beginning, a Union infantry private earned $11 per month. He was shortly raised to $13, and in 1864, to $16.

His Confederate counterpart started at $11 and received no raise until 1864 when he was given $18. By that time, however, Confederate money was almost worthless.

Officers fared somewhat better. A Federal infantry colonel received $95 base pay but was given extra sums for rations and body servants, raising his total to $194.

ON THE PENINSULA

IN THE spring of 1862, the Union launched a major effort in Virginia. Called the Peninsular Campaign, it was an unsuccessful attempt to capture Richmond. The outcome of the operation was largely determined by the character of the man who planned it, General McClellan (above.)

Brought to the capital by Lincoln shortly after Bull Run, made general-in-chief upon the retirement of Scott, McClellan's first task was to turn the mass of recruits that flooded Washington into an efficient fighting force. It was a job he did well.

The thirty-five-year-old general excelled at plans and training, discipline, paper work, and mounting tremendous reviews. True concern for his men's welfare brought him their admiration and respect. A handsome face, courtly manner, and firm seat on a horse made him a popular hero. To Robert E. Lee, he was the best of the Yankee generals.

But McClellan was an enigma. Often arrogant to superiors, he displayed overwhelming ambition and self-assurance. Procrastination was his greatest enemy. Having created a superb army, he was reluctant to commit it to battle.

McClellan's aptitude for avoiding action was a galling irritant to Lincoln in early 1862. The build-up of a tremendous army at Washington was no secret to either North or South. Union patriots wanted action and put pressure on Lincoln for an offensive.

The obvious target was the Army of Northern Virginia, encamped at Manassas Junction, dangerously near Washington. As McClellan dallied, the Rebels saw their time was running out. They burned and abandoned Manassas and withdrew to new positions behind the Rappahannock River. The Northern general-in-chief rode to the ruined junction March 8, claimed a bloodless victory, and returned to Washington.

Lincoln's patience was nearly exhausted. He proposed a plan of offensive action and ordered McClellan to carry it out or submit one of his own. The President favored direct overland attack on the enemy capital. McClellan vetoed Lincoln's ideas and countered with a grandiose scheme for moving his army to Virginia by water.

102

The proposal called for loading troops on transports at Washington, dropping down the Potomac into Chesapeake Bay, and landing at Fort Monroe on the tip of a peninsula formed by the York and James rivers. From the fort, the army would drive some seventy miles up the peninsula to Richmond.

The plan appeared to have merit. The Union would pick its own battleground, troops could move up good roads, and would have a secure line of retreat through Fort Monroe. Naval forces could guard the over-water supply line. Lincoln agreed to the project, stipulating that the general move by March 18, leaving behind a force sufficient to protect Washington from any Rebel thrust.

McClellan was temporarily relieved of over-all command and made general of the offensive force, the Army of the Potomac. Five corps were available. The I and V, under McDowell and Major General Nathaniel P. Banks, remained near Washington for screening operations. The remaining three, the II under Brigadier General Edwin V. Sumner, the III under Brigadier General Samuel P. Heintzelman, and the IV under Brigadier General Erasmus D. Keyes, all prepared for embarkation.

Four hundred vessels jockeyed at Potomac docks to load more than 100,000 men; 14,500 animals; and almost 350 guns. The over-water movement was uneventful and, as the enormous army began to disembark at Fort Monroe, McClellan arrived to take field command on April 2. Infantry, cavalry, artillery, and baggage trains moved out on the road to Richmond.

After making twenty miles, Union troops were abruptly halted by Rebel defenses built around Yorktown. At this old Colonial village, General John B. Magruder, with 13,000 men, held back McClellan's initial 53,000 for a month.

He did it by deception: marching troops back and forth to make them look triple their number, setting up logs as fake artillery, and generally bedazzling the Union general. Completely deceived, McClellan became overcautious. He halted, laid siege to Yorktown, and waited for his forces to build up.

Magruder held out as long as he thought prudent, then evacuated Yorktown on May 3, yielding command to the recently arrived General Joseph E. Johnston. As the Rebels fell back, McClellan pursued and fought them at Williamsburg. In this, the first real battle of the campaign, casualties for both sides totaled 3,900.

After Williamsburg, Johnston pulled back into the Richmond defenses. McClellan moved up the peninsula to establish his base at West Point, near the head of the York River.

Between the York and the city of Richmond runs a meandering river called the Chickahominy. McClellan placed some of his troops north of this stream, in a position to make contact with McDowell's I Corps, which Lincoln had promised to send overland as soon as possible.

The remaining Federal forces were deployed south of the Chickahominy, facing Richmond five miles away. In the evening, Yankee soldiers could hear bells from the churches and see their spires through the haze.

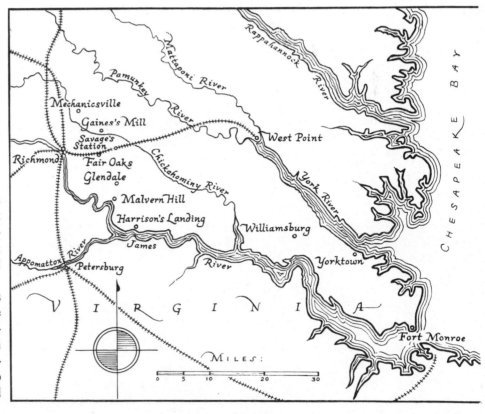

IN THE face of the enemy, McClellan again fell prey to unwarranted fear of Confederate strength and bombarded Lincoln with pleas for reinforcement. The President ordered McDowell south with 40,000 men. But mounting danger in the Shenandoah Valley forced Lincoln to cancel the order and McDowell never arrived.

McClellan's forces, however, continued to build up. For greater flexibility, he reformed his army. Taking one division each from the II, III, and IV Corps, he created two new corps, the V under Brigadier General Fitz-John Porter and the VI under Brigadier General William B. Franklin. When the reorganization was completed, the Union leader had two corps south of the Chickahominy near a railroad station called Fair Oaks, and the three remaining ones north of the stream.

The sight of a Union army split into two parts by a rapidly rising river was tempting to Confederate General Johnston, who saw a chance to apply superior pressure at a sensitive point. On May 31 he hurled 32,000 men at the 19,000 Yankees south of the Chickahominy to begin the two-day battle known as Fair Oaks or Seven Pines.

The initial attack pushed Union forces back. Across the river, Sumner heard the firing and anticipated a command to aid his comrades. McClellan gave the order and sixty-six-year-old General Sumner safely moved his forces over the stream to help check the Rebel advance.

The reinforcements saved the day, and a series of counterattacks on June 1 forced the Confederates to break off the action. Fair Oaks was considered a draw, although Union casualties topped 5,000 (below) and the Rebels lost approximately 6,100. Johnston was severely wounded in the action, and his services were lost to the South for some time. He was replaced by General Robert E. Lee, who retained command of the Army of Northern Virginia until the war's end.

Much of the Peninsular Campaign was fought over heavily wooded swamp country, and McClellan's soldiers learned to use the shelter of the trees to advantage. By mid-1862, the Army of the Potomac knew the value of cover and abandoned parade ground tactics on the battlefield.

LEE wanted information about McClellan's position, and on June 12, dispatched a force of 1,200 cavalry under General J. E. B. Stuart on a scouting mission. Three days' rations and sixty rounds of ammunition were issued to each man, and, for secrecy's sake, rumors were circulated to the effect that the expedition was bound for northern Virginia.

The force rode to Ashland, then turned east and moved well behind McClellan's troops. Fighting as they traveled, the horsemen got their information, cut up a railroad, and picked up prisoners.

Stuart was beginning the adventures that were to make a Confederate legend. Once the intelligence Lee requested was in hand, he went out on his own. Moving south, he crossed the peninsula, turned toward Richmond, and rode back into the capital. His trip had taken him completely around McClellan's army.

During "Stuart's Ride," Confederate cavalrymen skirmished with a division of the Fifth U.S. Cavalry at Tunstall's Station, but the engagement failed to halt the Rebel horsemen.

105

AFTER Fair Oaks, McClellan moved all troops but the V Corps south of the Chickahominy and built defensive positions between that river and a desolate area below it called White Oak Swamp. The Union leader had all but given up on McDowell's arrival, and rightly so. Clever Confederate feints so frightened Washington that McDowell was kept near the capital as a defensive screen.

McClellan was thinking in terms of moving his major base south across the peninsula to the James River. He had sent some supplies by water to Harrison's Landing, on the James, and had his men scout roads across the peninsula. Meanwhile, being only a few miles from Richmond, he dug in to wait and see what happened.

Lee, watching McClellan's static defense, called a council of war to plan aggressive action. With his top commanders, Major Generals Stonewall Jackson, James Longstreet, A. P. Hill, and D. H. Hill, he discussed his project. This involved throwing the bulk of his army against the Union V Corps, north of the Chickahominy. Once the corps was crushed, McClellan's base and communications would be so threatened that he would fall back rapidly.

There was one great risk. With the greater part of his force operating north of the river, Lee would be forced to leave a comparatively small group (20,000 men) standing between McClellan's 80,000 and Richmond. But Lee knew his opponent and trusted to McClellan's procrastination to avoid trouble south of the river. He was correct.

Southern troops struck on June 26 and the Battle of Mechanicsville developed. The V Corps fell back in order that night. This was the first of the series known as the Seven Days' Battles.

June 27 saw the second in the series, Gaines's Mill (above). Porter had taken up defensive positions along a creek and was there hit hard by A. P. Hill. He stemmed the tide of Hill's attack successfully, but Longstreet delivered another Confederate blow and Jackson came in to help.

Porter called for aid and received one division from Franklin. It was not enough. The V Corps broke, crossed the Chickahominy, and burned its bridges. That night McClellan decided to retreat across the peninsula to Harrison's Landing, along narrow roads through White Oak Swamp. On the twenty-eighth, as the Army of the Potomac was in motion, Lee repaired the bridges and started in pursuit.

The Union retreat, well planned and intelligently carried out, depended on strong rear-guard actions to hold off the Confederates. Savage's Station, on June 29, was the scene of the third engagement, but it was inconclusive. During the battle, the Union army destroyed its stores and finished crossing the swamp.

The fourth clash, Glendale, began on June 30 with an attack on the flank of McClellan's retreating troops. Through lagging staff work, the Rebels never committed enough men for victory. They were checked long enough for the Union army to reach an elevation called Malvern Hill.

As infantrymen lay awaiting enemy attack, Battery D, Fifth U.S. Artillery, blasted the enemy at the Battle of Glendale. Field guns, emplaced to take advantage of the terrain, fire from a crest. Behind them are the portable caissons, which carry ammunition and spare wheels for the cannon.

MALVERN HILL is a high, flat plateau looming up in front of Harrison's Landing and protecting it. At Malvern, on July 1, the Union army turned to fight Lee.

McClellan picked Porter and his V Corps to defend the height. The general was offered such troops as he wished along with the artillery of the entire army.

His defensive position was ideal. He had the military advantage of height. Swampy ground below forced the enemy to concentrate in a single area for attack. Porter's field guns were lined up hub to hub. There were siege cannon behind him and river gunboats on the James to back him up. And he had an army that had been beaten back but not defeated.

The latter fact was not clear to Lee, who thought he was facing an all-but-crushed enemy. The Confederate leader deployed his troops and ordered fourteen brigades to attack.

For most of the day, Rebel troops felt out Yankee positions. Skirmishers pushed forward and Confederate batteries sent an occasional shell over the Union line. Porter's men held their fire to conceal their strength and placement.

Lee attacked at 5:30. As Rebel troops moved out they met one of the severest artillery barrages of the war. Confederate infantry and artillery were blown to bits.

Brigade after brigade of riflemen came up the hill into a blanket of shrapnel, grape, and canister (right). Those who survived the Union guns were cut down by musket fire from the 14th New York, which received the brunt of the Rebel charge, and other regiments garrisoning the long defense line.

A few isolated Rebels reached the Union line, to be captured immediately, and Federal soldiers counterattacked from time to time in an effort to take Confederate colors. In a short while the attack crumbled. Lee withdrew at dusk, leaving more than 5,000 killed and wounded on the slopes.

Malvern Hill was a Union victory; but McClellan, despite the advice of his generals, made no attempt to follow up. He ordered the defensive positions abandoned and, by July 2, was encamped at Harrison's Landing. Lee withdrew to Richmond.

MCCLELLAN'S soldiers put the torch to their stores and brought wagon loads of wounded into Harrison's Landing (below). The Seven Days had been costly ones. Union casualties topped 15,000, while Confederate losses were over 20,000.

Neither side achieved victory. McClellan saw the Richmond steeples but failed to take the city. Lee saved his capital but was unable to destroy the Army of the Potomac.

That army was the finest force the Union had put together since war began. The fault lay not in the troops but in their handling, for it was McClellan's reluctance to risk his men that sounded the death knell of the campaign. Accurate figures are lacking, but it appears the Union general may have once had as many as 150,000 men while the peak Confederate strength was 95,000. McClellan, however, acted on the false asumption that the enemy numbered 200,000 or more.

Lee took risk after risk, but poor staff work and lack of coordination among his generals cost him dearly. His audacious plans were often shattered as out-of-position generals arrived hours late for crucial attacks. At Malvern Hill, the Southern leader had made a fatal tactical error.

To both governments, the Peninsular Campaign was an expensive failure. Lincoln and Davis called for full accountings from their leaders and began to plan their next moves.

Lee remained in the Richmond area. Freed from Federal siege, the capital's population rejoiced. McClellan called for reinforcements so he could open a new offensive. His request was refused, and in August he began to embark his troops so they could be used elsewhere.

JACKSON'S TERRITORY

DURING the Peninsular fighting, a magnificent action was taking place slightly north and west. It had a great deal to do with McClellan's defeat.

This was the Valley Campaign, today a classic in military textbooks. Stonewall Jackson, in this action, struck again and again at superior Union forces in the Shenandoah Valley. Over a three-month period he dazzled them, defeated them, and left them in helpless confusion as he withdrew.

One of the South's greatest officers, Jackson was a West Pointer who had fought in the Mexican War and taught artillery tactics at Virginia Military Institute. He was plain, unassuming, and shabby. Devoutly religious in a stern, Puritanical manner, he carried a Bible in his saddlebags, nestling up against the lemons he sucked in moments of contemplation. He was one of the greatest tacticians ever born.

Lee, running the military from Richmond, had need for such talent as McClellan began his gigantic move. Jackson's troops, some 20,000 in the Shenandoah Valley, were chosen to harry the North.

Union forces were in the area in strength.

McDowell, at Fredericksburg, had 40,000 men and was ready to join McClellan for the drive on Richmond. In the valley, opposing Jackson, was Banks with 20,000. He had the task of containing his Rebel opponent. To the west, in the mountains of western Virginia, Frémont (brought in from his former command in Missouri) had 15,000 men for an eventual push to the southwest.

McClellan had been calling for McDowell's 40,000 and stretched out his troops to meet them as they came overland. Lincoln, feeling Washington was reasonably secure, decided to let McDowell answer this request. To replace the Washington defense troops, a portion of Banks's force was removed from the valley.

Lee saw that McDowell's arrival to assist in the Peninsula Campaign would give McClellan overwhelming power. He ordered Jackson to move through the valley, attack the Federal forces, threaten Washington, and force Lincoln to call McDowell back.

Banks moved to chase Jackson from the valley. In early March, Jackson moved out of Winchester in the northern portion of the area, and Banks moved in.

The Shenandoah Valley Saw Much Fighting throughout the War
But Never Such Brilliant Tactical Movements as Those of Jackson

BANKS chased Jackson a short distance, then, feeling he had fled the valley, broke off the pursuit. The stage was set for Stonewall's offensive (lower right).

It came in a series of thunderbolts, smashing Union forces right and left. Daring, audacious, unorthodox, Jackson became a master at striking where least expected. His men covered the length of the valley five times in three months, following rail lines, crossing through gaps in the mountains, exploiting the element of surprise. For their speed in marching (up to forty miles in twenty-four hours) the troops were called "Jackson's foot cavalry."

Jackson hit Banks at Kernstown, March 23, and lost the battle. It was to be his only defeat, but he turned it into an advantage. Banks, frightened by the attack, called his troops back from Washington. Confederate strategy was working.

Banks started all over again to drive Jackson from the valley, and Frémont sent troops south toward Staunton. Stonewall entrained his men, let it be known they were going to Richmond, then secretly reversed his course at night and went west. He fought Frémont's men northwest of Staunton, May 8, and beat them.

In the next two weeks he crossed the valley again, drove far north, and fell upon a dumbfounded Banks at Front Royal and Winchester in late May. Banks was crushed and driven back all the way across the Potomac.

Now, as Lee had planned, Washington was truly alarmed. McDowell's advance to McClellan was canceled and half his men were sent to the valley to stamp out Jackson. A force from Banks was ordered to join a force from Frémont and back Jackson up against the Potomac. Stonewall slipped away.

The Rebel general was now more than a menace; he had become a seemingly indestructible force. Lincoln dispatched some 45,000 men to trap the valley fox.

McDowell's task force moved on Front Royal. Brigadier General James Shields drove south through the valley, east of the Massanutten Mountains, to cut off Jackson's retreat from the Potomac, while Frémont moved south, west of the mountains.

Stonewall raced them both and won. He picked his battleground at the upper, or southern, end of the valley and waited. On June 8, Frémont's detachment was soundly thrashed at Cross Keys (page 111). The following day, at Port Republic, one of Shields's columns was smashed.

Within a few days, Jackson (right) moved from the valley and joined Lee for the Seven Days' Battles. His brilliant footwork had tied up almost 100,000 Union soldiers for weeks and kept a substantial force from joining McClellan.

Jackson's tactical success largely derived from his own clear military principles:

"Always mystify, mislead, and surprise the enemy if possible; and when you strike and overcome him, never let up in the pursuit so long as your men have the strength to follow; for an army routed, if hotly pursued, becomes panic-stricken and can then be destroyed by half their number. . . . Never fight against heavy odds, if by any possible maneuvering you can hurl your own force on only a part, and that the weakest part, of your enemy and crush it."

113

LEE DEMOLISHES POPE

BY SUMMER of 1862 it was apparent the Union was winning in the west and losing in the east. Lincoln, thinking in terms of staff changes, looked to the Mississippi area for his appointments.

The President felt the need for a man in Washington to coordinate military affairs. There had been no such office since Mc-Clellan was detached to lead the Army of the Potomac. Halleck, with his bookish background of military theory and a string of western victories behind him, seemed a logical choice. He got the job July 11.

Scattered throughout Virginia were the armies of Frémont, Banks, and McDowell, which had chased Jackson in vain. Lincoln consolidated these forces into one group called the Army of Virginia. Pope (above), victor at New Madrid and Island No. 10, was called east and given command. Frémont resigned in a huff and faded from the war picture. The other generals held on to see what fate would bring.

It brought, in Pope, a brave but noisy braggart. After his West Point and Mexican War background, he had explored the West, as Frémont had. Success along the upper Mississippi made Pope a public figure, but the nation was soon sorely disappointed in his attempts at leadership in a major campaign.

It was Pope's misfortune to come up against the South's supreme champion. Lee (right) had come in during the middle of the Peninsular Campaign. From this time on, he was to lead the Army of Northern Virginia, finest fighting force in the Confederacy.

Lee's background was impeccable; he was of the "first families of Virginia" and his father, "Light-Horse Harry" Lee, had been a famous general.

Robert E. Lee, following West Point, became Chief Engineer of the field army that fought the Mexican War and, after that, Superintendent of the Military Academy. Love for his native Virginia kept him within the Confederacy he served so well.

He was near perfection in almost every way. Kind, courteous, loyal, generous, thoughtful, he became the idol of his men. For one so gentle, he was a superb warrior. His agile mind and the power of making quick decisions under pressure turned defeat into victory in many cases. Lee was audacious, taking a risk when the odds made it worth while; refraining from one if there was little to gain.

Together, Lee and Jackson made an overwhelming fighting team. This was the team Pope faced. But before action began, there was a certain jockeying of forces.

McClellan, upon the failure of the Peninsular Campaign, remained at Harrison's Landing, preparing to continue his offensive. He still cried for reinforcements, and Halleck went to visit him. As usual, McClellan was the victim of enormously inflated figures concerning the enemy's strength. He passed his concern on to Halleck.

It appeared from McClellan's estimates that Lee, at Richmond, had a force potentially greater than McClellan's and Pope's armies put together. Further, this force was between the two Union armies and theoretically could destroy each of them in turn.

The estimate was completely false, but it led to action. Halleck, over McClellan's bitter objections, told that general to abandon the attempt on Richmond and send his army north. There it would serve as a shield to Washington and, meanwhile, portions of it could be fed into Pope's new Army of Virginia.

The breakup of the huge fighting force began in August, troops going to Fredericksburg or Alexandria. Unit by unit, McClellan's men were siphoned off for other duties until he was a general without an army.

Lee had remained in Richmond, held there by the possibility of McClellan's striking for the city. He was watching his opponent closely and, seeing no signs of action, detached Stonewall Jackson to go up into Virginia and see what Pope was up to. When he saw McClellan begin to move out, Lee made preparations to join Jackson.

That general had already made contact with the enemy. Pope, gathering 50,000 men along the line of the Rappahannock, was pushing southwest toward Gordonsville, a rail junction connecting Richmond with the rich Shenandoah Valley. Jackson was below the Rapidan River, between Pope and Gordonsville, with 14,000 men. As he waited, he was sent a reinforcement of 10,000. Strengthened, he cautiously moved north.

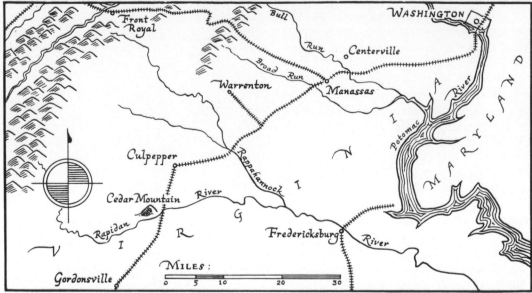

JACKSON'S force met Pope's at the foot of Cedar Mountain on August 9. Banks, of Pope's command, attacked at once and for a time held the advantage. Then Jackson flanked him, rolled up his line, and sent him reeling back under cover of his guns. Pope's men settled down along the Rapidan's northern bank. Jackson, not wishing to tangle with the entire Northern army, withdrew south of the river. The campaign to be known as Second Bull Run had begun.

When Lee moved to join Jackson, the Union cavalry spotted the advance and notified Pope, who retreated to make his defense line along the Rappahannock. Lee was coming north with all possible speed, anxious to engage Pope before reinforcements from McClellan's disbanding army were poured in. After he joined Jackson, his cavalry brought in a captured Yankee report showing Pope's forces would soon be increased until he had 100,000 men. Speedy Confederate action had become essential.

High water in the Rappahannock prevented Lee's crossing and made a perfect defense barrier for Pope. At this point Lee reacted characteristically, taking a long chance with a maneuver frowned on in textbooks: splitting your army in half in the face of a superior enemy.

Holding his own position, he sent Jackson and his troops up the Rappahannock, to the northwest, until they could find suitable fording places and cross the river. The Rebels went up river, crossed, and carried out a long, curving movement that placed them behind the Bull Run Mountains. The following day they came through Thoroughfare Gap in the mountains and fell upon Manassas Junction, scene of the first Civil War battle and now Pope's supply dump.

News of the depredations finally convinced Pope there was a major force in his rear, and he fell back on Manassas. Jackson had moved out a few miles and bivouacked to wait Lee.

Lee arrived to support Jackson, and Second Bull Run was fought on August 29 and 30. On the first day, Jackson exposed himself and awaited Pope's attack, which hit hard but did not break the Confederate line. Jackson, however, rearranged his defenses somewhat; and Pope, mistaking the movement, telegraphed Washington he had the Rebels on the run. The Union leader, at this late hour, was still unaware that Lee had come up and taken positions on Jackson's right flank.

On the thirtieth, as Pope renewed his attack, Lee released 30,000 men under Longstreet to send the Northern troops staggering back. Enfilading artillery fire and the infantry push ended the battle with a clean-cut victory for the South.

Inflicted a Crushing Defeat at the Scene of a Former Union Debacle

At Cedar Mountain (above) Jackson capitalized on his temporary numerical superiority to win a sharp victory. But at Second Bull Run, Union reinforcements, shown going into action below, could not swing the tide against the outnumbered but extremely well-generaled Confederates.

AMPHIBIOUS VICTORY

THE Union tasted stinging defeat in Virginia during 1862, but the war in Atlantic waters was going well for the North.

Hatteras Inlet had already been secured, a foothold on the threshold of North Carolina's inland coastal waters. The inlet opened into the vast waters of Pamlico Sound, not yet fully exploited by invading forces. North of Pamlico was Albemarle Sound, another inland area of equal importance.

A narrow neck of water called Croatan Sound connected the two, and Roanoke Island lay in the center of this passageway. To control the entire inland system, Northern forces would have to pass through Hatteras Inlet to Pamlico, then break through narrow Croatan Sound to Albemarle.

Lincoln and McClellan approved a major expedition under Brigadier General Ambrose E. Burnside. The general would have three brigades (15,000 men), and a big fleet under Flag Officer Louis M. Goldsborough.

Union contractors pulled together a flotilla that Burnside described as "motley," a considerable understatement. The need was for shallow-draught vessels that could maneuver easily in shoal waters. Eighty boats and ships were gathered.

The mongrel squadron assembled at Fort Monroe on January 9 to the sound of martial music. Morale was high among the troops.

On the eleventh, the fleet went to sea (below) and headed south. After a stormy passage, a rendezvous was made on the thirteenth off Hatteras Inlet.

There the storm increased, and before the vessels could gain the shelter of Pamlico Sound they were struck by gale winds. From the rigging of his vessel, Burnside rallied his men (left), and the flotilla rode through the disturbance with the loss of only two ships.

IMPROVISED dredging deepened Hatteras Inlet and the Burnside Expedition sailed through on February 4. Orders were given to advance on Roanoke Island the following day.

Confederate forces had constructed three small forts on the upper portion of Roanoke Island, to cover Croatan Sound. Opposite, on the mainland, was a battery of seven guns. In the sound itself, a group of piles and sunken ships partially obstructed the channel; and behind this barrier was the "mosquito fleet," a small group of lightly armed vessels.

Northern forces moved on February 5, were slowed by heavy weather, and engaged the enemy on the seventh. Naval vessels in the van engaged the forts all day and laid down fire on the Rebel fleet. One Confederate ship was destroyed; the rest, running out of ammunition, retreated to the inland harbor at Elizabeth City in Albemarle Sound.

As the fight went on, troops came ashore south of the forts, and the entire force was landed by midnight, to bivouac in a cold, cheerless rain. Southern forces had retreated up the island and taken up a defensive position across a swampy area that ran from shore to shore. A single causeway ran up the island through the swamp; where it reached the Rebel lines it was blocked by a small, three-gun fort.

On the morning of the eighth, the 25th Massachusetts led the advance and was joined by the 10th Connecticut in a frontal demonstration. Floundering through swampland, the 21st Massachusetts, 51st New York, and 9th New Jersey struck on the right. On the left, the 23rd and 27th Massachusetts with the 51st Pennsylvania drove through wooded marshes to put pressure on the enemy.

Shortly after the 4th Rhode Island and 9th New York came up, Union forces charged the earthwork from two positions and took the fort (right). Confederate soldiers retreating north were soon surrounded, and the engagement ended as an unqualified Yankee success. Union losses were small,

and the expedition captured five small forts with thirty-two heavy guns, along with 2,675 officers and men.

On February 10, the Union fleet entered Albemarle Sound and sailed to Elizabeth City in pursuit of the Confederate vessels that had withdrawn on the first day of action. They lay under the guns of a small battery. It was brushed aside by Yankee

ships, which captured or destroyed five of the six Rebel gunboats. Elizabeth City was taken, as were other towns; and the northernmost of the two great sounds fell under Union control.

Pamlico Sound, to the south, was open to Union shipping, but capture of important shore points was necessary before it could truly be classified as Northern-held territory.

121

MONITOR VS. VIRGINIA

WHILE Burnside planned his next move, the most famous naval battle in American history exploded a short distance away.

The scene was Hampton Roads, a huge naval basin lying between the mouth of the James River and Chesapeake Bay. Fort Monroe, major Union base for the Peninsular Campaign, lay just north of the roads. To the south, in Confederate hands, was Norfolk.

There, at the captured Gosport Navy Yard, Southern artisans had created one of the first major armor-plated warships. Christened *Virginia,* she was built around the hull and engines of the Union *Merrimac,* burned and sunk by the Yankees.

Raised and repaired, the one-time Federal ship was given a new superstructure in the shape of a casemate with slanted sides, covered by 2-inch iron plates. Through ports in the casemate peered six 9-inch Dahlgren guns and four more of lighter caliber. A 1,500-pound ram projected from the bow.

Awkward and ungainly, unable to negotiate rough waters, and with undependable engines, *Virginia* lacked speed and maneuverability. But she had slugging power and stamina on March 8, as she sallied forth from Norfolk.

Five Union ships lay in Hampton Roads: the steam frigates *Roanoke* and *Minnesota,* the sailing frigates *Congress, St. Lawrence,* and *Cumberland.* The latter carried twenty-four guns; the rest had forty or fifty each.

Virginia, under Flag Officer Franklin Buchanan, took on the fleet. *Cumberland* opened the action. Her shot bounced harmlessly off the 263-foot monster's iron flanks. *Virginia* backed; then, under a full head of steam, drove her ram deep into *Cumberland*'s side (above). As the Yankee ship reeled, Buchanan deluged her with shellfire and called for surrender. She refused, was rammed again, and sank.

Congress was run aground by her captain, after battling several small Confederate vessels that had accompanied *Virginia.* The latter stationed herself off the stern of the Federal ship and poured in hot shot until the white flag appeared.

Roanoke, St. Lawrence, and *Minnesota*

all ran aground. After a leisurely survey of the situation, which she controlled completely, *Virginia* chose *Minnesota* as her next target and buffeted her heavily until nightfall. Union fire from all ships engaged had been heavy, but even full broadsides left no more than slight dents in *Virginia*'s armor.

She returned to Norfolk for the night; and the North, in the face of this revolution in naval warfare, reached near panic. At a special Cabinet meeting, War Secretary Edward M. Stanton warned that the new ironclad could fight every Union vessel, one at a time, and win; then move in to attack Northern seaports and river bases.

While the Cabinet worried and wondered, the North's own contribution to the naval revolution was on her way to Hampton Roads. When *Virginia* came out the following morning to finish the job, a strange new vessel was guarding *Minnesota*.

Monitor, produced by the fertile brain of designer John Ericsson and the speedy work of a Greenpoint, New York, shipyard, was no match for *Virginia* in size or ugliness. She measured 172 feet, had a flat deck almost flush with the water, a tiny pilot house near the bow, and a slender smokestack near the stern. Amidships was a heavy, round, revolving turret carrying twin 11-inch Dahlgren guns and covered with 8-inch armor plate.

The dawn fog burned off on March 9; and as *Virginia* steamed forth, *Monitor,* under Lieutenant John L. Worden, moved to attack. *Virginia* opened fire; her shells bounced off. *Monitor* replied with the heavier guns whose projectiles cracked her opponent's 22-inch wooden casing under the armor and sent crew members spinning but caused no permanent damage.

The pounding lasted two hours. *Virginia* tried ignoring *Monitor* and turned her attention to *Minnesota.* Her guns damaged the wooden ship severely; but each time she tried to ram, *Monitor* appeared and fought her off (below). Twice *Virginia* went aground and *Monitor* poured in solid shot and shell with no effect. The Rebel vessel had broken her steel ram on *Cumberland*; nevertheless she tried head-on collision with her smaller opponent, but *Monitor* was more agile and twisted away easily.

Tired crews and commanders called it a draw; and each ship steamed to its dock, battered but unconquered. They did not fight again. Both ships were innovations; each appeared to have met its match.

In a matter of weeks, Johnston retreated, Norfolk had to be abandoned, and *Virginia* was blown up. *Monitor* perished in a storm off Cape Hatteras at the end of the year.

Direct attack with bayonet and clubbed rifle (above) carried Rebel positions at New Berne. Rain and fog limited artillery support, and the one-day action turned into an infantry affair. Burnside's troops, the "Coast Division," had a solid string of victories behind them, and their superb morale helped make the frontal assault a success. Capture of Forts Macon and Pulaski depended not on infantry but on siege artillery, such as the heavy mortar (below) shown being sighted for use.

Coastal Operations in 1862 Resulted in an Impressive List of Successful Engagements for the Northern Amphibious Forces

AT ROANOKE, eighty miles from the battle, a Union officer heard gunfire from the *Monitor-Virginia* combat March 9 as he watched Burnside prepare for the strike at Pamlico Sound. Picked as the main objective was New Berne, a city some distance up the Neuse River, with rail connections to the interior.

On March 11, thirteen regiments of infantry with six artillery pieces embarked, their ships making a rendezvous with naval vessels at Hatteras Inlet. By the thirteenth, foot soldiers were going ashore sixteen miles below their target.

The main Rebel defense line lay between a railroad and the river. Yankee gunboats in the Neuse cooperated with the infantry. On the fourteenth, Union soldiers attacked in three main groups. It was give-and-take fighting throughout the day, but the Northern combination of strength and morale proved too much for defending troops. The North won the field.

The last important point in the North Carolina coastal system was Fort Macon, on Bogue Island, forty miles southeast of New Berne. It controlled the southern inlet to Pamlico Sound.

As the Confederate leader in the fort refused surrender demands, Union troops moved artillery into positions surrounding the island and laid siege to the work. There was no hope for the Rebels, who surrendered March 26, giving the Union command of a vast complex of inland waterways.

Farther south, General Sherman of the Du Pont Expedition that had taken Port Royal, South Carolina, was preparing a siege against Fort Pulaski, Georgia, guarding the entrance to the Savannah River. Pulaski lay on Cockspur Island in the river's mouth, surrounded by Tybee, Bird, Venus, and other islets. Mortars and rifled artillery emplaced on these islands smashed the fort's walls to bits and it fell to Union forces April 11.

The only major Northern setback in this area during spring and summer took place at James Island, South Carolina, which helped guard Fort Sumter. Union troops attacked Confederate works in the Battle of Secessionville June 16 and were repulsed (below).

UNIFORMS

Wilson's Zouaves.   Duryee's Zouaves.   De Kalb Zouaves.   Rhode Island Officer.   Massachusetts Officer.   Michigan Officer.   Colonel New
     Pennsylvania Officer.

2d New York State Militia.   1st Michigan.   13th Brooklyn.   12th New York.   Marine Artillery, R. I.   New York 55th Zouave Corps.   1st Pennsylva

UNIFORMS OF UNITED STATES

New Jersey Officer. - New York Line Officer.   Rhode Island Artillery Officer.   Hawkins's Zouaves.   M'Chesney's Zouaves.   Fire Zouaves.

achusetts 6th.   5th Massachusetts.   71st New York,   New Jersey State Militia,   1st Rhode Island,   5th New York German Rifles,

VOLUNTEERS AND STATE MILITIA.

129

INFANTRY.   UNIFORMS OF REGULAR CONFEDERATE TROOPS.   CAVALRY.   ARTILLERY.

Volunteer Infantry of Virginia.   1st Regiment Maryland Line.   South Carolina Light Infantry.   Hampton Legion.   Rockingham Battery Artillery.   Gentlemen of the First Independent Cavalry.

Louisiana Zouaves.   Washington Artillery of New Orleans.   Mississippi Rifles.   Heavy Infantry of Georgia.   Alabama Light Infantry.   Marine Battery, Manassas Junction.

Black Horse Cavalry.   Dragoon Guards, 14th Regt., Va. Cavalry.   Mounted Rifles, North Carolina.   Virginia Cadets.   Greyson Dare-devils.   Kentucky Rifle Brigade.   Tennessee Sharp-shooters.

CONFEDERATE ARMY.

131

A BEWILDERING variety of uniforms appeared on the backs of soldiers reporting for duty in 1861. Unprepared for the tremendous influx, the Union Quartermaster Department could not clothe all volunteers. The newly created Confederate government was even more helpless.

Individual states came to the rescue. As companies were raised for service within their boundaries, state governments procured and issued handsome uniforms that dazzled the belles of Washington and Richmond when the war was young.

Standardization did not then exist. Northern troops (pages 128-129) wore clothes displaying a wide variety of color and cut. Men from Wisconsin often came in cadet gray. Certain Vermonters wore gray trimmed in emerald green. New York, Massachusetts, and Pennsylvania favored blue.

Southern soldiers (pages 130-131) made much the same appearance. Gray, blue, and brown uniforms came from Georgia and the Carolinas. The Kentucky Rifles reached the scene in fringed buckskin.

Many units turned to the colorful European armies for inspiration. There was a rash of Zouaves in North and South, wearing uniforms patterned after the famed French Algerian units. The Zouave craze started before the war as Elmer Ellsworth raised a militia unit in Chicago during 1860, dressed it in the French manner, and sent it touring the country to give fancy drill exhibitions.

Ellsworth's Zouaves became famous and their baggy trousers, red sashes, and distinctive headgear were known far and wide. When war broke out, Ellsworth became a colonel and brought his men into service as the 11th New York Volunteers, or Fire Zouaves (pages 126-127). Additional Zouave units soon blossomed above and below the Mason-Dixon line. Many were content to copy Ellsworth's uniforms. A few learned the complicated Zouave drills, as well.

Other organizations became equally picturesque. Highlanders appeared in plaid "trews," leaving their kilts at home. The Garibaldi Guard dressed in imitation of the Italian Bersaglieri. There were Chasseurs, Blenker's Germans, and an outfit christened

Les Enfants Perdu. The Brooklyn Phalanx, Sixth Pennsylvania Lancers, and Zagonyi Rifles of the North were to challenge, on the field of battle, such Southern units as the Louisiana Tigers, Tennessee Sharpshooters, Black Horse Cavalry, and the Hampton Legion.

High-spirited companies in glamorous clothes gladdened the public eye and appeared regularly in the illustrated papers. They were in the minority. Many fighting men arrived in their own clothes, to be outfitted when uniforms were available. If this was impossible, they would fight in everyday dress.

By 1863, the Union had a standardized blue uniform. Issued to each infantry soldier were a cap, blouse, overcoat, dress coat, trousers, shirts, drawers, socks, and shoes. Equipment included a shelter half (two of these buttoned together would make a pup tent for two men), woolen blanket, rubber blanket, knapsack, haversack for food and canteen. Cavalrymen and artillerymen received somewhat similar issue, but were given boots instead of shoes.

The Confederacy attempted somewhat the same procedure but severe shortages hampered their quartermasters. Clothes and equipment were passed out when received; when this was exhausted, soldiers made do on their own. Confederate gray cloth was soon used up and homespun material, dyed a butternut brown, took its place. Rebel soldiers, who had been "Johnnies" and "graybacks" to the Yankees, became "butternuts" late in the war.

Hot weather and heavy marching taught troops to eliminate equipment in a hurry. Dress coats and overcoats disappeared. Knapsacks were often discarded and possessions carried in blanket rolls that could be slung over the shoulder. Sometimes the haversack was thrown away and the knapsack retained, or the canteen disposed of in favor of a tin cup. Cooking and eating utensils of the simplest kind accompanied each man.

Veteran Union troops took on the appearance of the soldier shown at upper left, his equipment pared to a minimum, the battered coffeepot probably the most valuable of what remained. Confederate vet-

erans (lower left) traveled even lighter. A hat, shirt, trousers, and shoes made up their clothing; a knife and a tin cup their cooking gear; a blanket or two their shelter.

Under the stress of travel and combat, the white belts of the 7th New York and the trim blouses of the Hampton Legion went into oblivion. In the field, troops lacked distinction. Because this could cause confusion, corps badges came into being among Northern troops, reputedly at the instigation of Major General Philip Kearny.

In March, 1863, General Joseph Hooker ordered the badges to be worn by members of the Army of the Potomac, and the custom soon spread. Each corps had a patch of distinctive shape, and differences in color indicated divisions within the corps (page 134). The blazes were worn on the cap.

Pets accompanied every army. Dogs were common; raccoons, turtles, and owls more exotic. Perhaps the best-known pet was "Old Abe," the bald eagle who, on his special perch, went into battle with the 8th Wisconsin (upper right).

133

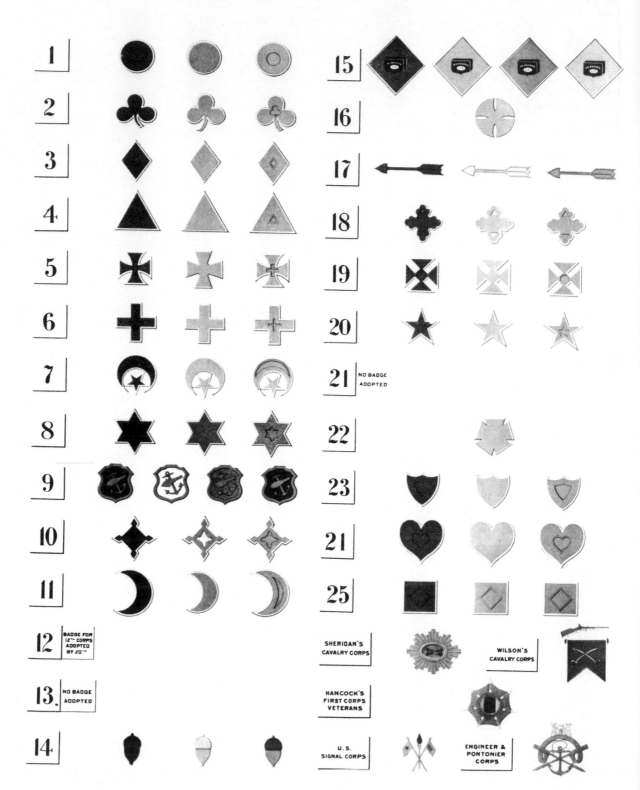

134

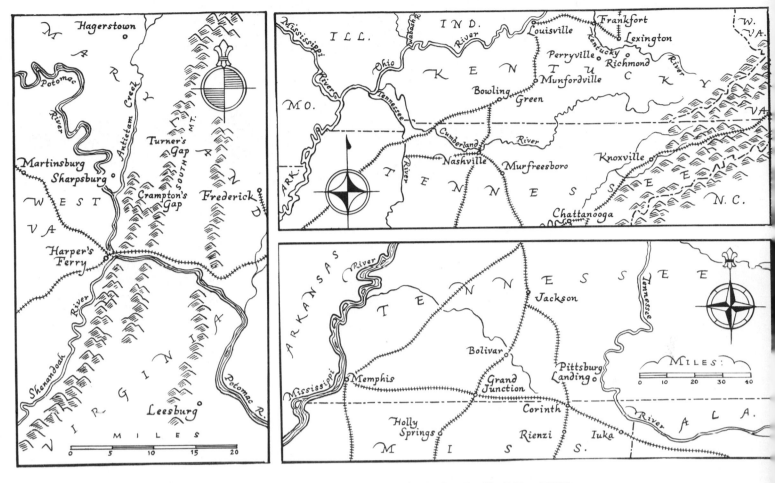

THE TRIPLE OFFENSIVE

ID-1862 saw the Confederacy in high spirits. McClellan's irresistible force had been stopped. The leader who replaced him had been soundly thrashed. In the east, the South was winning the war.

In late summer and early autumn, the South planned three offensives. One was to invade Maryland, one Kentucky, one to roll up Grant's army.

The North was disheartened. News of western victories had a tonic effect on the nation, but the eyes of the people were drawn almost magnetically to the Virginia battlefield. There, between Washington and Richmond, victory was a necessity if the Northern will to fight was not to be drained away by failure after failure.

In this area, Lincoln had a disillusioned army and no commander. Pope, after Second Bull Run, had been relieved and sent west to watch over the Indians.

To solve his command troubles, the President turned once again to McClellan and asked him to reconstitute the Army of the Potomac that he had trained so well and used so badly. The choice was unpopular in the Cabinet. But the venom in high places was drowned by the cheers of troops who venerated their former leader. With McClellan once more in the saddle, morale was restored and the Army of the Potomac became a dangerous fighting body.

Union troubles in the west lay not in command but in troop dispersion. Halleck had collected an enormous force to take Corinth; before leaving for his Washington command post he broke it up.

Buell, with the Army of the Cumberland, had been sent to capture Chattanooga. Sherman, with one division, was at Memphis. Grant remained in western Tennessee, guarding the rail line from Memphis to Corinth.

Upon losing Corinth, Beauregard had been replaced by General Braxton Bragg, who now commanded troops facing Grant. He knew of the Northern troops' dispersion and made plans accordingly.

DRIVE TO MARYLAND

THE Southern public saw Lee's invasion of Maryland in September as the most important move of the Confederate triple offensive. One success in the eastern theater of war was still worth two in the west, and the South was collecting eastern victories like scalps.

Also, there was a strong feeling that Maryland secretly sympathized with the South and would welcome Rebel troops as deliverers rather than invaders. And the state was rich in food and forage for men and beasts.

A successful push through Maryland would bring Lee into Pennsylvania. From there he could frighten the North by advancing on Philadelphia, or flanking Baltimore and Washington. Such a move might have far-reaching effects on the peace party already calling for an end to the war.

There was also the reaction abroad to consider. If Southern troops could show they

were not only far from being overrun but actually capable of powerful offensive action, France and England might recognize the South officially.

Lee crossed the Potomac into Maryland on September 5 and moved north to Frederick. One bubble burst then and there: the Marylanders did not immediately rally round the Confederate flag.

Sentiment, at the moment, was less important than tactical considerations. West of Frederick lay a sixty-five-mile barrier called South Mountain, a continuation of the Blue Ridge. Two main passes pierced it: Turner's Gap and, a few miles south, Crampton's Gap.

Lee planned to take his forces through the gaps, which would bring him to the northern limit of the Shenandoah Valley. This would be his line of communication as he moved north.

There was one drawback: Harper's Ferry lay in the valley, athwart the potential communication line. The general determined to capture its garrison of 10,000 Yankees and rifle it of supplies.

This was a dangerous move, for he knew McClellan would pursue him and possibly catch him with his army separated. But he knew his man. Banking on McClellan's caution, Lee marched his troops through Crampton's Gap and split them up.

Special Order 191 sent two Rebel forces south to take Harper's Ferry from two sides, stationed another force at Boonsboro, and indicated Lee himself with Longstreet would proceed north to Hagerstown, near the Pennsylvania border.

With the reborn Army of the Potomac, McClellan was following on Lee's heels and arrived in Frederick, to plaudits from the citizenry, soon after Lee's departure. There, the gods of war smiled on the Union leader. A lost copy of Special Order 191, wrapped around three cigars, was found in a field by an enlisted man, who bucked it to McClellan. The general had Lee's complete plans,

saw the Southern army was split four ways, and needed only to speed through the gaps to catch and destroy Lee's troops piecemeal.

The old fear of numbers held him back. McClellan had 87,000 men against Lee's 51,000. But his intelligence estimate indicated the Southern force to be tremendous, and Little Mac once again had "the slows." After losing twenty-four hours in deliberation, he marched against the passes September 14.

Lee, seeing McClellan's intention, moved like a whirlwind. Longstreet was sent flying back from Hagerstown, D. H. Hill ordered from Boonsboro to protect the outlets of the passes, Stonewall Jackson ordered up from Harper's Ferry.

The Confederates got artillery up and peppered the oncoming Union forces (left) throughout the fourteenth, in the Battle of South Mountain. All day they held the passes, gaining precious time; but by evening the Union had won through and McClellan was face to face with Lee.

McClellan showed extreme caution in committing his troops on South Mountain, but once they faced the enemy, fighting became a vicious hand-to-hand affair. The Rebels suffered 2,700 casualties to the Union's 1,800, but they held back a vastly superior Union force for an entire day.

To open the battle, Hooker's troops easily forded Antietam Creek (above). When Burnside attempted to cross the stream farther south, he met Rebel fire controlling paths leading to the bridge. Units of the 51st New York and 51st Pennsylvania made the first crossing (below).

Tremendous Concentration of Firepower in a Relatively Small Area Made Antietam a Death Trap for Thousands of Men

LEE arrived from Hagerstown to hear Harper's Ferry was his. Jackson had sent the prisoners south and was moving at top speed to join his commander. This information canceled any thought of retreat. Lee and Jackson, the old team, were going to hold their ground.

As his battleground, the Confederate leader picked an area around the little town of Sharpsburg. Antietam Creek lay across his front, a natural barrier the Federals would have to cross before attacking. A few miles to his rear was the Potomac.

Lee had two large commands to fight the battle: one under Longstreet, the other under Jackson. McClellan had six corps: the I under Major General Joseph Hooker, the II led by Sumner, the V under Fitz-John Porter, the VI under Franklin (this one had an extra division attached), the IX led by Burnside, and the XII under Major General Joseph K. F. Mansfield.

With overpowering odds on his side, McClellan once again presented his opponent with the gift of time. By the fifteenth, the passes through South Mountain were secure. The Union army did not move; neither did it venture forth until the evening of the sixteenth, for reconnaissance.

On either of these two wasted days, Lee could have been hit while his troops were still scattered. Jackson's men were driving up from Harper's Ferry but had not arrived.

Confederate troops were strung out from north to south behind the line of Antietam Creek, taking advantage of forest, orchard, and gently rolling country; but there were no truly strong defense points in the entire position. On the evening of the sixteenth, Union patrols probed the defenses, then fell back to await the morning.

McClellan planned his main attack on the Confederate left, at the top of the Rebel defenses, with another attack on the Confederate right. When both flanks had been rolled back, he intended to use reserves to smash through the center.

On the morning of the seventeenth, just after dawn, Hooker struck the Rebel left with stunning force. Slashing through woods and a cornfield, his men moved up the slope to an old Dunker Church, pressing back the Confederates of Jackson's command. Advancing elements hidden in the corn lost alignment for a few moments and, when they emerged, were caught in flanking fire. Men fell by hundreds under concentrated rifle and artillery fire, and the Union pulled back.

Rallying again, the Yankees came forward. Jackson called for support. When it arrived, he smashed the Union advance back once more, Federal troops taking losses up to 25 per cent. In little more than an hour, the first phase of the battle was over, Rebels and Yankees holding positions on each side of the Hagerstown road and blazing away across the highway.

Hooker struck at 6:00 A.M. At seven-thirty, Mansfield came to his assistance, hitting the enemy slightly below Hooker's position. Mansfield was killed almost immediately, but his troops pressed on in the face of murderous Confederate fire. Rebel reserves under Brigadier General John B. Hood stopped the Yankee advance, but only for a moment. As Hood reeled back, the Federals took the Dunker Church, the high point in the immediate vicinity. Farther advance was checked by Stuart and D. H. Hill, who fell on the Northern flanks.

Both sides paused to breathe. Union losses were severe. Rebel losses were worse.

By nine McClellan sent in another corps, under Sumner. With a portion of his force, the Union general smashed against the Dunker Church sector and was gaining ground when disaster struck his flank and rear. Two new Confederate divisions under Major General Lafayette McLaws and Brigadier General John G. Walker slashed the Union column and trapped it, knocking out 2,000 men in a matter of minutes. Fresh from Harper's Ferry, Walker and McLaws pursued the fleeing Federals, who took shelter under their artillery.

THE attack of Walker and McLaws ended the first phase of Antietam, along the Confederate left, about ten o'clock. By ten-thirty action was resumed in the Rebel center.

Sumner had lost part of his force. Two divisions were left. These he ordered against D. H. Hill, whose men had taken shelter in a sunken road south of the Dunker Church. This became the battle's crux—a vantage point from which the Southern troops poured out a murderous fire. The road was christened "Bloody Lane," and before it Union bodies piled up in mounds.

Major General Israel B. Richardson, commanding Sumner's First Division (New England and New York troops) led the push against this wall of fire. Adroit maneuvering put his men on the Confederate flank. As they fired down Bloody Lane, the entrenchment became heaped with Confederate bodies, and the Rebel line broke and ran. Richardson was killed; his men pursued the enemy, assisted by new troops from Franklin's VI Corps. Fighting carried into the streets of Sharpsburg, but the pace was more than mortal man could stand. By noon, the blazing battle for the Rebel center died out.

One more engagement was to come. At the south of the battle line, on the Confederate right, a bridge spanned Antietam Creek. During the morning, Burnside had made several attempts to move his IX Corps over the structure but was heavily repulsed each time. By afternoon, most of the force opposing him had been put into the battle to the north, and he crossed the stream.

Burnside's crossing was made at 1:00 P.M. It took two more hours until the incoming troops were arranged to his satisfaction. By three, the fresh Union force moved out to take high ground commanding Sharpsburg and infiltrate the town (upper right).

Once more, time played into Confederate hands. A. P. Hill, after a gruelling seventeen-mile march from Harper's Ferry, came up to strike Burnside's flank in the nick of time. The red-shirted commander pressed his men vigorously and Burnside fell back,

calling upon McClellan for reinforcements. The situation was stalemated as the sun went down to end the long day's battle.

Lee was fought out. Night would give him time to pull the remnants of his army together and fall back across the Potomac. Losses were enormous on both sides, but McClellan had almost two fresh corps for battle the following day, to bring certain defeat to the Confederates.

There was no action on the morrow. Neither was there retreat. All day long on the eighteenth, Lee collected his torn and battered forces and awaited McClellan's at-

tack. The Army of Northern Virginia did not flee from its foe, and Robert E. Lee was standing his ground. It was an audacious dare and a colossal bluff. It worked.

Victory could have been McClellan's for the taking. He stalled and called for reinforcements, in the familiar pattern. It was the last piece of procrastination in his military career.

On the night of the eighteenth, Lee moved back across the Potomac onto friendly soil. McClellan did not pursue.

The Battle of Antietam (called Sharpsburg in the South), on September 17, was the bloodiest single day of the war. From sunrise to sunset, almost 24,000 men fell on the field. Of these, 4,800 were killed. Many received wounds that later proved fatal. Losses were about equally divided between the opposing sides.

The North counted Antietam a victory, for the Maryland invasion had been stemmed and the Confederate offensive halted. The victory was incomplete. Once again, the Army of Northern Virginia had escaped. It could hardly be called intact, but it was an army in being, capable of being restored to its former power.

ATTACK IN KENTUCKY

Munfordville was fortified by Federal troops to protect a river crossing, and Bragg (top), while moving through Kentucky, dispatched a force to take the location. Union fire hurled the Rebels back for a brief time as the Yankees refused a surrender demand. Bragg sent reinforcements and on September 14 the outnumbered garrison was forced to cease fire and capitulate.

GENERAL Bragg created a daring plan that, like Lee's, had political overtones. He would withdraw troops from central Mississippi, move them to Mobile, Alabama, and there put them on trains for Chattanooga. From the Tennessee city, he could invade Kentucky, which would rise to greet its liberators.

The long rail movement was successful, and Bragg beat Buell to Chattanooga. Buell had been plagued by raids upon his rail lines by two of the South's best partisan cavalry leaders, Nathan Bedford Forrest and John Hunt Morgan.

Bragg left Chattanooga with 27,000 men on August 28. He was to have effective assistance from Major General Edmund Kirby Smith, who made a separate attack from east Tennessee, crossed the Kentucky border, and captured Richmond on August 30. By September 2, he had Lexington, and his scouts were probing for Louisville and even Cincinnati, Ohio, as he waited for Bragg.

That general was driving north for Louisville. Buell, alerted at last, was reaching for the same objective, marching somewhat to the west of Bragg.

At Munfordville, the Rebel leader captured a Union garrison, then halted. Instead of taking Louisville, or fighting Buell, Bragg moved northeast toward Frankfort, Kentucky's capital. There he was to rendezvous with Kirby Smith and carry out the political part of his mission, the installation of a Confederate governor in the state.

Bragg's deflection of course enabled Buell to enter Louisville (above), to the immense relief of its inhabitants. It also cost Bragg the campaign. The new governor was installed with proper ceremony, but Kentuckians did not rise to join Confederate ranks as expected. Guns brought north to arm them lay unused.

As the Southern leaders dabbled in politics, Buell himself weathered a political storm, then moved to meet the enemy and cut off possible retreat. Dry weather had reduced the water supply of both armies, and pickets, seeking pools in a creek bed, clashed, warning Bragg that Buell was almost upon him.

Miscalculating enemy strength, Bragg attacked near Perryville on October 8. In a fierce battle, he gained ground, only to be pushed back as Union strength was felt. With 3,100 killed and wounded, Bragg abandoned the state and retired to Tennessee. The second Confederate offensive had failed.

143

ACTION IN MISSISSIPPI

GRANT and the Army of the Tennessee held the Memphis-Corinth railroad with forces at those cities and others farther north at Bolivar and Jackson. Stretched almost to its limit, the army was further weakened by troops drawn off to go to Buell's assistance.

Against the defense line was to break the third Southern offensive, under Major Generals Earl Van Dorn and Sterling Price. Both were in Mississippi, the former near Vicksburg, the latter at Tupelo. Between them, they had over 30,000 men.

In September they moved north, and Price occupied the Mississippi city of Iuka, about twenty miles southeast of Corinth and practically in Grant's front yard. The Union leader had not determined enemy strategy but decided to strike swiftly, while the Rebel forces were separated.

Major General William S. Rosecrans left Corinth with 9,000 men and moved south of Iuka to strike from below; Major General E. O. C. Ord, with about the same strength, was to come in from the north. Rosecrans struck September 19 and Price fought back hard (above). Ord was late and did not join the battle, which lasted until dark. That night, Southern troops made their escape from the area and joined Van Dorn. Union attempts at pursuit were foiled by heavily wooded country.

The next Confederate drive was for larger stakes. In Van Dorn's words:

"I determined to attempt Corinth. I had a reasonable hope of success. Field returns at Ripley showed my strength to be about 22,000 men. Rosecrans at Corinth had about 15,000, with about 8,000 additional men at outposts, from 12 to 15 miles distant. I might surprise him and carry the place before these troops could be brought in . . . it was necessary that this blow should be sudden and decisive."

Rosecrans, commanding at Corinth, knew of Van Dorn's plans and prepared for attack. The town was protected by two concentric series of fortifications started by Beauregard and partially completed by Rosecrans. The Union leader posted three divisions in the outer works to await the Rebels.

They struck hard, on the Union left, October 3; and fighting spread across the entire front. In the Yankee center, troops slammed back the Rebel charge and poured out in pursuit of the enemy. Speedy action on the part of Southern leaders sent their forces pouring into the hole thus temporarily opened; and the Rebels found themselves taking Corinth's defenders in the flank. Union men hung on; but enfilading fire was too much, and they slowly fell back from the outer defense perimeter. By nightfall they retired into the inner works and darkness halted the battle. Van Dorn counted the day a victory.

October 4 broke hot and clear, the thermometer at 94 as Van Dorn's skirmishers advanced to feel out Yankee defenses. Confederate strategy was to strike the Union left and divert power to that area; then send Price storming through the middle.

Stiff fire held back the Rebels on the left

as Price made his move. Yankee artillery wreaked havoc on wave after wave of assaulting infantry and broke the charge, but Rebel soldiers penetrated positions on the Union right and entered Corinth.

A street battle found its way to Rosecrans' headquarters, but Van Dorn was weakening fast and Union reserves pushed him out of the city (below) just as fresh Yankee troops came down from the north. The Confederate army fell back, defeated.

Corinth was a hard-fought battle in which great individual bravery was apparent. The sides had about 22,000 men each, but fortifications and their reserves to the north gave the Yankees the advantage.

Union losses totaled 2,500. Confederate casualties were 4,200. Van Dorn lost his command. The third and last Confederate offensive ended in defeat.

EMANCIPATION

FAILURE of the Confederate triple offensive brought military operations to a near halt; and autumn, 1862, was a comparatively tranquil period for North and South. The major event of this time was a political one. On September 22, Lincoln issued the Emancipation Proclamation.

Its essence stated "That on the 1st day of January, A.D. 1863, all persons held as slaves within any state or designated part of a state the people whereof shall then be in rebellion against the United States shall then be, thence-forward and forever free. . . ."

In simple terms, Lincoln's proclamation said a formal order would be issued at the start of the following year, freeing slaves in the Confederacy. On face value, the document seemed relatively worthless, for it could not be enforced until Federal troops penetrated Confederate territory. But the proclamation had powerful overtones.

When the war began, Lincoln pointed out his major aim was saving the Union, and he promised not to interfere with the Southern way of life. The Emancipation Proclamation

did away with the promise. Abolition of slavery had become a major issue, and this fact was formally declared to the world.

The President had planned his move for a long time. His own opinion of slavery as a moral wrong was a contributing factor. Need for a single cause to unite the North, in the face of military defeats, spurred the action. The effect abroad had been considered. England and France were sympathetic to the South, giving it financial and military aid. Once slavery had been made a major war issue, neither could afford to throw its prestige behind a nation that fought to retain that outmoded, barbarous institution.

Lincoln discussed emancipation with his Cabinet before he issued the document. Seward made one point: If the decree were issued while the North was in retreat, it might be looked on as a last, despairing cry for help. Wait for a Union victory, was Seward's advice, then issue the proclamation on the heels of it.

Antietam gave Lincoln his chance. Calling his Cabinet together, he stated his resolve:

146

"Gentlemen, I have, as you are aware, thought a great deal about the relation of this war to slavery, and you all remember that, several weeks ago, I read to you an order that I had prepared upon the subject, which, on account of objections made by some of you, was not issued . . . When the rebel army was at Frederick I determined, as soon as it should be driven out of Maryland, to issue a proclamation of emancipation such as I thought most likely to be useful. I said nothing to any one, but I made a promise to myself and to my Maker. The rebel army is now driven out, and I am going to fulfill that promise. I have got you together to hear what I have written down. I do not wish your advice about the main matter, for that I have determined for myself."

Minor changes were suggested by the Cabinet, and Lincoln made them. The government sat back to watch results.

They were not all good. The South became united as never before. In the North, opinion was split. Republicans lost heavily in the off-year elections, and the Democrats picked up thirty-two seats in the House of Representatives, possibly as a result of the proclamation.

Overseas, reaction was all the President hoped for. Liberals and progressives showered Lincoln with messages of congratulations, and a great mass meeting in London praised the American President highly. In the face of such popular opinion, foreign governments could no longer openly espouse the Confederacy.

With the proclamation behind him, Lincoln settled back again to the business of war. Lee was in the Shenandoah Valley, at Winchester, refitting and reorganizing his army. Jackson and Longstreet were made lieutenant generals and each officially put in charge of a corps.

McClellan, still deluded by Lee's phantom numerical superiority, would not advance. In late October, with more than 100,000 men, he crossed the Potomac and began to grope for the Confederate army in Virginia.

Lincoln's Cabinet at the time of the Emancipation Proclamation is shown at upper left, posed with Victorian rigor. Members, from left to right, included Edwin M. Stanton, War; Salmon P. Chase, Treasury; Gideon Welles, Navy; William H. Seward, State (seated in foreground); Caleb B. Smith, Interior; Montgomery Blair, Postmaster General; Edward Bates, Attorney General.

While Lee was resting in Virginia, he sent Jeb Stuart's cavalry on a raid deep into Yankee territory. Taking 1,800 men, the Rebel cavalier rode north through the Shenandoah Valley, crossed the Potomac into Maryland, penetrated Pennsylvania as far as Chambersburg, and came home.

FREDERICKSBURG

LINCOLN tolerated McClellan's apathy in the face of decision for more than a year. He cajoled, pleaded, and commanded, with little effect. Rudeness and insubordination were overlooked, in hope the mercurial general would produce victories.

In early November, the President's patience cracked, and McClellan was relieved of duty. Hearing the news, Lee expressed regret. "We always understood each other so well," he said. "I fear they may continue to make these changes till they find someone I don't understand."

Burnside (above) took over the Army of the Potomac. He was a flashily handsome man with elaborate whiskers that became a national fad, and a silver tongue. Burnside attended West Point, fought in the Mexican War, helped run a railroad, and invented a rifle before 1861. In the war he fought at Bull Run and captained the successful expedition against North Carolina coastal waters. He came late into battle at Antietam and showed no great drive when he arrived. Burnside appeared to have some knowledge of strategy; he was no tactician.

The North was calling for action as the new leader took over, and he proposed a drive southeast to take the city of Fredericksburg, then a continuation of the drive to Richmond. The plan was simple, unsubtle, and obvious. Its success depended on reaching Fredericksburg before Lee discovered the plan.

The Colonial city that was Burnside's objective lies just below the Rappahannock River, a major waterway running southeast from the Blue Ridge Mountains to empty into Chesapeake Bay. At Fredericksburg, the line of the river is almost from north to south, and the city occupies the western bank. It is in a shallow plain along the river bank, but the ground rises to heights back of the town. Across the stream, on the eastern bank, is the little settlement of Falmouth, on a plain near the river, backed up by rising land known locally as Stafford Heights.

While Northern strategy was being planned, the Army of the Potomac lay near Warrenton, a little south of Manassas. Scarcely thirty miles to the southwest, Confederate pickets guarded the fringes of their army at Culpepper Court House. This was the eastern end of the Rebel force; the rest of it stretched west in a thin line that ran over the Blue Ridge into the Shenandoah Valley.

Lee's strength had been built up during the rest period, and he had about 72,000 men ready for battle in two corps, the I

148

under Longstreet, the II under Jackson. The Confederate corps was a much larger unit than its Federal counterpart.

Burnside had six corps, 106,000 men, organized under a newly-devised structural plan. They were assembled in the Right Grand Division under Sumner, the Center Grand Division led by Hooker, and the Left Grand Division under Franklin.

Northern troops moved out in mid-November, reached the Fredericksburg area, and went into camp at Stafford Heights, across the river from the city. Lee's cavalry picked up the move, and the Rebel general sent Longstreet, with two divisions, to occupy the ground above Fredericksburg and keep an eye on the Yankees.

It gradually became apparent that the entire Army of the Potomac was on the move, and a major battle impended. Lee pulled his men back across the mountains and sent the Army of Northern Virginia into the Fredericksburg sector.

By late November, the two armies faced each other across the Rappahannock, a formidable barrier. Lee held Fredericksburg and the heights behind it; Burnside the little settlement of Falmouth and the high ground that backed it up. Completely lost to the North was the element of surprise. Victory would have to come from a pitched battle.

Burnside's first move depended entirely on his ability to lay pontoon bridges across the Rappahannock so he could strike the enemy. At this point, the Northern services of supply halted the campaign. No pontoons appeared. Red tape or muddleheadedness had misdirected the heavy wooden boats. It was more than two weeks before cumbersome wagons approached (below), bearing the pontoons that could make crossing the river a reality.

Burnside (mounted, in foreground) laid down a powerful barrage on Fredericksburg, throwing tons of metal into the city, but without wiping out the sharpshooters who were holding up his engineers. Volunteer storming parties crossed the river in pontoons to eliminate the Rebel menace.

WHILE Yankee generals awaited their pontoons and fretted for action, Confederate forces used the twenty-odd days presented them to erect an awesome defense system.

Just north of Fredericksburg the hills begin at the river and run around behind the town in a crescent. Lee pulled most of his troops out of Fredericksburg and set up his defense system on Taylor's Hill, Marye's Heights, and Telegraph Hill, all part of the gently rolling slopes. Longstreet's men looked down on Fredericksburg; Jackson's were below the city where the ridges began to level off. On the extreme Confederate right, to close the gap between hills and river, Stuart's cavalry was posted. One brigade, Mississippi troops under Brigadier General William Barksdale, remained in the city.

In front of Marye's Heights, a canal and drainage ditch marked the end of the plain and the start of rising ground. Behind the ditch was an old sunken road with a shoulder-high stone wall in front of it. Longstreet put some 2,500 men in back of this natural barrier.

Across the Rappahannock, Brigadier General Henry J. Hunt, the Union artillery chief, placed 147 guns on Stafford Heights. They could not reach Rebel hilltop positions, but commanded the city and flat ground that led to the slopes.

Two Southern cannon shots from Marye's Heights on the morning of December 11 signaled that Union troops were about to make their river crossing. Coming to the river's edge, they launched their pontoons, anchored them, and began construction of planked roadways over the wooden scows.

As the temporary bridges reached out into the Rappahannock opposite the town, Barksdale's Mississippi sharpshooters opened fire on the engineers from their foxholes in

Rugged Terrain and Twenty Days' Labor Enabled the Rebel Army to Build a Magnificent Defense System above Fredericksburg

Fredericksburg. Federals toppled into the river and new soldiers came up to continue the construction.

Burnside ordered Hunt's artillery to open on the city with every available gun. For more than one hour the barrage continued, making the earth tremble with concussion. Union shells blew old Colonial buildings to bits, set fire to wooden structures, and gradually leveled the city.

Southern sharpshooters lay face down in their holes and most of them escaped injury. As the barrage lifted and Burnside sent his men forward with the pontoons again, Rebel fire lashed out as before.

Control of the city by troops on the ground was the only answer to this stalemate to Federal forces. Sumner piled his men into boats and sent them across the river. Many men used pontoons, rowing them across (below). As the Yankees landed, Longstreet pulled back his sharpshooters.

Sumner's men, their bridgehead secured, streamed into smoking Fredericksburg and warmed themselves at the embers of de-

stroyed buildings. For the rest of the day, and most of the next, Yankees poured into the ruined city.

Below the city, Federal forces had an easier time. Franklin's soldiers laid their bridges without encountering major resistance, although ice in the river created obstacles. On the eleventh and twelfth, the Northern force crossed in strength.

By evening of the twelfth, the "grand divisions" of Sumner and Franklin were in battle positions on Confederate-held soil. Some from Hooker's division were with them; the rest remained across the river in reserve.

Burnside's original plan had been to strike hard below the city (away from the highest hills and the well-defended sunken road) in his first attack. He changed his mind during the night and ordered only a limited offensive to take place in this area the following day.

Major General George G. Meade, with one division, was to open the ball. Two more divisions were to follow him for support.

AS OPPOSING troops moved into position, they ran into menacing weather. Snow, sleet, and icy winds kept men close to their fires. On the morning of December 13, fog shrouded the forces, who moved phantomlike in a weird, unearthly setting.

Longstreet, high on a hilltop, saw the mist burn off at ten o'clock and looked down at the panorama spread out before him:

"Franklin's 40,000 men, reinforced by two divisions of Hooker's grand division, were in front of Jackson's 30,000. The flags of the Federals fluttered gayly, the polished arms shone brightly in the sunlight, and the beautiful uniforms of the buoyant troops gave to the scene the air of a holiday occasion rather than the spectacle of a great army about to be thrown into the tumult of battle. From my place on Lee's Hill I could see almost every soldier Franklin had, and a splendid array it was. But off in the distance was Jackson's ragged infantry, and beyond was Stuart's battered cavalry, with their soiled hats and yellow butternut suits, a striking contrast to the handsomely equipped troops of the Federals."

The scenic tintype vanished with the mist. Meade struck on Jackson's front, south of the city. He was brought up short by artillery fire from twenty-one-year-old Major John Pelham, a Confederate youth who was a wizard with cannon. Yankee guns across the river took up the fight and silenced Rebel artillery. Meade then punched a salient in the Southern line but lacked the strength to exploit it and was stopped by Generals Jubal A. Early and A. P. Hill.

At Fredericksburg, Sumner and Hooker hurled their men against the ditch and sunken road protecting Marye's Heights (right). The first wave was stopped dead by stinging fire from well-protected Rebels in their entrenchments.

The second wave met a similar fate. So did the third. Oncoming soldiers tripped over fallen comrades and picked their way through the groaning wounded.

Six charges were made against rifle fire from behind the stone wall and plunging

artillery fire from the heights. Assaulting men walked into murder on December 13. They had no chance; they had not had a chance since the attack against impregnable positions had been planned.

Longstreet saw it all:

"Before the well-directed fire of Cobb's brigade, the Federals had fallen like the steady dripping of rain from the eaves of a house. . . . The dead were piled sometimes three deep, and when morning broke, the spectacle that we saw upon the battle-field was one of the most distressing I ever wit-

nessed. The charges had been desperate and bloody but utterly hopeless."

Night on the battleground was a thing of terror. Wounded men froze to death on the cold ground. A Union officer heard ". . . a smothered moan that seemed to come from distances beyond reach of the natural sense, a wail so far and deep and wide, as if a thousand discords were flowing together into a key-note weird, unearthly, terrible to hear and bear yet startling with its nearness. . . ."

Burnside's stubbornness and inflexibility carried him to utter, brutal defeat. Ordering rank after rank into the very jaws of death cost him almost 13,000 men (the Rebels lost less than half that number).

For two days, the general held his ground, making frenzied plans for attacking again to wipe his record clean. He was disuaded by cooler heads and moved back across the river.

Soundly whipped by the Army of Northern Virginia, the Army of the Potomac retreated through slush, snow, and mud. It was the nation's best-trained fighting force; its men were brave and experienced; but leadership was woefully lacking.

153

ROSECRANS VS. BRAGG

FOLLOWING the unsuccessful expedition into Kentucky, Bragg led his Confederates to Murfreesboro in the central portion of west Tennessee and went into camp. Thirty miles northwest, the Army of the Cumberland was in quarters at Nashville.

A new commander took charge: Rosecrans, the victor at Corinth, chosen to replace Buell, despite some objections in Washington. Buell's reluctance to tackle east Tennessee had exhausted the patience of Lincoln and Halleck.

Rosecrans (above) was a West Point graduate and served as an engineer in both military and civilian life. A genial, hearty man, his book learning was impressive, as was his conduct on the battlefield. The troops were for him.

Rosecrans' superiors in the capital did not appear to share this regard. Once in office, the general displayed the same reluctance to advance that had brought about Buell's dismissal. He would move, he said, once sufficient supplies had been accumulated, and all the Washington telegrams in the world would not hurry him.

There was logic in his attitude, but it was hard for anyone but a field commander to understand. The Yankee general occupied an area in which Rebel cavalry was having a field day. Horsemen, regular and partisan alike, made sweeping raids on Rosecrans' supply lines, destroying provisions and slashing communications.

Forrest went west to annoy Grant; Morgan, now a brigadier general, operated in the Tennessee-Kentucky country with special attention to trains and wagon columns supplying the Army of the Cumberland. It was because of this constant danger to communications that Rosecrans insisted on building up his stores before moving on Bragg.

When the build-up was completed to Rosecrans' satisfaction, he began his offensive, leaving Nashville on December 26. As he moved, Brigadier General Joseph Wheeler, Bragg's cavalry chief, circled behind the massive Yankee columns in a whirlwind raid. While advance units of the Union forces were taking positions at Murfreesboro on December 29, Wheeler's 2,500 struck their rear, capturing 1,000 prisoners and most of the army's meat.

December 30 saw Rosecrans on his chosen battleground northwest of Murfreesboro. Between the city and the Union troops, Stone's River ran north and south. It was a shallow stream, easy to ford.

Bragg chose the river as, roughly, his defense line. His force numbered 35,000 in two corps under Generals Leonidas Polk and William J. Hardee. One additional division was attached.

Most of Bragg's men were deployed west of the river. Hardee was to the south, on the Confederate left. Polk held the center and right. On the extreme right, some Confederate troops lay east of Stone's River.

Rosecrans faced Bragg with 41,000 in three corps, called Right Wing, Center Wing, and Left Wing. Major General Alexander McDowell McCook held the Right Wing, to the south, facing the Confederate left. Major General George H. Thomas commanded the Center Wing; Major General Thomas L. Crittenden, the Left.

Rosecrans and Bragg had similar plans. Each intended to strike the other's right flank. The first to move would probably win.

On December 31, at dawn, Hardee hit the Union right with sickening force. His 20,000 smashed two divisions and threw them hopelessly out of position. The Federal center held firm, acting as a pivot on which the Yankee line was swung back like a minute hand moving from six to nine o'clock.

The third division of McCook, Brigadier General Philip H. Sheridan commanding, stopped the Rebel advance after much ground had been lost. Thomas, from the center, moved in to help Sheridan. Crittenden started from the north, his offensive plans canceled.

Sheridan moved his artillery into frontline positions for point-blank fire with canister and grape. He ordered a counterattack, and his troops lunged with fixed bayonets. Rosecrans, behind the lines, fed in troops as rapidly as they arrived. Hardee's powerful offensive halted.

By midday, Sheridan's men, short of ammunition, were forced back as the battle slowed. At dawn the Union line ran from north to south. Hardee's drive had doubled it back on itself so it formed a V pointing south. If Bragg could crack the point of the V, he could split the Federals in half and roll one big segment up against the river.

Rebel reserves were called up and formed for the major attack, which came at 2:00 P.M. Thomas, commanding the Union defenses, held his ground under heavy pressure. Over and over again, his men hurled back the Rebels. Crittenden's men streamed in to help. Sheridan fell on the Rebel flank. There was even a weary Union counterattack as the winter night came down.

Both armies rested and succored their wounded as Bragg telegraphed news of a New Year's victory to Richmond.

The 78th Pennsylvania and 21st Ohio capture a Rebel battery of two 12-pound Napoleons, two howitzers, and a 6-pound rifled cannon by direct assault. A Union soldier bayonets the color bearer of the 26th Tennessee in the arm as he reaches for the battle flag, a prized combat trophy.

BRAGG spoke too soon. The Union had been smashed back and severely drubbed, but not broken. New Year's Eve saw a council of war over candlelight in the Federal tents. Many of Rosecrans' staff urged retreat. Thomas and Sheridan fought against it and carried the day.

No action took place on New Year's Day. At the northern sector of the line, a Union division and two additional brigades crossed Stone's River and took up positions on the eastern bank. Bragg's cavalry, meanwhile, noticed activity along the road to Nashville and reported the Union army was retreating.

On January 2, Bragg found the Federal force east of the river, in an excellent position to flank him. Surprised, he sent Breckinridge to drive the Yankees back.

The Rebel attack came with a rush and bowled over Yankee troops. As they were being forced into the river, pursued by the victorious Rebels, a thundering artillery barrage broke out. Major John Mendenhall placed fifty-eight Union guns on a high bank west of the river, so situated that they could pour down fire into Rebel ranks on the eastern shore. The barrage, at the rate of a hundred shells per minute, blasted the Confederate advance.

Union soldiers rallied. As they pressed Breckinridge back, Thomas prepared for a general advance. Brigadier General James S. Negley ordered his men to ford the river and assist their comrades on the eastern bank. The 18th and 21st Ohio, and the 19th Illinois, swept through the stream (left) to break up the Rebel push.

Bragg re-formed his forces and threw them in to halt the Federal rally, but it was too late. Renewed in strength, the Yankees fanned out. The Confederate general called for retreat.

Both sides claimed victory at Murfreesboro. The North took the city but at tremendous cost, and Bragg fell back thirty-five miles, south to Tullahoma.

Casualties, in proportion to the number of troops engaged, were shocking. Rosecrans lost 13,000 men, more than 25 per cent of his force; Bragg's casualties almost reached 12,000, a loss of more than 30 per cent of his army.

157

WEAPONS

Gilbert Gaul

THE Civil War was a rifleman's war. Expert use of artillery often helped bring victory, but in the long run, the infantry remained queen of battles. Union snipers (above) on their lonely vigils, or Confederate companies beating back Yankee attacks (right), found the guns they carried with them to be their best friends.

Firearms available in North and South at the war's beginning varied widely in type and quality. In the early days, purchases from abroad increased the variety of rifles and muskets in the field. Ammunition wagons were forced to carry five or more different kinds of cartridges, and critical shortages developed at crucial times.

In 1862, the North achieved a satisfactory degree of standardization, and by the following year was able to discontinue foreign purchase. Indirectly, the Confederates reached the same standardization by stripping battlefields of Northern arms.

The basic weapon manufactured in the North and used by both sides was the Springfield rifle, model 1861. This was a muzzle-loader, fired by percussion cap, shooting a .58 caliber bullet. It was an accurate gun with high enough muzzle velocity to give it solid hitting power.

The grooves in its rifled bore gave the 1861 model accuracy and penetration. Its projectile was a Minié ball, a lead slug with a conical nose and a hole in its tail. When the rifle was fired, gas from the explosion entered the hole and expanded the ball slightly, squeezing the soft lead into the spiraled grooves.

The squeezing process guaranteed that the projectile would pick up rotation from the grooves. The spinning motion kept the ball on a true course. Expansion of the Minié ball's base also made a tight seal within the barrel, so there was little gas leakage. Because of this, the bullet was pushed from the barrel with the full force of the powder explosion.

The Minié ball used in the Springfield was more than one-half inch in diameter and about an inch long. It could kill at half a mile. The soft lead expanded when it hit bone, and caused a terrible wound.

The Springfield was accurate up to 250

or 300 yards, and a good man could get off two shots per minute. To achieve this speed, a soldier had to work fast, for there was much to be done before his rifle could be fired.

Springfield ammunition was one-piece, a paper cartridge containing powder and ball. In action, the infantryman tore the cartridge open with his teeth, poured the powder down the barrel, pushed in the bullet with his thumb, drew his ramrod and forced the projectile down, put the ramrod back in its tube, pulled back the hammer, put a percussion cap on the nipple beneath the hammer, and was ready for firing.

The Springfield 1861 was popular with both Yankees and Confederates, as were the later models of 1863 and 1864. Earlier Springfields, model of 1855, were used at the start of the war by the North but their specialized priming systems functioned poorly in wet weather.

Antiquated smoothbore muskets, caliber .69, were carried by many Southern soldiers in 1861. Some Rebels got .54 caliber rifles.

Such arms were eventually replaced by captured Springfields and British .577 caliber Enfields. The Confederacy bought 400,000 of these dependable rifles, and the North also purchased them in large numbers.

Breech-loading rifles, some of them repeaters, were available in 1861, but found small favor with Colonel James W. Ripley, the Union Chief of Ordnance. His objections mentioned their large initial price, complicated mechanisms, the need for special ammunition, and the possibility the troops would burn ammunition too fast because the rifles fired rapidly.

Despite objections, the breech-loaders found their way into the Union army, many purchased by states or individuals, and eventually, by the Ordnance Department. Rebel soldiers complained that the Yankees loaded their repeaters on Sunday and shot them all week.

Famous breech-loaders were the Sharps single-shot, the Spencer, carrying seven cartridges in its magazine, and the Henry, which held fifteen shells at a time.

THE rumble of field artillery as it went "into battery" to set up its guns and open fire (upper left) was a reassuring sound to foot troops. Horse-drawn field guns, on light, wheeled carriages, accompanied the infantry into battle. Artillerymen rode their guns and the ammunition-carrying caissons (lower left); there were a few batteries of "horse artillery," in which every man had his own mount.

As with small arms, field guns varied in kind, depending on whether or not their barrels were rifled. Especially favored by both armies were the 3-inch U.S. rifle, made of wrought iron and firing a 10-pound shot, and the Napoleon 12-pounder, which had a bronze barrel.

The 3-inch rifle far outranged the Napoleon, was more accurate, and delivered its shell with greater hitting power. But gunners had trouble with projectiles. Some shells, coated with lead to insure a tight seal within the gun, left lead particles behind to foul the grooves. Those shells that carried copper rotating bands (which theoretically expanded into the grooves at the moment of firing) often malfunctioned.

Smoothbore Napoleons were murderous at close range. Their bronze construction made them tough and they wore well in the field.

Rifles and Napoleons both fired solid shot, useful against enemy guns and fortifications. Both could also handle exploding shells, some filled with shrapnel balls. The smoothbore Napoleons could efficiently employ grape and canister. These were cases carrying slugs or iron balls. They were blown open by the firing charge, scattering the small projectiles like shotgun pellets. At ranges of a few hundred yards, case shot could cut troops to shreds.

Case shot from the Napoleons was effective to about 700 yards. Loaded with other projectiles, the guns had only about half the range of the 3-inch rifles. Nevertheless, McClellan's chief of artillery specified that two-thirds of the guns for the Peninsular Campaign be these smoothbores.

Similar in appearance to field artillery, but heavier and built on sturdier carriages, was siege artillery (below). Trains of this weighty ordnance, which could fire projectiles up to 100 pounds and more, were drawn into position so the guns could hammer enemy fortifications.

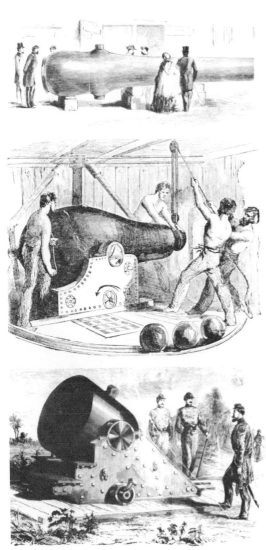

TRULY big guns made their mark during the Civil War. Seacoast forts were defended by huge cannon, and troops attacking such structures employed guns that threw an impressive weight of metal. Ironclads and monitors carried monster weapons.

The famous Confederate floating battery used against Fort Sumter (opposite page, below) was armed with 32- and 42-pounders. Coastal citadels like Sumter were often defended by Columbiads (opposite page, above). These were 8-, 10-, and 12-inch guns, some of which could hurl a 128-pound shell 5,000 yards.

Massive weapons were difficult to move and demanded special carriages. Within forts, the barbette mount, with a traverse carriage, was often used, as on the 8-inch howitzers shown below. Such guns were positioned to fire just over the top of a protecting parapet. Small wheels, running on a semicircular track behind the gun, enabled it to be pivoted over a wide arc.

Proud of its gigantic guns, the North's Ordnance Department occasionally displayed its creations. The public gathered in awe to see exhibitions of such weapons as (left, top to bottom) a Rodman gun, a 15-inch monster destined for a monitor turret, and a 13-inch mortar of the type used to hurl projectiles into the Rebel lines at Petersburg.

FACED with a rapidly growing Union navy, the Confederacy went underwater to cut the enemy fleet down to size. A group of ingenious weapons for use against ships sprang from Southern hands.

Mines, usually called "torpedoes," were widely used. Commander Matthew F. Maury, after pleading his case for months, was put in charge of a bureau responsible for underwater warfare and given a budget to develop his weapons.

Rebel torpedoes, made from beer kegs, old boilers, demijohns, or barrels, came into being. Filled with powder, they hung beneath or just at the surface and were exploded by percussion caps set off by passing vessels. Barrel torpedoes (lower right) were used in pairs. Joined by cable or chain, two barrels (with powder-filled boilers attached underwater) floated downstream to entangle Union ships.

Some Confederate torpedoes were exploded chemically, the shock of contact breaking a tube of sulphuric acid that set off the detonation. Others were attached to electric wires running to shore. Observers watched until Union ships neared the torpedo, then sent current through the wires to cause the explosion.

By the war's end, the Federal fleet had worked out torpedo sweeping techniques to clear explosive-strewn rivers. Areas such as the entrance to Mobile Bay were heavily mined by the Rebels, and the monitor *Tecumseh* met death there. Other monitors, *Milwaukee* and *Osage*, suffered a like fate in later days. In all, Confederate torpedoes sank thirty-one Union ships including seven ironclads.

Submarines played a part in the Southern attempt to neutralize Yankee shipping. The first crude craft were driven by propellers turned by hand cranks. When submerged, the craft obtained air through a rubber tube floating on the surface (bottom). In theory, the submarines were to come up under an enemy ship and attach a torpedo with a delayed fuse to the vessel's hull through a waterproof gasket, then escape before the explosion.

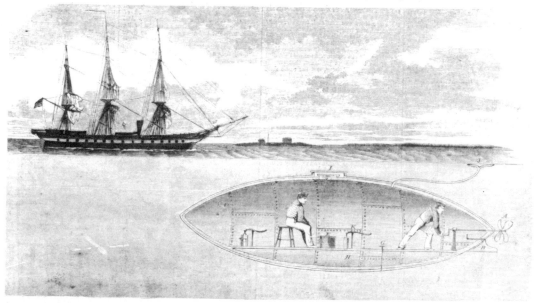

166

1863

VICKSBURG BESIEGED

FOR the first six months of 1863, Union forces in the west strove for a major objective: complete control of the Mississippi River.

The only obstacle remaining was a stretch of water between Confederate-held Vicksburg on the east bank, and Port Hudson, Louisiana, two hundred river-miles to the south. This water area was the link joining Louisiana, Texas, and Arkansas with the Confederate states to the east.

Across this part of the Mississippi poured food, men, and munitions to be transshipped to points throughout the Confederacy. Union control of this river line would isolate the three western states and slow their flood of supplies to a trickle.

The key to the area was Vicksburg, magnificently endowed for defensive fighting. Facing the river, the city sat on a chain of two-hundred-foot bluffs that ran for miles along the bank. Behind the city, the bluffs sloped sharply into an area split by ravines and dotted with patches of heavy woods.

Lieutenant General John C. Pemberton, defending the Vicksburg area, made the most of the natural strong points. From the cliff along the river front, forty heavy guns frowned down on passing craft. Above and below the city, miniature forts emplaced in the bluff were connected by a semicircular line of artillery positions and rifle pits.

North of these man-made defenses, an immense natural shield protected Vicksburg in the form of eight thousand square miles of swamp, bayou, and inundated forest. This huge, desolate area, the lowland between the Mississippi and Yazoo rivers, was impenetrable by troops in any number and could not sustain heavy equipment.

Musing over these barriers in autumn, 1862, Grant prepared his first plan. He would move south along the Mississippi Central Railroad and draw Pemberton's troops out to battle. Simultaneously, Sherman would leave Memphis with 30,000 men and go down the Mississippi by boat, land in the Vicksburg area, and strike the skeletal force Pemberton left behind.

Rebel action shattered the plan. As Grant was moving, Confederate General Earl Van Dorn swept up behind him, took his main base at Holly Springs on December 20, burned stores, and disrupted communications. At the same time, Nathan Bedford Forrest's hard-riding cavalry raided Union communications in western Tennessee, destroying railroad tracks and tearing down telegraph lines. Grant's army stalled, and he lost touch with Sherman.

The latter had moved down river (with the aid of Admiral David D. Porter's fleet), then turned and gone up the Yazoo, disembarking to attack Chickasaw Bluffs on Vicksburg's northern flank. Alert and well-protected troops poured down a withering fire. Sherman, stopped in his tracks, retreated after losing 1,700 men on December 28 and 29.

In this action, and under Grant's orders, Sherman had used troops of General John A. McClernand, a political appointee in constant disagreement with Grant. McClernand sped down river to rejoin the force that had been spirited away from him, raged at Sherman, then paused to consider a suggestion from the latter.

It was this: re-embark, move up the Mississippi and Arkansas rivers, and attack Fort Hindman at Arkansas Post. The post was forty miles up the Arkansas River, which joins the Mississippi seventy-five miles north of Vicksburg. From Fort Hindman, Sherman argued, Confederates could come down river to threaten Union shipping on the big river. A quick thrust could capture the fort and perhaps help the nation forget the Chickasaw Bluffs repulse.

McClernand was short on military ability but long on opportunism. Seeing a chance to command an amphibious force, with almost certain victory, he adopted the plan immediately.

On January 4, McClernand officially took over the expedition. His troops were named "Army of the Mississippi," which was his own idea, and divided into two corps under Sherman and Brigadier General George W. Morgan. The force numbered at least 29,000 and was assisted by Porter's fleet of three ironclads and six gunboats.

The new army landed near its objective January 10, and ironclads laid down fire on the fort (upper left). Some 4,600 fighting men made up the Confederate garrison.

The following day, army and navy both bombarded Fort Hindman for four hours. Under heavy fire, the garrison's commander flew the white flag. McClernand's casualties were more than 1,000, but he took over 4,000 prisoners. The operation was a side show, but had some strategic significance in that it crippled the Rebel position in Arkansas.

Vicksburg, however, remained secure. In mid-January, Grant came down river to take command, establish headquarters at Milliken's Bend, and attempt to reduce the stronghold. For this effort he had three corps under McClernand, Sherman, and Major General James B. McPherson.

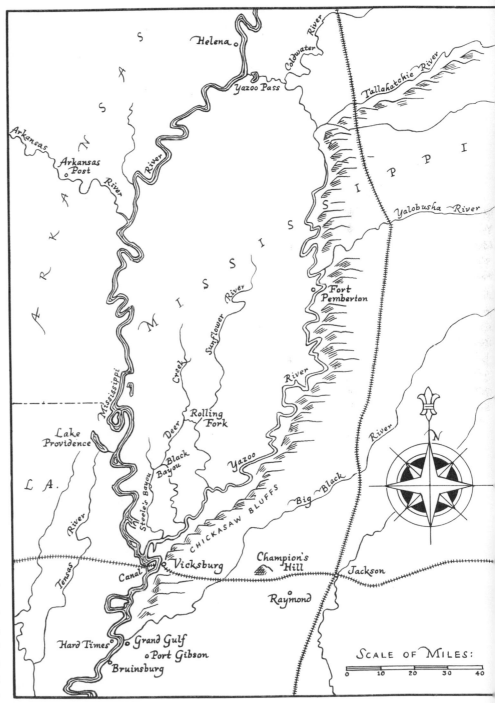

Union troops in the foreground (above) cut through a levee to divert the Mississippi, as a work force behind them blasts holes in the earthen retaining wall. River steamers (below) made brave attempts to force passage of the flooded lowlands, folding their stacks for easier progress.

GRANT'S army occupied a fifty-mile strip along the Mississippi's western bank. The tactical problem was to cross the river (while avoiding Vicksburg's guns) so the city could be attacked from the rear.

Attempts were made at four different places in early 1863. At times, all were made simultaneously. None succeeded.

First came the Vicksburg Neck Canal. A channel was dug across the neck of a peninsula opposite the city (below) in hopes the river would change its course and flow through the canal, isolating Vicksburg and opening a waterway that would help land troops south of the city. Spring floods washed out the operation in March.

Next was the Lake Providence route, utilizing a body of water west of the river and north of Vicksburg. Levees were cut and blasted so the Mississippi would flow into the lake. Transports were to run this passage, go south through a chain of rivers and bayous to the Red River, then into the Mississippi, from which they could land troops south of the citadel.

This meant a detour of more than four hundred and fifty miles in enemy country through passages clogged with stumps and obstacles. It was abandoned in March.

The last two attempts, through meandering waterways north of Vicksburg, were based on hope that transports could negotiate swamps and flooded forests and put troops ashore above the city.

The Yazoo Pass Expedition saw transports move through the pass, then down the Coldwater and Tallahatchie rivers in an attempt to enter the Yazoo. At this junction point, the Confederates turned a few square yards of dry land into tiny Fort Pemberton. The fort's guns stopped the steamboats.

Finally, Admiral Porter led a small fleet north up Steele's Bayou and Deer Creek with the intention of crossing over and dropping down the Sunflower River and the Yazoo to high land above Vicksburg.

The Rebels felled trees and blocked channels to impede progress. Under threat of Confederate attack, Porter called for Sherman's troops, which were nearby. The army broke up enemy fire, then guarded Porter's ships as they slowly and ignominiously steamed backward through the swamps to end the last amphibious expedition.

GRANT'S plan to take Vicksburg had three parts: (1) march down the western bank of the river to some point below the city, (2) have Porter's boats run south past the Vicksburg guns, then ferry the soldiers across the river, (3) feint with a force north of the city, to divert Pemberton.

In late March, McClernand's XIII Corps moved down to New Carthage, followed by McPherson's XVII. On the night of April 22, Porter ran past the Vicksburg batteries (above). Gunboats, transports, and coal barges, illuminated by Confederate fires on both banks, took a stiff bombardment but came through with the loss of only one transport.

Meanwhile, Sherman's XV Corps went up the Yazoo and demonstrated near Haynes's Bluff, twelve miles above Vicksburg. On April 17, Colonel Benjamin H. Grierson led 1,000 cavalry on a six-hundred-mile raid through Mississippi, smashing communications and terrorizing the countryside.

Such diversions were immensely effective, and at dawn on April 30, the Mississippi crossing began, from below Hard Times Plantation to Bruinsburg, thirty-two miles below Vicksburg. By noon McClernand had 18,000 men ashore and was moving inland.

The Confederates, numbering several thousand men, took up strong positions on a plantation just outside Port Gibson. McClernand deployed his troops for battle. Grant inspected the field, ordered up McPherson, who had a portion of his corps ashore, and soon had news of a Yankee victory on May 1. Port Gibson was occupied the following day.

Union troops streamed across the river (right). Sherman came downstream. Grant arrived at Grand Gulf on May 3, then determined to move on Jackson, Mississippi's capital, fifty miles to the northeast, to forestall General Joseph E. Johnston's coming through that point to reinforce Pemberton.

Grant's decision to cut himself off from a base, abandon his communication line, and live off the country was military heresy. He was testing the possibility of carrying only ammunition and staple rations, letting his troops scour the country to gather food for men and forage for animals. The risk was enormous, for he might have been encircled and starved into surrender. But his experiment worked, astounding his superiors and establishing an important military precedent.

*Grant Was Tired of Futile Fumbling
And Took the Biggest Chance of His Career to
Conquer Vicksburg and Give the Nation a Victory*

Success Bred Success as Grant Beat Johnston Back to Take Jackson, Then Turned and Drove Pemberton into Vicksburg

FOR the drive on Jackson, Grant placed McClernand on the left flank, along the Big Black River, Sherman in the center, and McPherson on the right. Fighting through heavy woods (below), Federal forces met the Confederates at Raymond and defeated them May 12. Two days later, Sherman and McPherson pushed Johnston's 6,000 out of Jackson, wrecked the city, and turned toward Vicksburg.

Grant led the advance, probing for Pemberton, who had reached for Grant's communication line, found nothing, and stopped to make a stand at Champion's Hill between Jackson and Vicksburg. Dug in on seventy-foot heights, Rebel forces occupied strong defensive positions as Union troops hit them on May 16.

Grant feinted to draw off Pemberton's reserves, leaving a gap for McClernand's troops, who were to strike the major blow. The latter general moved too slowly and was stopped dead. A stiff battle developed, raging for four hours until Union men turned the enemy's flank and routed him. Champion's Hill cost the Union 2,400 casualties; the Confederate figure was about 3,900.

Retreating, Pemberton stopped briefly on the seventeenth in an attempt to hold the bridgehead over the Big Black. He was blasted loose and entered the Vicksburg trenches on May 18 with Grant at his heels.

As Grant stood at the Big Black, awaiting action on the seventeenth, a messenger reached him with orders from Halleck telling him to return to Grand Gulf, cooperate with Banks in reducing Port Hudson, then return to Vicksburg. The Union leader ignored the order and prepared to attack Pemberton in Vicksburg as soon as he could.

As the Vicksburg Campaign developed with successes such as that at Champion's Hill (above), Banks was still faced with the strong garrison at Port Hudson. Farragut pounded the position with naval guns (below) but achieved no results. Banks then laid siege to the fortress.

GRANT felt Pemberton was fought out. Accordingly, he ordered a general assault May 19, with every expectation of victory.

Surprisingly stiff resistance hurled Union troops back with a loss of 900. The Confederate spirit was far from the breaking point. Once the troops had stopped retreating and occupied strong defenses, they dared Yankee attack.

Neither Grant, his generals, nor his men were in a mood to be halted. The Union chief knew Johnston was in his rear, with an army almost approaching his own in size. The possibility of the Rebel general's arrival could not be ignored. Grant was anxious to dispose of Pemberton, then turn on Johnston and drive him from the state.

In addition, he knew the temper of his troops. After their successful march, they were sure the works before them would crumble in the face of a determined attack. Grant decided to try on May 22.

Sherman's troops were to the north of Vicksburg, around Haynes's and Snyder's Bluffs. McPherson held central territory on both sides of the Vicksburg-Jackson Road. McClernand, to the south, held the Warrenton area near the river.

The signal gun spoke at 10 A.M., and a vicious, swirling battle developed at once. Well-placed Rebel artillery, double-loaded with grape and canister, raked the Union infantry. Over and over again, Federal soldiers gained a slope, a ditch, a parapet, only to be stopped in their tracks by vigorous counterattacks.

The 22nd Iowa, of McClernand's corps, spearheaded the attack on Fort Beauregard, one of Vicksburg's main defenses (right). Scaling ladders put men on top of the ramparts where rifle butts and bayonets became the chief weapons for hand-to-hand combat.

Grant, pulling back his men, received a message from McClernand, saying he had major enemy positions and renewed Union pressure would win the day. Sherman and McPherson were ordered to renew the assault. They did, found McClernand's statement completely unfounded, and fell back to break off the battle. Grant counted his losses for the single day at 3,200.

FOLLOWING the costly failures of May 19 and 22, Grant gave orders to dig in, and Union forces settled down to starve out the city. A continuous chain of trenches, rifle pits, and gun emplacements, some thirteen to fifteen miles in length, started at Haynes's Bluff in the north, ran around the rear of Vicksburg, and reached the river at Warrenton, south of the city.

Federal soldiers not in the immediate firing line carved living quarters into the sides of hills and gullies, improvising rough lean-tos from timber and canvas (above). Active troops pitched tents, cooked rations, washed clothes, and cleaned rifles within sight and sound of the guns (right). To shield themselves from the blazing sun, the Yanks built light, open-sided structures topped with leafy boughs.

Once the city was invested, Grant reopened permanent supply lines, and the troops did not lack rations, ammunition, or equipment. Drinking water was something of a problem, as was the sweltering heat of a Mississippi summer, which brought plagues of chiggers and mosquitoes, followed by the inevitable malaria. Monotony, the portion of all troops, was broken by pouring fire on the enemy.

Vicksburg was subjected to continuous bombardment. Federal cannon hammered steadily at Confederate works (before the siege ended, Grant had 220 guns). From positions across the Mississippi, huge 13-inch mortars hurled shells into the city. At night, Union mortar boats crept close to the river bank and lobbed their projectiles in amongst sleeping soldiers and civilians.

Yank troops dug steadily on parallels, the zigzag trenches that brought Union positions closer and closer to the enemy works. Mud-filled barrels, called sap rollers, were pushed ahead of the diggers to absorb enemy fire. Snipers on both sides were active, and casualties from their fire ran from ten to a hundred per day.

Within Vicksburg, ringed in and cut off from outside help, soldier and civilian suffered alike. Yankee fire forced women and children from their homes to take shelter in hastily dug caves. Shells destroyed the newspaper office, a Baptist church, the city hospital's drug supply. Rations grew short. The people ate mule meat and rats, ground up field peas to make a flour substitute, and boiled tree buds to serve as vegetables.

Inside the city, Pemberton lived on the hope that Johnston, somewhere in the Jackson area, would arrive and relieve the city. In mid-May, Johnston had advised Pemberton to abandon Vicksburg and save his troops. The siege ended that possibility. Johnston finally despaired of gathering enough force to aid Pemberton and advised him to surrender.

Grant was fully alert to the possibility of an attack by Johnston. To ward off such a potential blow, he detached Sherman from the siege and had his troops dig in near the Big Black River, facing east.

Grant found the siege period useful to clean house and rid himself of McClernand, who had posed continual problems by his insubordination, self-glorification, and ineptness in action. Without consulting Grant, McClernand issued public congratulations to his soldiers for their part in the assault on May 22, intimating it was poor support that had lost them the battle. Grant seized upon this order as an excuse to relieve McClernand (with Washington's approval). He was replaced by Major General E. O. C. Ord.

As Grant was changing his command structure, reinforcements continued to pour in until he had 71,000 men. He knew attrition and starvation were bringing Vicksburg to its knees and it was only a question of time before the city surrendered. But his army was increasing daily, and Grant pined for action. He called his officers together and, after consultation, picked July 6 as the tentative date for an all-out offensive.

Pemberton, too, brought his staff together, to sound them out. The general asked each officer present to vote on whether or not he should surrender. All but two voted to give in. Pemberton spoke of cutting his way through the enemy in a last desperate dash to bring out his force, but in the end agreed to seek surrender terms.

IN THE last days of the siege, as Union positions were pushed closer and closer to Confederate works, mining operations were carried out.

One of the major mining attempts of the Vicksburg siege took place June 25, at a strong Confederate hilltop position. More than a ton of powder was placed under Rebel lines by Union sappers, the explosives spread through three underground channels.

At three o'clock, the mine was to be exploded. Heavy artillery fire was ordered to follow up the explosion. Infantry stood ready to move into the gap in enemy lines.

Troops stood to their parapets as the mine went off (below), lifting the top off the hill and forming a sizable crater. Two Yankee regiments swarmed into the crater and up the other side to press the Rebels back. Taking cover behind their own steep parapets, the Confederates quickly halted Union attackers.

By late June, the no-man's-land between Yank and Rebel positions had shrunk so much that hand grenades could be used with accuracy.

PEMBERTON flew the white flag on July 3. Grant came in to meet him and called for unconditional surrender, which Pemberton refused.

After a few hours, Grant softened his demand and proposed the Confederates stack arms, sign paroles promising not to bear arms, and return to their homes. Pemberton accepted.

The surrender became official as Grant and Pemberton met on July 4 (left). The Union army entered the city in triumphal procession that day, parading past the shell-riddled courthouse before the eyes of a silent populace (above).

Grant took more than 31,000 prisoners, 172 guns, 60,000 rifles and muskets, and much ammunition. For this bounty the Union paid with over 1,500 dead, 7,400 wounded, and 450 missing in action.

Vicksburg gave the nation a major victory in the west, opened the Mississippi, split the Confederacy in two, and made Grant's reputation as the leading Union general. It may well have been the most important campaign of the Civil War.

181

*Confederate Raiders Carried War to the Homes of Western
Civilians in the Days That Followed the Vicksburg Campaign*

Morgan's riflemen laid down fire as his main force stormed over the covered bridge at Cynthiana, Ky., to meet Yankee militia called out to stop the Rebel raiders (above). Men of the raiding force stole horses, fired barns, and destroyed some property in the course of their long ride, but traveled too fast to carry out mass depredation. The picture below shows the Lawrence massacre, perpetrated just before dawn by Quantrill's men, who, drunk on captured liquor, fired the town.

NEWS of the Vicksburg surrender quickly traveled down river, and the besieged garrison at Port Hudson yielded to Banks on July 8, giving him 6,300 prisoners. The capitulation was followed by a general lull in western fighting, but summer and fall saw Rebel raiding bands strike at civilian areas in the North.

Among the best-known raiders was the dashing John H. Morgan, a brigadier general. He had been harassing Union communications from Tennessee bases when he received orders from Bragg to invade Kentucky, threaten Louisville, and cut a railroad used by Rosecrans. Gathering 2,500 mounted infantry, Morgan moved out in July, ignored his orders, and launched a thousand-mile sweep northeast through Kentucky, Indiana, and Ohio.

The group cut telegraph wires and rail lines, levied tribute from local citizens, stole horses and food, and showed war to the Ohio farmers. Yankee militia was turned out and gunboats sent up the rivers. Morgan fought stiff engagements with heavy losses along the way, and eventually split his force. Some men escaped into Kentucky; many were killed or captured. About 350 remained with their leader, who took them north almost to the Pennsylvania border where Federal troops caught them July 26. Morgan was imprisoned at Columbus, Ohio. He escaped, and was killed in Tennessee in 1864.

The ugliest customer among the raiders was William C. Quantrill, a border ruffian from Kansas who raised a band of guerrillas to burn and pillage their way through Kansas and Missouri. In August, he took 450 men into Lawrence, Kansas; killed 150 people; and razed the town. Two months later he carried out a similar raid at Baxter Springs.

By September, the Confederates had abandoned Little Rock, Arkansas, and fallen back to the southern part of the state, where another sweeping raid was being planned. Colonel Joseph O. Shelby, with 800 cavalry, ripped into Missouri on September 27, cutting a thousand-mile swath. He destroyed a million dollars' worth of property and made it home after losing most of his men.

Meanwhile, plans for action in the west were taking shape. For diplomatic reasons, Lincoln was anxious to take Texas. Banks was given units with which to do the job. Loading his force on ships, he left New Orleans and struck at Sabine Pass (on the Texas-Louisana border) September 8 but met with failure. The next move took him down the curving Gulf Coast to the Rio Grande River where it was the border between Texas and Mexico. He landed to capture Brownsville, Texas, on November 6.

Banks then worked his way back up the Gulf Coast, taking Corpus Christi, Aransas Pass, and Pass Cavallo, and was heading for Galveston when orders brought his operation to a halt. Banks's first objective, Brownsville, was economically important to the South, for cotton from there could be taken across the Rio Grande by ferry (below) to Mexico and there sold for gold, which the Confederacy desperately needed.

PRISONS

LIST OF UNION SOLDIERS

Buried at Andersonville.

COPIED FROM THE OFFICIAL RECORDS AT WASHINGTON.

NOTE.—The * denotes a Corporal; e † a Sergeant. The figures on the left indicate the number of the grave.

NEW YORK—*continued.*

512 Rafferty, M, 132, Co G, died Apr 12.
2534 Rafferty, P, 5 cav, Co M, died June 26.
11330 Rafferty, T, 5 artil, Co B, died Oct 23.
4593 Raker, L, 1 cav, Co E, died Aug 3.
3751 Ranch, J, 100, Co D, died July 22.
10875 Randall, John, 99, Co A, died Oct 13.
6503 Ralinger, J, 47, Co D, died Aug 22.
6794 Rangheart, John, 100, Co A, died Aug 25.
7778 Rastifer, John, 100, Co A, died Sept 4.
4216 Rattery, John, 104, Co I, died July 29.
10937 Ray, C, 3 cav, Co B, died Oct 14.
10246 Ray, R S, 154, Co A, died Oct 3.
4336 Raynard, F, 125, Co F, died July 30.
3435 Rattersboom, J, 3 artil, Co K, died July 17.
2880 Ramsay, Isaac, 86, Co I, died July 4.
1265 Ramsay, Hiram, 31, Co K, died May 21
2186 Reamer, W C, 111, Co B, died June 19.
2820 Redman, J, 3 artil, Co K, died July 3.
11695 Reddo, D V, 8 cav, Co M, died Oct 31.
7232 Reed, F A, 64, Co E, died Aug 30.
8574 Reed, J, 149, Co H, died Sept 12.
406 Reed, S G, 13, Co D, died April 6.
6041 Reed, W D, 146, Co H, died Aug 18.
10232 Reed, W J, 41, Co I, died Oct 2.
8492 Reed, William, 14 artil, Co I, died Sept 11.
7369 Reetz, John, 52, Co A, died Aug 31.
5694 Reeve, G, 152, Co C, died Aug 15.
1680 Reeves, John, 57, Co H, died June 6.
10467 Redmond, J, 43, Co C, died Oct 7.
10911 Regler, W H, 22 cav, Co M, died Oct 14.
9122 Reiley, P O, 164, Co B, died Sept 18.
7195 Renback, C, 29, died Aug 29.
12455 Rebman, J, 59, Co C, died Jan 15, '65.
8431 Rencermane, J R, 5 cav, Co B, died Sept 11.
9320 Randall, A B, 76, Co F, died Sept 20.
3352 Remsen, C, 2 cav, Co M, died July 15.
8209 Reynolds, O, 155, Co E, died Sept 8.
6799 Reynolds, O S, 85, Co E, died Aug 25.
10265 Reynolds, Samuel, 92, Co H, died Oct 3.
6350 Reynolds, Wm, 140, Co I, died Aug 21.
6546 Reidy, J D, 65, Co I, died Aug 23.
4318 Rice, F,* 39, Co I, died July 30.
3077 Rich, T D, 24 battery, died July 9.
12289 Rich, J, 82, Co C, died Dec 15.
3561 Richey, R, 66, Co C, died July 18.
2427 Rider, E, 178, Co E, died June 24.
8005 Rhenevault, R H, 21, Co B, died Sept 6.
11904 Rehm, W, 7 artil, Co C, died Nov. 7.
3891 Richistine, C*, 132, Co D, died July 24.
5317 Richards, A, 52, Co D, died Aug 11.
5674 Richards, A, 41, Co E, died Aug 14.
12343 Richards, A, 9, Co C, died Dec 7.
3682 Richards, H, 47, Co E, died July 21.
7578 Richards, N J†, 146, Co C, died Sept 2.
4240 Richardson, H M, 20 cav, Co M, died July 29.
12193 Ricker, M, 2 artil, Co M, died Nov 29.
8155 Rickhor, J, 85, Co E, died Sept 8.
415 Rikel, Robert, 125, Co G, died April 7.
12282 Riley, I, 73, Co E, died Jan 2 '65.
2885 Riley, J, 99, Co C, died July 4.
5021 Riley, John, 176, Co C, died Aug 8.
6347 Riley, John, 39, Co D, died Aug 21.
11163 Ripley, F A, 152, Co C, died Oct 19.
11760 Ripp, W, 42, Co B died Nov 3.
3514 Rising, C, 76, Co F, died July 18.
10310 Risley, George W, 47, Co G, died Oct 4.
2558 Ritcher, F†, 132, Co D, died June 27.
7245 Ritson, S, 18 cav, Co E, died Aug 29.
9224 Ritzmillin, John, 115, died Sept 19.
1775 Roach, F, 99, Co F, died June 9.
1842 Roach, Charles, 85, Co E, died June 11.
2354 Robberger, PH, 46, Co B, died June 23.
11195 Roberson, C A, 122, Co B, died Oct 20.
2346 Robertson, W H, 134, Co B, died June 24.
8554 Robertson, W M, 96, Co B, died Sept 12.
9970 Robinson, H, 39, Co K, died Sept 28.
7607 Robinson, A, 111, Co I, died Sept 2.
3680 Robinson, H C, 95, Co I, died July 21.
6419 Robinson, John, 115, Co A, died Aug 22.
27 Robins, L,* 154, Co K, died Mar 8.
7663 Roberts, A, 173, Co C, died Sept 3.
7585 Rockwell, N C, 14 artil, Co D, died Sept 2.
3813 Rockfellar, R E, 85, Co D, died July 23.
11342 Rockfellar, H, 15 artil, Co M, died Oct 23.
3959 Rock, F, 6 artil Co F, died July 25.
4350 Rogers, A, 7 artil, Co I, died July 31.
6059 Rogers, A, 125, Co H, died Aug 18.
5791 Rogers, G, musician, 85, Co F, died Aug 15.
3011 Rogers, James, 132, Co H, died July 7.
4287 Rogers, H C, 85, Co C, died July 30.
8369 Rogers, H J, 2 artil, Co E, died Sept 10.
4912 Rogers, M, 43, Co D, died Aug 6.
7208 Rogers, O S,† 85, Co C, died Aug 29.
6824 Rogers, Thomas, 12, Co F, died Aug 25.
11772 Romer, F, 9, Co A, died Nov 3.
8468 Rook, G, 6 artil, Co E, died Sept 11.
9963 Rooney, John, 152, Co G, died Sept 28.
9102 Rooney, M, 132, Co F, died Sept 18.
8922 Rooney, P, 2 artil, Co C, died Sept 16.
5569 Root, A N, 85, Co C, died Aug 14.
2998 Roots, W T, 120, Co H, died July 7.
1735 Root, Legrand, 24 battery, died June 8.
10278 Rose, A, 16, Co L, died Oct 2.
9550 Rosecrans, J E, 125, Co H, died Sept 23.
8171 Ross, C, 23 cav, Co A, died Sept 8.
3874 Ross, E, 3, 111, Co I, died July 24.
5591 Ross, David, 27, Co D, died Aug 14.
6741 Ross, G, 76, Co K, died Aug 24.
9751 Ross, A, 1 cav, Co M, died Sept 25.
11963 Ross, J H, 121, Co G, died Nov 11.
5929 Rosenberger, John, 4, Co D, died Aug 17.
3616 Rosser, Lewis, 84, Co A, died July 20.
2924 Rosenburg, J, 30, Co A, died July 5.
8737 Rosson, Chas, 24 cav, Co E, died Sept 14.
12259 Roswell, J, 93, Co K, died Dec 10.
727 Ross, Jacob, 151, Co A, died April 25.
1940 Row, W J, 120, Co B, died June 14.
5097 Roth, Louis, 39, Co D, died Aug 9.
8504 Rothwell, M,* 20 cav, Co M, died Sept 12.
3722 Rouge, Wm, bugler, 12 cav, Co F, died July 21.
7709 Rowbotham, R, 11 cav, Co L, died Sept 3.
5857 Rowell, J E, 70, Co G, died Aug 16.
3492 Rowell, L N, 99, Co H, died July 17.
59 Roberts, A B,† 8 cav, Co B, died Mar 18.
2609 Ruddin, C, 120, Co H, died June 28.
867 Rudler, Wm, 120, Co M, died May 3.
40 Rue, Newton,† 5 cav, Co A, died Mar 13.
8667 Runey, F, 69, Co H, died Sept 13.
12635 Russ, John, 2, Co K, died Feb 10, '65.
8856 Russell, J,* 7 artil, Co A, died Sept 15.
5094 Ryan, D, 106, Co D, died Aug 8.
8599 Ryan, J, 95, Co E, died Sept 12.
8741 Ryan, J, 22 cav, Co E, died Sept 14.
7258 Ryan, Owen, 12, Co A, died Aug 30.
4762 Rynoch, John, 66, Co I, died Aug 5.
6413 Ryson, John, 7 artil, Co L, died Aug 22.
6206 Ryne, J M, 39, Co E, died Aug 9.
684 Rush, John, 111, Co E, died April 23.
7234 Sackett, R S, 85, Co G, died Aug 29.
1929 Sadley, M, 77, Co H, died June 14.
1880 Safford, B J, 24 battery, died June 12.
11870 Salsbury, H, 1 artil, Co M, died Nov. 6.
10652 Salisbury, E, 16, Co D, died Oct 11.
10923 Samlett, —, 13 cav, Co I, died Oct 14.
10880 Samet, W, 15, Co H, died Oct 13.
3769 Sampson, J, 106, Co K, died July 22.
346 Sanders, Charles,* 9 mil, Co A, died April 2.
3818 Sanders, J, 99, Co C, died July 23.
9857 Sanders, J, 12 cav, Co A, died Sept 27.
4423 Sandford, P O, 7 artil, Co L, died July 31.
2341 Sanghin, J, 12 cav, Co F, died June 23.
7740 Sawyer, J, 2 cav, Co L, died Sept 3.
11232 Sayles, A, 22 cav, Co E, died Oct 21.
3612 Seaman, A,* 85, Co H, died July 19.
10856 Seaman, A, 2 artil, died Oct 13.
1372 Sears, F, 2 cav, Co H, died May 25.
6120 Seagher, J, 8, Co M, died Aug 19.
4325 See, Henry, 11, Co K, died July 30.
8824 Seeley, A J, 140, Co A, died Sept 15.
11374 Seeley, C B, 15, Co H, died Oct 24.
4256 Seeley, Thomas, 100, Co F, died July 29.
10027 Segam, Ed, 5 cav, Co K, died Sept 29.
4204 Seigler, George, 10, died July 29.
7458 Seigle, John R, 120, Co K, died Sept 1
11886 Selson, H, 59, Co C, died Nov 6.
3457 Serrier, R, 40, Co C, died July 17.
1746 Serine, C, 4 cav, Co M, died June 8.
629 Settle, Henry, 99, Co H, died April 19.
9828 Seyman, F, 1 cav, Co A, died Sept 27.
5951 Seard, Louis, 77, Co E, died Aug 17.
6888 Schayler, J W, 21 cav, Co M, died Aug 26.
10794 Schadt, Theodore, 160, Co A, died Oct 12.
3557 Scheck, B, 2 cav, Co G, died July 18.
3190 Schemerhorn, H, 120, Co G, died July 12.
11965 Schempp, M, 7 artil, Co F, died Nov 11.
2795 Schermashie, B, 170, Co A, died July 2.
1325 Schlotesser, J, 91, Co H, died May 24
11515 Schlotesser, J,† 1, Co L, died Oct 26
9578 Schmaker, John, 39, Co B, died Sept 23.
10291 Schmaley, J, 1, Co G, died Oct 16.
10550 Schmeager, A, 39, Co A, died Oct 9.
5311 Schneider, Charles, 39, Co A, died Aug 11.
8595 Schockney, T T, 24 battery, died Sept 12.
8796 Schofield, J, 7, Co H, died Sept 15.
2441 Scholl, John, 54, Co D, died June 25.
11422 Schriber, H, 59, Co I, died Oct 24.
7814 Schroder, G, 7 artil, Co E, died Sept 4.
8550 Schrum, J, 15 artil, Co K, died Sept 12.
1070 Schrimer, Wm, 20, Co B, died May 13.
4280 Schware, F, 12 cav, Co K, died July 30.
6613 Schwick, A, 66, Co G, died Aug 23.
4859 Scott, J C,† 85, Co K, died Aug 6.
6857 Scott, P C, 14 cav, Co G, died Aug 26.
8622 Scott, W W, 2 cav, Co F, died Sept 13.
8290 Sibble, W, 148, Co G, died Sept 9.
4362 Sick, R, 5, Co E, died July 31.
4557 Sickler, E, 7 artil, Co E, died Aug 2.
3210 Sickles, A, 120, Co D, died July 12.
11950 Siddell, G, 40, Co H, died Nov 10.
12284 Simmons, A, 8, artil, Co H, died Dec 13.
6364 Simmons, C G,† 85, Co B, died Aug 21.
8316 Simon, H, 146, Co B, died Sept 10.
6284 Simons, H L,† 85 Co E, died Aug 20.
142 Simondinger, B, 155, Co I, died Mar 24.
242 Simpson, D, 99, Co H; died Mar 30.
6345 Sisson, P V,† 22 artil, Co M, died Aug 21.
10067 Shaat, J, 50, Co A, died Sept 30.
201 Shae, Pat, drummer, 61, Co M, died Mar 28.
4801 Shaffer, M, 7 artil, died Aug 5.
4584 Shaffer, J, 66, Co E, died Aug 2.
782 Shafer, H, 103, Co F, died Apr 28.
6747 Shaughnessey, J, 6 cav, Co A, died Aug 24.
4446 Shannan, E, 6 artil, Co H, died Aug 1.
5645 Shank, S W, 24 battery, died Aug 14.
290 Shaw, Alexander, 3 artil, Co K, died Apr 1.
9667 Shaw, T I, 15 cav, Co M, died Sept 24.
12814 Shaw, W, 7 artil, Co F, died Mar 25.
7660 Shay, John, 69, Co B, died Sept 3.
3360 Sheldon, M, 7 artil, Co B, died July 15.
4247 Shepardson, L,* 22 cav, Co E, died July 29.
5474 Shaw, J, 2 cav, Co E, died Aug 13.
7798 Shuler, Chas, 52, Co G, died Sept 4.
8335 Shaw, M, 76, Co D, died Sept 10.
9924 Sheppard, W H, 9, Co F, died Sept 28.

139 Smith, Wm, 99, Co H, died March 24.
325 Smith, Wm, 3 artil, Co K, died April 2.
532 Smith, Wm, 104, Co A, died April 14.
812 Smith, Wm, 106, Co B, died April 30.
7550 Smith, Wm, 2, Co L, died Sept 2.
10164 Smith, Wm, 76, Co K, died Oct 1.
12394 Smith, H, 7, Co C, died Jan 5, '65.
3708 Snedegar, A J, 111, Co D, died July 21.
7173 Snyder, A, 25, Co E, died Aug 29.
4448 Snyder, B, 2, Co B, died Aug 1.
10076 Snyder, Wm, 1 dragoons, Co E, died Sept 30.
1319 Sombeck, Geo, 52, Co I, died May 23.
5169 Somers, John, 2, Co E, died Aug 9.
2773 Sopher, James, 132, Co F, died July 2.
2403 Sopher, S, 102, Co K, died June 24.
4352 Sotter, J M, 47, Co C, died July 31.
3534 Southard, H, 5 cav, Co C, died July 18.
10526 Southard, N, 2, Co H, died Oct 8.
11346 Southard W A, 18, Co I, died Oct 23.
2877 Souther, Henry, 69, Co K, died July 4.
8124 Southworth, R, 22 cav, Co E, died Sept 8.
10488 Skall, S, 7 artil, Co L, died Oct 7.
12029 Skeeley, T, 56, Co H, died Nov 15.
9954 Spark, G,† 16 artil, Co C, died Sept 28.
6975 Sparks, E, 10, Co B, died Aug 27.
5421 Spaulding, H, 1 cav, Co F, died Aug 12.
5567 Spellman, John, 66, Co B, died Aug 13.
10712 Spencer, A, 93, Co D, died Feb 28.
10989 Sperry, A, 51, Co F, died Oct 16.
3532 Span, James, 147, Co H, died July 18.
5982 Spanbury, S, 14 artil, Co C, died Aug 17.
5821 Sprague, E H, 10 battery, died Aug 16.
3593 Sprague, J, 85, Co I, died July 19.
10780 Sprig, James A, 24 cav, Co E, died Oct 11.
4877 Sprink, A, 146, Co F, died Aug 6.
9035 Strats, John, 15, Co A, died Sept 17.
889 Stacey, John, 99, Co I, died May 4.
4574 Stadler, J,† 39, Co A, died Aug 2.
10078 Stancliff, A B, 106, Co H, died Sept 30.
2570 Stanton, H H, 22, Co E, died June 27.
5187 Stark, J D,* 100, Co A, died Aug 9.
11740 Starkweather, L, 146, Co E, died Nov 2.
12650 Star, C, 15, Co D, died Feb 13.
7381 Stanton, L H, 7 artil, Co K, died Aug 31.
2520 Stark, J H, 121, Co A, died June 26.
1698 Stanley, J C,* 85, Co C, died June 7.
10290 St Dennis, L, 16, Co F, died Oct 4.
9903 Stewart, Peter, 5, Co B, died Sept 27.

21.
3976 Tanner, M, 1, Co E, died July 25.
4326 Tanschivit, Ed, 15 artil, Co E, died July 30.
7019 Tell, Wm, 59, Co C, died Aug 27.
9143 Thompson, A, 9, Co D, died Sept 18.
133 Terry, Aaron,† 12, Co K, died March 24.
9064 Teneych, M, 14 artil, Co E, died Sept 17.
4909 Tewey, J, 99, Co H, died Aug 6.
6445 Terwilliger, D R, 85, Co D, died Aug 22.
10352 Thomas, J, 2 cav, Co D, died Oct 5.
3598 Thomas, H,† 88, Co D, died July 19.
3711 Thomas, W, 3, Co H, died July 21.
4619 Thomas, J, 85, Co G, died Aug 3.
10361 Thearer, J, 1 battery, died Oct 5.
8161 Thompson, C W, 85, Co K, died Sept 8.
4781 Thompson, J, 39, Co H, died Aug 5.
5510 Thompkins, Ira, 6 art, died Aug 13.
5524 Thompson, P, 10, Co E, died Aug 13.
6730 Thompson, N B, 146, Co A, died Aug 24.
5784 Thompson, J, 104, Co G, died Aug 15.
2613 Thompson, T, 12 cav, Co F, died June 28.
320 Thompson, Daniel, 142, Co E, died April 2.
3538 Thresh, G, 5 cav, Co K, died July 18.
5147 Thruston, N E, 85, Co C, died Aug 9.
11235 Thornton, J, 14 art, Co L, died Oct 21.
6309 Thorpe, W C, 82, Co I, died Aug 20.
4293 Thurston, G W, 85, Co E, died July 31.
12843 Thayer, G, 70, Co E, died April 22, '65.
679 Thierbach, P M, 39, Co D, died April 22.
11230 Tilton, H, 24 artil, died Oct 20.
8283 Tillitson, N P, 51, Co A, died Sept 9.
8849 Timerson, Wm, 7 artil, Co I, died Sept 15.
2680 Timmish, —, 85, Co C, died June 30.
659 Tiner, David, 79, Co E, died April 21.
10422 Townsend, W, 111, Co B, died Oct 6.
8068 Townsend, L, 22 cav, Co G, died Sept 7.
3883 Townsend, John, 52, Co A, died July 24.
535 Townsend, Geo M, 111, Co F, died April 14.
9050 Tohnson, E, 22, died Sept 17.
4774 Toney, L, 100, Co D, died Aug 5.
10727 Tolal, Pat, 164, Co K, died Oct 11.
5833 Tonner, L, 5 cav, Co G, died Aug 16.
6047 Tobias, A, 120, Go G, died Aug 18.
2112 Toomey, J F,* 85, Co I, died June 17.
12465 Tourney, P, 99, Co B, died Jan 16, '65.

THE name Andersonville was synonymous with horror during the latter part of the Civil War. Largest of the Southern prisons, the huge open pen was a living hell for Union captives inside its stockades.

More than 45,000 prisoners were confined at Andersonville. Almost 13,000 died there, not to mention those who were removed to meet their end in other camps throughout Georgia and the Carolinas.

Inadequate food, polluted water, indescribable sanitary conditions, primitive medical care, and constant exposure to the elements all took their frightful toll. Scurvy, acute diarrhea, dysentery, and gangrene were the major killers.

Disease was brought on by starvation rations and foul living conditions, stemming from overpopulation of the prison. Built in late 1863 and early 1864, Andersonville had been intended for 10,000 men at most.

Camp Sumter, as it was officially called, lay on a rail line connecting Albany and Macon, about sixty miles southwest of the latter city. A double stockade of squared tree trunks enclosed twenty-seven acres of barren ground. In the beginning, barracks were planned for the camp; but the sudden influx of prisoners, starting in February, 1864, swamped the authorities and shelters never appeared.

Rations fell off steadily as Andersonville's population increased. Unsifted corn meal, filled with husks and eaten raw, was each man's daily portion. The spare diet and accumulating filth brought disease. Doctors could do little. Day by day, prisoners carried their dead outside the stockade. The men who survived carried memories of Andersonville all their days.

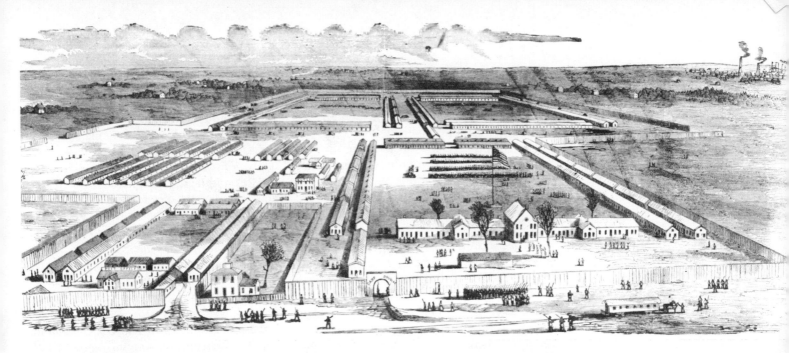

ANDERSONVILLE was the worst of prisons, North or South. Others, for temporary periods, were almost equally bad. At Camp Douglas (above), near Chicago, 10 per cent of the Rebel prisoners died during one month of 1863.

Neither North or South set out to practice calculated cruelty on its captives. Both sides were victims of the lack of preparation for a long war.

Housing for captured men in large number was not in Yankee and Rebel plans. Neither was a ration system nor medical care. Converting existing structures, or building from the ground up when there was no other way, both governments did what they could, but it was never enough.

Confusion arose from the agreement for handling prisoners, which changed several times during the war. At the outset, captives were paroled and sent home after promising not to take up arms again. This system was economical, as it eliminated housing and feeding responsibilities, but there was no way of assuring paroles would be kept.

In July, 1862, Northern and Southern governments agreed to exchange or parole all prisoners within ten days of their capture. For a time, the prisons were almost empty.

After the Emancipation Proclamation, as Negro troops joined the U.S. Army, Jefferson Davis decreed that all Negro slaves captured bearing arms, and their white officers, would not be treated as prisoners of war but delivered to the states to be punished by their laws. Because of these strong words, and other considerations of his own, Halleck ordered all exchanges stopped in May, 1863.

The order was not always obeyed to the letter, but the prisons soon began to fill again. By 1864, Grant took a firm stand against exchange: "We have got to fight until the military power of the South is exhausted, and if we release or exchange prisoners captured, it simply becomes a war of extermination."

Despite the seesaw policies of both governments, muster rolls climbed steadily in the major prisons. About 215,000 Confederates, captured on the field (upper left) were confined by the Yankees. In Rebel jails, 195,000 Northerners served their time.

Libby Prison, at Richmond (lower left), held Federal officers. At nearby Belle Isle, in the James River, a tent city accommodated enlisted men. Other Confederate prisons were Castle Thunder, at Petersburg, Virginia; Castle Pinckney, in Charleston Harbor; an abandoned cotton factory at Salisbury, North Carolina; and various camps and stockades in Georgia, South Carolina, Alabama, and Texas.

Largest of the Northern prisons was Point Lookout, Maryland, a tent camp. The worst was Fort Delaware, in the river of that name. Others existed in Lake Erie; on an island in the Mississippi; at Elmira, New York; and in New York City, Boston, Indianapolis, Washington, St. Louis, Baltimore, and Columbus, Ohio.

189

PRISON life was miserable, debilitating, and often fatal. More than 30,000 Union prisoners died in captivity. The Confederate death toll was approximately 26,000.

The fortunate men who lived through incarceration found conditions varying widely from place to place. In one Southern institution, Captain Frank E. Moran of the 73rd New York Volunteers saw prison life at its brightest:

"A minstrel troupe was organized. . . . A number of musical instruments were purchased, forming a respectable orchestra. . . . Refreshing music often enlivened the place where the weary-souled prisoner had laid down for the night. . . . Chess, checkers, cards, or such other games occupied much of our time. . . . It was not infrequent to see a lively breakdown at one end of the room and a prayer meeting at the other; to hear the loud tum of the banjo mingling with the solemn melody of the doxology."

Farther south, Private John McElroy, 16th Illinois Cavalry, looked at captivity through different eyes:

"Let me describe the scene immediately around my own tent . . . as an example of the condition of the whole prison: I will take a space not larger than a good-sized parlor or sitting room. On this were at least fifty of us. Directly in front of me lay two brothers.

. . . They were now in the last stages of scurvy and diarrhea. Every particle of muscle and fat about their limbs and bodies had apparently wasted away, leaving the skin clinging close to the bone of the face, arms, hands, ribs, and thighs—everywhere, except the feet and legs, where it was swollen tense and transparent, distended with gallons of purulent matter. Their livid gums, from which most of their teeth had already fallen, protruded far beyond their lips. To their left lay a Sergeant and two others of their company, all three slowly dying of diarrhea. . . . To my right was a handsome young Sergeant of an Illinois Infantry Regiment, captured at Kenesaw. His left arm had been amputated between the shoulder and the elbow, and he was turned into the stockade with the stump all undressed, save the ligating of the arteries . . . he had not been inside an hour until the maggot flies had laid eggs in the open wound, and before the day was gone the worms were hatched out, and rioting amid the inflamed and supersensitive nerves . . ."

Extreme conditions such as described by McElroy produced living skeletons, with wild, vermin-ridden hair, such as the men shown (right) after being picked up by Federal troops near Wilmington, North Carolina, late in the war.

The amount of misery and degradation

brought about by prison life depended on the geographical location of camps, food available, water supply, medical care, and the character and quality of camp commandants and guards.

Southern soldiers, in Elmira, New York, or on Johnson's Island, in Lake Erie's Sandusky Bay, suffered through bitter northern winters. Yankees in the South cringed under the blistering sun of Georgia and South Carolina.

Climate worked its worst discomfort in the big tent cities, north and south, and through the open-pen stockades peculiar to the Confederacy. Most Northern camps boasted barracks to shield men from the weather. Below the Mason-Dixon line, prisons were sometimes created from ship chandlers' lofts or tobacco warehouses, which permitted a rough degree of comfort.

Food was the major source of complaint on both sides. The breakdown of Southern transportation often kept Yankee troops from receiving adequate rations.

Transportation was never a valid excuse for food shortages in Northern prisons, but many Confederates went hungry. Diaries and letters mention spoiling bacon and hard crackers as the full rations for temporary periods, and speak of constant hunger among prisoners.

Inadequate water supply cursed many locations. In the stockades, a single brook might serve thousands. Enclosed prisons sometimes had but a single "hydrant" for all their occupants (left). At the dreaded Fort Delaware, Southern inmates depended on standing rain water or visits from a small water boat that filled the prison tanks at intervals.

IN OCTOBER, 1861, the government at Washington appointed Lieutenant Colonel William Hoffman as Commissary General of Prisoners. He held the administrative post throughout the war. The South delayed such an appointment until 1864, when Brigadier General John H. Winder was given a somewhat similar position, less well defined than that of Hoffman.

Choosing staffs to run the prisons and men to guard them challenged the administrative chiefs. Volunteer troops and their officers had enlisted for action in the field, not to act as jailers. In the North, the Veteran Reserve Corps, made up of disabled soldiers, produced guards. Raw, untrained soldiers often drew the guard assignments turned down by their more experienced comrades. Negro troops were sometimes used.

Conscripted militia furnished guards for Southern camps. As the need for manpower haunted the South, in 1864, every able-bodied soldier went into the lines. The very old and very young took over posts at the prisons.

Guards and prisoners often struck up relationships built around trade and barter. Money, buttons, boots, and miscellaneous equipment were turned over to captors who provided food in return. Many guards were friendly, some were cruel, most were callously indifferent.

Charges of cruelty and indifference were often leveled at prison commanders. In some cases, the accusations sprang from fact. In others, the alleged harshness resulted from red tape and material shortages.

After the war, the collective sins of prison commanders fell on the head of Captain Henry Wirz, the Confederate chief at Andersonville. Brought to trial, he labored mightily in his own defense. His efforts failed and conviction for "murder in violation of the laws and customs of war" among other points followed. On November 10, 1865, Wirz was hanged (below).

HOOKER OUTFOUGHT

LINCOLN had achieved a major victory in the west during the first half of 1863. Hoping to repeat the performance in the difficult eastern theater, he found a new leader for the Army of the Potomac.

Burnside, after his defeat at Fredericksburg, called upon the President to fire several high-ranking officers or accept his resignation. Lincoln chose the latter. "Fighting Joe" Hooker took his place.

Hooker, after West Point, served with Confederate General Jackson in the Mexican War. Since 1861, he had fought on the Peninsula and at Second Bull Run, Antietam, and Fredericksburg. The general was a fine fighting man, hard, handsome, addicted to beauty and the bottle. His men respected him.

They were a downcast lot when the new leader took over, an excellent army that could not win. Hooker arranged a furlough system, improved living conditions, drilled his soldiers hard. Desertions diminished. Morale climbed. In the spring, the refurbished Army of the Potomac, over 100,000 strong, looked across the Rappahannock at Lee, who held Fredericksburg.

Hooker created a master plan to crack Lee's force once and for all. It was brilliant and depended only on determined execution to become a complete success. But the Union general was up against a supreme tactician.

All went well for the Union at the start. The master plan had four parts to make full use of seven infantry corps and one of cavalry.

Part one called for a sweeping Yankee cavalry raid behind Lee's lines to cut his communications. Part two sent the V, XI, and XII Corps up the Rappahannock, to the northwest, to ford the river, then march down and take Lee from the rear. Part three indicated Corps I and VI would demonstrate in front of Fredericksburg, to hold Lee's attention. Part four placed the II and III Corps a short distance up the Rappahannock, to cross when called and come to the assistance of either group as needed.

If Lee fought at Fredericksburg, the up-river group would fall on his rear. If he turned to face that force, troops from Fredericksburg would do the same.

High water held up the cavalry, but Hooker's infantry corps, starting April 27, took positions as planned. The up-river force crossed the Rappahannock and a tributary, the Rapidan, and moved toward Lee. On April 30, they encamped at Chancellorsville, a tiny site marked by a crossroads and the old Chancellor mansion. Hooker arrived to take field command.

Lee had half Hooker's strength, as Longstreet was operating in the Atlantic coastal area. Most of this strength was sent up river while only one division remained to hold Fredericksburg in the face of Yankee troops already beginning to cross. The Confederate general, with immense numerical inferiority, did not consider retreat.

As he and Jackson met near Chancellorsville on May 1, the latter ordered an immediate attack. It took Hooker off balance and, despite his superiority, he fell back under this unexpected assault. Here, the Union leader faltered, and Lee quickly exploited his lack of confidence.

The maneuver planned by the Lee-Jackson team for May 2 may have been the most dazzling of the war. Even though up against Hooker's mighty numbers, Lee split his force and ordered Jackson to march south and west, then swing up to fall on the Union rear. Lee himself would demonstrate on Hooker's front, with two divisions to hold the attention of Hooker's three corps.

Jackson marched all day, cutting through a tangled mass of second-growth forest called the Wilderness. A little before sunset, the Rebel cheer lifted while tough Southern veterans fell on Hooker from behind. Under the thundering blow, the Union right collapsed as night fell. Confederate jubilation died under a tragic error. Stonewall Jackson was severely wounded when fired upon by his own men.

Jackson's Men Burst Forth from the Woods Like a Tornado to Strike

Lee's Total Force Was Inferior to Hooker's, but
He Applied Maximum Strength at Sensitive Points

MAJOR General J. E. B. Stuart left his cavalry to take field command of Jackson's troops and attacked again on May 3. Hooker, who had been reinforced by the II and III Corps, still was unable to hold his own. As he was watching the battle from the Chancellor home, his headquarters, a Confederate shell smashed into the mansion, and falling masonry knocked the Union general unconscious. He tried to retain command when brought back to consciousness, but the spark had gone out.

Under heavy artillery fire, Stuart's men joined up again with Lee's and began to drive the disheartened Yankees toward the the river. The III and XII Corps stood their ground against Stuart's rushing drive; at the Rappahannock, the V Corps held the ford to prevent Confederate troops from pocketing the Union army completely.

At Fredericksburg, Union forces were ordered up to smash Lee's rear. They took the city, and Marye's Heights, on May 3, and headed for Chancellorsville. Lee, with Hooker on the run, shuttled his troops over to meet this new offensive and fought the Battle of Salem Church on May 3 and 4.

Stopped short by Rebel power, Union soldiers fell back on Fredericksburg and hastily threw up defenses. The rear guard held off further Confederate attack as the remainder of the force fell back across the river.

Lee once more called in his men for a final thrust on Hooker's shattered command. There was no resistance. The massive Union army left the field and crossed the river to its old camp around Falmouth. The Union master plan had been crumpled by the daring of Lee and Jackson. More than 40 per cent of Hooker's men never fired their rifles.

Yankee soldiers carrying captured battle flags marched 2,000 prisoners back with them (below). But the Army of the Potomac once more tasted disillusion and defeat.

Hooker placed over 97,000 men in action; Lee, 57,000. The Union counted casualties of 17,000 against 13,000 for the Confederacy. Brilliant tactics and personal courage on the part of Hooker were not enough. In trouble, he had hesitated. Lee, when in trouble, usually advanced.

At Chancellorsville, the South won the day, but at a terrible price. On May 10, Stonewall Jackson died.

NORTHERN INVASION

EXCEPT for the shattering action at Chancellorsville, the spring of 1863 was a quiet one in the eastern theater. Confederate troops had proved they could hold their own, but time was favoring the North. Decisive Southern action seemed necessary. Lee projected another offensive into Yankee territory.

Once loose in Maryland and Pennsylvania, the Rebels could again threaten Washington, Philadelphia, and Baltimore. Their presence might help the Northern peace party in its demand for a negotiated settlement of the war. At the very least, Lee's soldiers would send Northern credit tumbling.

Of immediate importance was the supply problem plaguing the Confederacy. The government at Richmond suggested Lee would find ample food for his men and forage for his animals in the Keystone State.

Europe awaited a significant Confederate victory. Queen Victoria's government still favored the Southern cause. In France, a loan, secured by cotton, was floated for the South. One stunning triumph on Northern soil could bring open recognition from overseas.

Jefferson Davis, because of the heavy Federal troop concentration along the Rappahannock, feared for his capital. A move by Lee into the North might force withdrawal of these threatening troops.

Davis and his Cabinet approved the offensive, and Lee prepared to move. Reorganization had given him three corps.

On June 3, gray-clad troops left Fredericksburg, heading west toward the Blue Ridge Mountains. Union cavalry struck at Brandy Station on June 9 in a whirlwind action, but the march was not interrupted.

Lieutenant General Richard S. Ewell slipped through the Blue Ridge passes and moved north through the Shenandoah Valley, smashing a Union garrison at Winchester. A. P. Hill followed. Longstreet marched up the eastern side of the range, then entered the passes and joined the main body in the Valley. By June 25, Lee had crossed the Potomac (foreground above).

Lee's Massive Army Posed an Ominous Threat to Northern Cities in Its Path, and Many Inhabitants Took to the Highways

Harrisburg appeared to be the first major objective of Lee's army, and citizens fell out to dig fortifications around the city. Shops closed, railways sent rolling stock away, and housewives hid their valuables. Lincoln called out the militia in Pennsylvania, Maryland, West Virginia, and Ohio.

AS LEE'S 75,000 moved north, Major General Alfred Pleasonton kept his Union cavalry close to the advancing army. Yankee horsemen, having gathered experience in the past two years, were alert, enterprising, and pugnacious. Between skirmishes, they brought valuable information to Hooker.

Knowing Lee was headed north, the Union general proposed he strike south and capture Richmond. Lincoln quickly vetoed the suggestion and ordered Hooker north to shield Washington.

The ponderous Union army, 87,000 men, left the Fredericksburg area. Once under way, it moved with astonishing speed. Lee was swinging northeast in a great arc beyond the Blue Ridge. Hooker paralleled the move, marching in a shorter arc east of the mountains to keep between Washington and the enemy.

As he marched north, Hooker sent back pleas for reinforcements. When one of his requests was refused, he offered his resignation as commander. It was accepted at once. Major General George G. Meade replaced him June 28 and Lincoln gained a sound commander for the big battle to come.

Lee, at a crucial time, was about to lose the services of one of his brilliant leaders for a short period. J. E. B. "Jeb" Stuart, top cavalryman of the Confederacy, asked permission to make another of his well-known raids. Lee granted the request.

The Rebel raid was thrown off schedule by Hooker's rapid advance. Stuart's horsemen, blocked by the Union columns, were forced into detours and delays. After an agonizing wait, they crossed the Federal rear and drove north through Maryland and Pennsylvania. Their wide sweep carried them out of touch with Lee, and their usefulness as the "eyes and ears" of the army ended.

At a crucial moment of the campaign, Stuart's absence left Lee lacking important information. Without intelligence to the contrary, the Confederate commander assumed the Union army was far to his rear.

Feeling secure from attack, Lee's troops fanned out after crossing the Pennsylvania border. By June 28 they were deployed in a semicircle with Chambersburg at the left, Carlisle at the top, and York at the east.

Midway between Chambersburg and York and slightly to the south lay Gettysburg, placed at the junction of several main roads. The sleepy country town had not figured in the plans of either army. Southern troops were driving for Harrisburg, Northern forces pursuing them to bring on battle.

Things changed abruptly on June 28. A civilian scout brought Lee news that the Union army was north of the Potomac in force, near Frederick, Maryland. The rebel commander became alarmed for the safety of his communication line through the Shenandoah Valley and hurried to concentrate his scattered forces.

Cashtown, nine miles west of Gettysburg, was the rallying point. Longstreet and Hill came in from Chambersburg, while Ewell's men fell back from York and Carlisle. Establishing a strong defensive position, the Rebels awaited the Yankees' appearance.

Meade, almost upon his enemy, expected an attack by Lee. He set up defensive positions of his own at Taneytown in northern Maryland, along a watercourse called Pipe Creek, fifteen miles south of Gettysburg.

On June 30, Meade sent Brigadier General John Buford's cavalry toward Gettysburg to investigate the Rebels. The same day the Confederates, hearing shoes were available in the town, moved forward in brigade strength to round up the footwear they desperately needed.

Reaching an elevation near the city, Southern soldiers spotted the cavalrymen and withdrew to report their observations to A. P. Hill. The general sent Lee word he would approach Gettysburg the following morning to test enemy strength.

On June 28, Lee's men took Wrightsville, Pa. A small Federal force withdrew as the Confederates approached, firing the bridge over the Susquehanna before they retired. Southern leaders kept their men well under control and there was little looting, but the army foraged as it went.

GENERAL Robert E. Lee (above) took three large corps into battle at Gettysburg. Their commanders (left to right) were James Longstreet of the I, Ambrose P. Hill of the III, and Richard S. Ewell of the II. All ranked as lieutenant generals.

Lee and his leaders were West Point graduates and veterans of the Mexican War. By spring of 1863 they had seen much of the Civil War and were closely acquainted with the Army of the Potomac, which they had whipped more than once.

Longstreet was senior commander at Gettysburg, under Lee. Benign and patriarchal in appearance, "Old Pete" was rough and ready with his humor, joked in the army manner, and carried a heavy dignity. He was stubborn, never hesitating to criticize his superior on questions of tactics and strategy. When not convinced of an action's wisdom, Longstreet sometimes was slow to move his forces, bringing adverse criticism on himself. In battle, he was steady, nerveless, and a source of confidence to his men.

A. P. Hill was a soldier's soldier, fast-thinking and brilliant in tactical execution. At Antietam, he helped save the Confederate army from destruction. Explosive when aroused, Hill had an edgy temper and was a difficult associate. But he appeared at the right place, at the right time, in moments of crisis.

Ewell had a birdlike appearance, a bald head, sharp nose, and squeaky voice. Alert and nervous, he was a terrier when committed to battle but lacked the genius necessary to high command. Much of his experience was acquired in the West, where he fought Indians for years. Ewell put himself into the heart of battle when his troops were in action, and gained a wooden leg after Second Bull Run.

MAJOR General George G. Meade (above) became Lee's opposite number at Gettysburg.

A West Point graduate who fought in the Mexican War, he was badly wounded during the Seven Days but returned to take the field at Second Bull Run and Antietam, and command a corps at Fredericksburg and Chancellorsville. Crusty, serious, studious, he displayed great honesty.

Meade took seven corps to battle under major generals. Corps commanders were (top to bottom, left to right) Oliver O. Howard, the XI; Henry W. Slocum, the XII; John Sedgwick, the VI; John F. Reynolds, the I; George Sykes, the V; Daniel E. Sickles, the III; Winfield S. Hancock, the II.

Howard, a God-fearing man, lost an arm at Fair Oaks but returned to fight the Army of the Potomac's major battles until after Gettysburg. Slocum saw action at Bull Run,

and his solidity and personal bravery were evidenced in Virginia and Maryland.

"Uncle John" Sedgwick, rich in military experience, shed his blood for the Union more than once before Gettysburg. A superior soldier, he was respected by the officers and loved by his men.

Brave and brilliant, Reynolds had seen action in Mexico, on the Peninsula, and at Fredericksburg and Chancellorsville.

Sykes was a career soldier and a stern taskmaster. He covered the retreat from Bull Run, then met Lee's men in every major engagement after it. Sickles sprang from New York politics instead of West Point. Brave, opinionated, dashing, reckless, he was nothing if not colorful.

Hancock stayed close to his men under fire and was idolized by them in return. He had handled troops expertly for years, in Mexico and elsewhere.

201

Casualty figures soared during the battle, and some units were almost completely wiped out. Officers from corps commanders down fought at the front; many were killed or wounded (above). High ground seized by the Union provided excellent positions for later defensive fighting (below).

Once Commanders Opened Fire, the Huge Armies Were Committed

GETTYSBURG was a three-day battle. It began the morning of July 1 on an elevation west of the town.

Two of A. P. Hill's brigades swept down the Chambersburg Road to open the firing. They were met by Buford's cavalry, who gave an excellent account of themselves until the I and XI Corps arrived.

Reynolds had field command. He looked about him, saw the advancing Confederate strength, and sent Meade word of the desperate need for reinforcement, adding that Gettysburg was the place to fight Lee. Reynolds' judgment was sound; it was ended forever by a Confederate bullet at ten o'clock.

Troops poured in from both sides as battle began again. The I Corps, now under Major General Abner Doubleday, held ground west of Gettysburg in the face of frightful losses. Howard's XI Corps moved into the plain north of the city.

There he encounted heavy pressure from Ewell but the Yankee leader held and even counterattacked. It was futile in the face of Confederate power. Early pounded in from the northeast and the Rebels smashed the XI and sent it staggering back through Gettysburg.

The withdrawal exposed the I Corp's right flank. Under A. P. Hill's remorseless pounding, the corps crumbled and fell back to ground south of the city to join the shattered XI.

Ewell seized Gettysburg, then pressed toward Yankee defenses. Without cavalry scouts to tell him of Union strength, he decided to await reinforcement.

Meade, after hearing of Reynolds' death, sent Hancock to take field command. The general gathered a small force of cavalry and artillery, sped to the battlefield, and rallied the beaten Union forces as twilight ended the first day's battle.

Hancock surveyed the ground, found it admirably suited for defense, and sent Meade word that this was the place to meet the entire Confederate army, as Reynolds had advised. Meade arrived and Federal troops poured into the defensive positions Hancock had chosen.

These were on high ground that formed a fishhook shape. At the top of the hook was Culp's Hill and, at the bulge, Cemetery Hill. The long, curving shank was Cemetery Ridge, which ended in two elevations called Little Round Top and Big Round Top.

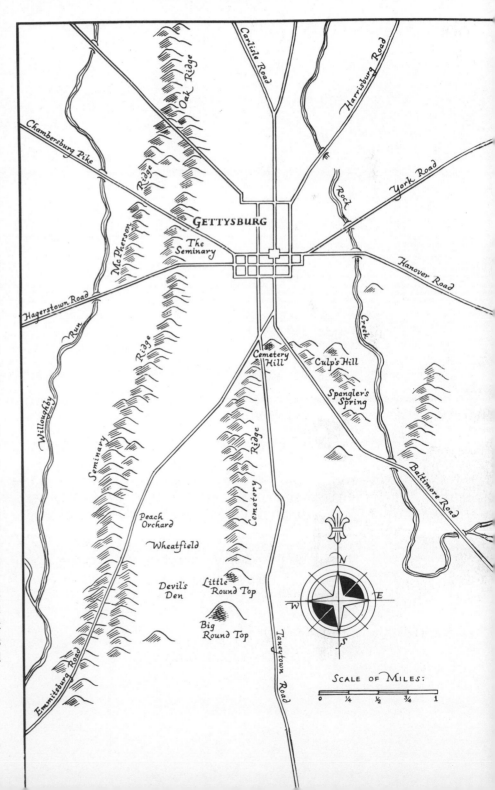

The Confederate Offensive on Gettysburg's Second Day Was Delayed

EWELL'S reluctance to attack on the afternoon of July 1 gave Meade time to consolidate his hilltop defenses. About one mile west, the Confederates occupied Seminary Ridge, a long rise named for the Lutheran college on its crest. Morning of July 2 saw the two armies facing each other.

Lee determined on the offensive that day. Longstreet was to strike the Yankee left; Ewell, the Yankee right. Longstreet did not favor the plan, and moved slowly.

Facing him was the Union III Corps, badly out of position. Sickles, ignoring Meade's orders, had moved his troops west of the hilly defense line into a peach orchard. The movement created a salient vulnerable from west, north, and south, and left Little Round Top unoccupied.

Longstreet blasted Sickles with artillery, then charged the salient. As the action commenced, Major General Gouverneur K. Warren, Meade's Chief of Engineers, saw Little Round Top was defenseless. He spurred his horse, seized the first troops he saw, and hurried them to the rocky hilltop.

Longstreet was also driving for the important height, from which he could enfilade the entire Union position. Texans and Alabamans met the 20th Maine and other Yankee units on Little Round Top in an explosive action. It was touch and go until Yankee reinforcements came up to hurl the Rebels back.

Below, Longstreet was cutting Sickles to pieces at the peach orchard, the wheatfield, and a rock-strewn wasteland called Devil's Den. The arrival of the V Corps stabilized the position and helped contain the attack.

On the Union right, upon the sound of Longstreet's guns, Ewell fired on Culp's Hill, weakened by the removal of troops sent to aid Sickles, and sent infantry to occupy former Yankee entrenchments.

Nearby, Early's men stormed Cemetery Hill at dusk (right) to fight a bitter engagement lasting until ten that night. Rebel troops took the crest temporarily, until Hancock's reserves drove out the Louisiana Tigers, leaving the position safe in Union hands.

Well-served Union artillery along important heights did much to smash Confederate attacks in the second and third days' fighting. By the time of Pickett's Charge, Yankee batteries of the II Corps had exhausted most of their long-range ammunition and momentarily ceased firing.

DAWN of July 3 promised a steaming summer day and action to match. On the Union right, artillery fire greeted the sun. Units of the XII Corps, returning from their march to relieve Sickles at Little Round Top, found Confederates occupying their former positions on Culp's Hill and controlling the water supply at nearby Spangler's Spring.

To drive them out, Yankee guns pounded the area. Infantry followed up the barrage, meeting stiff resistance. The action flowed back and forth all morning. By eleven o'clock, the Rebels had enough and fell back beyond Rock Creek as the Federals reached their objective.

During the previous night, Meade called a council of war. Lee had already struck him hard on both flanks. It was the Union leader's opinion that the next major Confederate attack would be aimed at his center.

Union observers found Meade's hunch was correct as they watched the Rebels build up for a powerful drive. Yankee defenses were put in readiness. Reserves from the flanks poured onto Cemetery Ridge and guns went into battery. Stone walls lining the elevation gave riflemen almost complete protection and troops deployed behind them.

In the enemy camp, Lee was outlining his plans to a bitterly protesting Longstreet. Apparently, Lee felt Meade had strengthened his flanks and weakened his center. This was to be the target of direct Confederate attack. An artillery barrage would signal the beginning, then infantry could cross the open fields and storm Union positions along the ridge south of Cemetery Hill.

To Longstreet, the plan was suicidal. "I have been a soldier all my life," he said to Lee. "It is my opinion that no 15,000 men ever arrayed for battle can take that position." Lee held his ground: "The enemy is there and I am going to strike him."

Major General George E. Pickett's division, not yet blooded at Gettysburg, was to lead the charge. His three brigades, under Richard B. Garnett, Lewis A. Armistead, and James L. Kemper, were part of Longstreet's corps. Additional brigades, from A. P. Hill, would join in the advance.

Field command was in Longstreet's hands, but much of the responsibility fell on his colonel of artillery, Edward P. Alexander. He would lay down the opening curtain of fire and, when it had taken maximum effect, give Pickett the signal to start.

Alexander gathered a hundred and thirty-eight guns, emplacing them all the way from the peach orchard to the Lutheran Seminary, the majority trained on the Union center. Hunt, the Yankee artillery chief, had more than two hundred pieces but could only crowd eighty into the crucial section of Cemetery Ridge. The remainder were placed on the flanks or kept in reserve.

Through late morning and early afternoon, unearthly quiet pervaded the haze-hung battlefield as the armies watched each other. At one o'clock, Rebel signal guns barked and Alexander's artillery let go.

The bombardment, a thundering, earth-shaking phenomenon, was heard in distant cities. Union guns held fire until they could range on Rebel muzzle flashes, then joined the chorus. For ninety minutes the countryside trembled with concussion.

Hunt slowed his fire to let the guns cool. Alexander interpreted the pause as a sign the Federals were heavily damaged. He was running low on ammunition, and desperately signaled for the Confederate charge.

The Rebel 15,000 moved out proudly. Fire ceased on both sides. Only the tread of the long gray lines ruffled the silence.

Then Yankee guns boomed from the flanks. The Rebel infantry, leaving a bloody trail of dead and wounded, reached the stone walls. Crashing volleys of rifle fire decimated their lines. Grape and canister spewed from Union guns at point-blank range.

For a moment, the Rebels stood on the ridge, then fell back, shattered by the murderous fire of Hancock's II Corps.

Placing his cap on the point of his sword, Armistead led the last gallant rush into the muzzles of Federal guns. He was mortally wounded, as was Garnett. Kemper was wounded and captured; Pickett miraculously survived the hail of Yankee fire and lived to fight again.

PICKETT'S Charge was the Rebel wave that broke against the Yankee rock to mark the end of Gettysburg.

As the struggle raged, another battle took place three miles east of Cemetery Ridge.

Jeb Stuart, after his sweeping raid, reached Lee on July 2, but his men were too worn for battle that day. On the third, Lee sent him to operate behind the enemy line and cut off Union retreat should Pickett's drive succeed.

Stuart swung around Gettysburg, drove south, and ran into Union cavalry under Brigadier General David McMurtrie Gregg. The forces clashed to open a three-hour battle that ended in Confederate withdrawal.

July 4 saw streaming rain pour down on the exhausted armies. By evening, Lee was organizing his retreat and beginning to move out. The march was a nightmare as the seventeen-mile-long wagon train of wounded men rocked and bumped over washed-out roads (left).

Lee's cavalry screen protected the withdrawing army from Yankee attack, fighting skirmishes in the process. The Southern army reached the Potomac, waited until the high water receded, then crossed over into Virginia and home.

Was a Long and Painful One for the Surviving Confederate Troops

GETTYSBURG was the greatest battle ever fought in North America and probably the most controversial. When the war ended, a host of leaders who had fought in the three-day struggle turned to pen and paper to justify their actions, express opinions, and offer second guesses on strategy.

There was much to discuss. Confederate tactics appeared deficient in imagination and certainly lacked the sharpness of execution that had marked the Army of Northern Virginia's earlier engagements.

Ewell's hesitancy to strike Union troops on July 1, once he had them on the run, looms as a lost opportunity. Longstreet's procrastination on July 2, when he did not move against Sickles until the afternoon, cost him Little Round Top.

Lack of coordination between the Confederate thrusts on the Union right and left July 2 was most unlike Robert E. Lee. Simultaneous pressure on both flanks might have forced Meade into difficult decisions, perhaps leading him to weaken his center, which faced A. P. Hill's III Corps.

The mystery of Pickett's Charge has never been explained satisfactorily. Lee was not in the habit of ordering suicidal actions, especially over the passionate objections of his leading corps commander. Fitzhugh Lee, the general's nephew, stated that the charge was not in accordance with Lee's entire plan, which had misfired along the way:

"A consummate master of war such as Lee would not drive en masse a column of 14,000 men across an open terrain of 1,300 or 1,400 yards, through a concentrated and converging fire of artillery, to attack an army of 100,000 on fortified heights, and give his entering wedge no support. Why, if every man in that assault had been bullet proof, and if the whole of those 14,000 splendid troops had arrived unharmed on Cemetery Ridge, there would still have been time for the Federals to seize them, tie them and take them prisoners before their supports could have reached them."

Lee never explained why Pickett's flanks were not supported or why he ordered the charge. With characteristic generosity, he took all blame for the failure upon himself.

Meade, too, kept his head up in adversity. He had clashed with Sickles, but the most penetrating criticism came from Lincoln, both angry and sorrowful that Meade had not capped his victory with capture of the Southern army.

The Rebel force had been available for the taking. Lee left Gettysburg July 4, but his movement was slow and tortuous. Rains had swollen the Potomac and he was forced to wait at Falling Waters until a pontoon bridge could be built. It was not until the thirteenth that crossings in strength could be made.

Lee protected himself with a weak cavalry screen that could have been penetrated by a determined Union force of any size. It was sufficient to halt Meade when he finally began pursuit after a delay of several days, with the fresh VI Corps. As he reached Lee's scouts, Meade informed Halleck he would move cautiously until he found out Lee's full strength.

The general-in-chief approved: "I think it will be best for you to postpone a general battle until you can concentrate all your forces and get up your reserves and reinforcements." Meade did as much. When he advanced on the fourteenth, the Rebels had escaped.

Halleck's next letter was less sympathetic: "I need hardly say to you that the escape of Lee's army without another battle has created great dissatisfaction in the mind of the President, and it will require an active and energetic pursuit on your part to remove the impression that it has not been sufficiently active heretofore."

It was too late. The quarry had reached cover. Lincoln burned and muttered of bad faith.

While military men and politicians argued over what might have been, the Gettysburg casualty figures gave the public an icy shock.

Union losses totaled just over 23,000, with 3,155 dead, 14,529 wounded, and more than 5,000 missing. The Confederate figure was 28,000: 3,903 dead, 18,735 wounded, and the remainder missing.

Address delivered at the dedication of the cemetery at Gettysburg.

Four score and seven years ago our fathers brought forth on this continent, a new nation, conceived in Liberty, and dedicated to the proposition that all men are created equal.

Now we are engaged in a great civil war, testing whether that nation, or any nation so conceived and so dedicated, can long endure. We are met on a great battle field of that war. We have come to dedicate a portion of that field, as a final resting place for those who here gave their lives that that nation might live. It is altogether fitting and proper that we should do this.

But, in a larger sense, we can not dedicate — we can not consecrate — we can not hallow — this ground. The brave men, living and dead, who struggled here have consecrated it, far above our poor power to add or detract. The world will little note, nor long remember what we say here, but it can never forget what they did here. It is for us the living, rather, to be dedicated here to the unfinished work which they who fought here have thus far so nobly advanced. It is rather for us to be here dedicated to the great task remaining before us — that from these honored dead we take increased devotion to that cause for which they gave the last full measure of devotion — that we here highly resolve that these dead shall not have died in vain — that this nation, under God, shall have a new birth of freedom — and that government of the people, by the people, for the people, shall not perish from the earth.

Abraham Lincoln.

November 19, 1863.

SOLDIERS marching to battle at Gettysburg noticed a sign posted at the graveyard that gives Cemetery Hill its name: "All persons found using firearms in these grounds will be prosecuted with the utmost rigor of the law."

By July 4, the firearms had been used and many of their owners were beyond reach of the law forever. On the slopes and in the valleys, bodies lay in profusion. Some were in shallow graves, some unburied.

Andrew Curtin, governor of Pennsylvania, visited Gettysburg and was appalled by these grim fruits of war. He suggested a common burial ground for dead heroes of the Federal Army and appointed an agent to see to the task.

David Wills, a local lawyer, purchased seventeen acres of land on Cemetery Hill in the name of Pennsylvania and engaged a landscape architect to design a memorial plot.

In a matter of months, some 3,500 bodies were brought together, identified whenever possible, and laid to rest in the new cemetery. The fallen were buried by states, each state appropriating funds for the purpose. A few years later, the memorial burial ground was turned over to the national government.

When reburial had been accomplished at

Gettysburg, a dedication ceremony was planned for November 19, 1863. It was an impressive occasion. Troops filed in to salute their departed comrades, country folk hitched their wagons and came to town for an all-day celebration, and the glittering gentry of the cities thronged the quiet town (above).

Official Washington was present in force. Lincoln had been invited as a matter of course, but not included in dedication plans. Protocol dictated that he be asked to say a few words, and the President assented.

Chosen as speaker of honor was the Honorable Edward Everett of Massachusetts, one of the most distinguished men in American public life.

For two hours he reviewed classical burial customs, offered a dissertation on war, dissected the action at Gettysburg, and played upon the chords of patriotism. A storm of applause followed the speech.

Lincoln arose, shuffled to the platform with notes in hand, and spoke for two minutes. In less than 300 plain words he laid his heart before the people and created an American classic. The audience produced a faint ripple of applause. Secretary of State Seward and Everett agreed the President had failed.

211

CHARLESTON RESISTS

FOR a New Year's Day present in 1863, the Confederacy received the city of Galveston, Texas. The gift was donated by Major General John B. Magruder, who had made his name the year before by holding up McClellan's peninsular advance at Yorktown.

In 1862, a small Union fleet arrived off the principal Texas port to blockade it, and a 300-man garrison of Massachusetts troops bivouacked on the wharf. "Prince John" Magruder, newly arrived at his Houston headquarters, determined to break the blockade.

The Rebel chief sent troops to points near the wharf, then mounted a boarding party on two steamers armored only with cotton bales. At dawn on January 1, Magruder's navy approached *Harriet Lane,* which sank one of the Southern vessels but was boarded by men from the other (above) and captured. Another Yankee ship, aground, was blown up. The remaining vessels withdrew, and the Massachusetts troops surrendered.

Southern victory was short-lived. Within a week a new blockading squadron appeared. One of its ships, *Hatteras,* was decoyed out to sea by the Rebel raider *Alabama* and sunk, but the blockade continued.

Sporadic action in the Gulf continued in 1863, but the major amphibious action of the year took place in the Atlantic and involved the Union attempts to reduce Fort Sumter and capture Charleston.

That city's defenses had been entrusted to General Beauregard after his return from sick leave. An able engineer, he went to work with a will to make his position impregnable.

Charleston, like New York, is on land that points into a spacious harbor. In this harbor, shielding the city, were Fort Sumter and the smaller Fort Ripley. Bordering the open waterway, above and below, lay fortified islands that could pour shot and shell on any fleet attempting direct entrance. Sullivan's Island is north; to the south are James, Morris, and Folly islands, all closely connected and slashed by swamp and bayou.

Beauregard set himself the task of strengthening existing forts, emplacing more guns, and creating new batteries. He found two gunboats, which, under his orders, harassed the blockading fleet.

Southern defenses met their first major test April 7. Encouraged by former successes in Atlantic coastal waters, the Union sent Rear Admiral Samuel Du Pont with his flagship *New Ironsides* and eight new monitors to engage Beauregard.

Steaming past Morris Island's guns, they cautiously approached Sumter and opened fire. In a two-and-a-half-hour artillery battle they caused little damage, were badly worsted, and withdrew. The twin-turret monitor *Keokuk* sank and others were disabled. Du Pont fired about 150 shots; Beauregard, more than 2,200. Southern batteries had been arranged to support each other and their cross fire was formidable.

Direct attack had failed and blockade runners still entered and left Charleston. The next attempt to seize the city was to be by land infiltration under troops assigned to Major General Quincy A. Gillmore.

Yankee forces had occupied Folly Island; on July 10 they moved north and crossed over to Morris Island, which protected the southern boundary of Charleston Harbor. Fort Wagner and Battery Gregg, well up the island, were the objectives.

The U.S. Navy stood offshore to lay down a heavy curtain of fire on Fort Wagner July 18 as Gillmore's troops undertook a powerful offensive. Once again, Beauregard held his own:

"The assault was terribly disastrous to the enemy. His loss in killed, wounded and prisoners must have been 3,000, as 800 bodies were interred in front of Battery Wagner on the following morning. . . . Our own loss during the bombardment and assault was 174, killed and wounded."

Thrown back, Union troops settled down to siege, helped by the guns of the navy. Wagner and Gregg were kept under almost continuous bombardment from July to September, Yankee troops working closer all the while. On September 6, Beauregard saw the end was near and removed his garrison, the Northern force entering on the following day.

In late August, Gillmore had announced that unless Forts Wagner and Sumter surrendered, he would shell Charleston. His threat was called. The general ordered a Parrott gun set up in the swamps of Morris Island, and it poured thirty-six shells into the city before it burst.

Neither threats nor shells could open the way to Charleston, which held out until 1865. Fort Sumter was slowly pounded to rubble but kept its flag flying almost to the end of the war.

Union vessels attacking Rebel-held Fort Sumter (below) April 7 were exposed to heavy fire from forts ringing Charleston harbor. Welles and Fox, jubilant after the repulse of *Virginia* in Hampton Roads, placed immense faith in the new monitors and hurried several to completion for the attempt on the important Southern port. Du Pont did not share their enthusiasm.

MOUNTAIN WAR

FOURTH of July, 1863, had proved a momentous holiday for the North. At Gettysburg, Lee began his retreat. Pemberton surrendered to Grant at Vicksburg. With major victories in east and west, Lincoln looked toward the center where Rosecrans was pressing Bragg.

The opposing generals had watched each other for months, Rosecrans at Murfreesboro; Bragg, to the southeast, at Tullahoma. Washington prodded the Union commander continually. He refused to move toward east Tennessee until given sufficient cavalry for thorough scouting operations in the territory he was to occupy.

This was the most spectacular terrain in the east. Chattanooga, Rosecrans' objective, lay below the Tennessee River, which came from the northeast, twisted by the city in a series of hairpin bends, and flowed southwest.

The river cut through the Cumberland Mountains, a wild and rugged range of towering heights, abrupt drops, sheer cliffs, and narrow, wooded valleys. Theoretically, the peaks were ideal positions for defensive fighting. In fact, the range offered protective cover and concealment to invading troops.

Running from northeast to southwest, the Cumberlands near Chattanooga formed a series of parallel ridges. Below the city and slightly west was Raccoon Mountain. Wills Valley lay just to the east, then came Lookout Mountain; another valley; Missionary Ridge; the valley containing Chickamauga Creek and Pigeon Mountain.

Chattanooga sat on Tennessee's southern border. Directly south was Georgia. Alabama lay southwest. Nestled in its mountains, the city was east Tennessee's most important strategic point.

Two major railroads reached it from the west. Two more ran east from the town. One stretched to Knoxville, a hundred miles northeast, then on into Virginia. The other ran southeast to Atlanta and the heart of Dixie. Capture of Chattanooga would present the North with a major junction.

Protection of the important rail center was Bragg's task, but his forces had been weakened for the South's attempt to save Vicksburg. With his remaining force, an army numerically inferior to Rosecrans', he stretched a protective cordon along the Duck River, near Tullahoma.

To break this line or by-pass it, Rosecrans had the XIV Corps under Thomas, the XX under McCook, the XXI led by Crittenden, and one corps in reserve under Major Gen-

eral Gordon Granger. On June 23, Union troops took the offensive.

Bragg, fearing for his left and the railroad line that bisected his center, concentrated weight in these areas. Rosecrans pressed hard on the sensitive points, but it was only a feint. Thomas swung wide around the Confederate right to flank Bragg's position.

The Rebels withdrew. Rosecrans followed up, passing through narrow defiles to seize strategic hills commanding Tullahoma. Bragg's position became untenable and he withdrew to Chattanooga.

The Union advance had been well executed and relatively bloodless, although mountains, scrub, and mired roads made progress painful and wearying. Rosecrans stopped at Stevenson, Alabama, to rest and plan a campaign that would take him across the Tennessee and through the mountains into Chattanooga.

Once again, Bragg was deceived. The logical invasion plan meant moving up the river to points above the city, then a sudden descent. To assure Bragg this was his plan, Rosecrans sent Crittenden upstream and had him shell the city from the north.

Meanwhile, as Bragg concentrated his men for a supposed thrust by Crittenden, Thomas and McCook crossed the river near Bridgeport, west and south of Chattanooga. Ignoring the city, they drove east across the mountains toward the railroad from Atlanta. His supply line threatened, Bragg evacuated Chattanooga September 8, and Union troops marched in the following day (above).

215

Shielded by a stone wall, the 19th and 24th Illinois repulsed a Confederate cavalry charge at Crawfish Creek (above) during the bitter Chickamauga fighting. The Union high command (lower right) was committing its forces well when Longstreet's break-through split the line.

CHATTANOOGA was captured by Crittenden's corps. A few days earlier, Burnside, with the Army of the Ohio, came down from the north to take Knoxville. The east-west rail line had been cut in two places, and Rosecrans, exultant, pushed on to smash and capture Bragg. It was the Union general's turn to be fooled.

Bragg spread word abroad that he was fleeing for Atlanta. In reality, he awaited reinforcements to make his force stronger than Rosecrans'. From Knoxville, Buckner brought a corps. Johnston sent troops from Mississippi under Breckinridge. Longstreet, detached from the Army of Northern Virginia, was on his way by rail with two divisions. Eventually, Bragg's troops numbered 66,000 against Rosecrans' 58,000.

The Union leader, advancing to seal off his enemy, had separated his force. Crittenden held the north, Thomas the center. McCook lay far to the south.

Bragg's powerful army, handled with skill, could crush Rosecrans' corps one by one, but Confederate intelligence was faulty and execution of commands lethargic.

Rosecrans' cavalry did its work well and the general saw his dilemma. As Bragg's army gathered in the area around Lafayette, Georgia, for the offensive, Rosecrans sped orders to his far-flung commanders.

Opposite Lafayette, Thomas prepared to hold the line. Crittenden moved south. McCook marched fifty-seven miles in thirty-six hours to reach his commander the night of September 17. With his force together once more, Rosecrans began to back cautiously toward Chattanooga. Bragg moved to cut him off.

Both armies went north through the valley of Chickamauga Creek September 18, and Rosecrans regrouped his corps, placing Thomas on the left. Union troops marched up the west side of the watercourse, Confederates the right. That night, most of the Southern army crossed the river.

Bragg hit hard the following morning and a hammering, all-day battle began. One by one, from north to south, Southern units struck their opposite numbers. They gained ground, lost it, gained it again, and halted in stalemate at twilight.

Rosecrans shortened his line and strengthened it that night. On the twentieth, Bragg tried again with the same pattern. Polk, on the right, smashed against solid Union positions, made a little ground, and was stopped.

As battle raged, Rosecrans ordered one unit in the Union center to change position. A garbled order pulled it suddenly out of line, leaving a gaping hole. Longstreet saw the opportunity and sent six divisions pouring through the opening to fan out behind Union positions and rout the Federal army.

Panicked, Northern soldiers streamed back toward Chattanooga. Only Thomas held his own, seeking high ground on Snodgrass Hill and forming a horseshoe defense position. With the aid of Granger's reserves he held off Rebel attack, saved the Northern army, and earned his nickname as the "Rock of Chickamauga." When the last Confederate drive had been repelled by bayonet, the doughty general pulled back into the city.

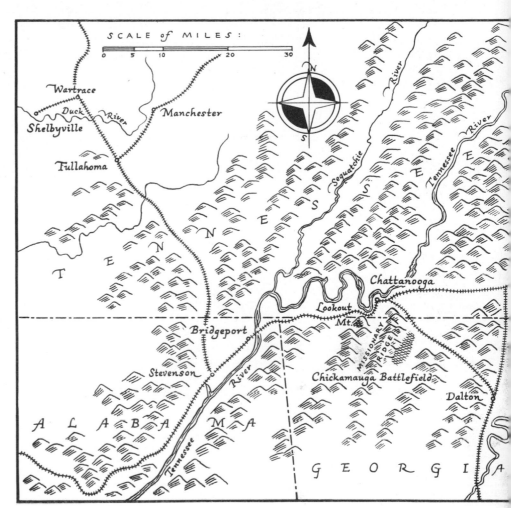

CHICKAMAUGA had been a blood bath. More than 28,000 dead and wounded fell on the battlefield, 17,000 of them Confederates. Bragg paid a tremendous price to win the day and trap Rosecrans' army.

But trapped they were, within Chattanooga, and the Rebel general settled down to siege. Starvation became a real possibility for Union troops occupying the city.

About thirty miles to the west lay Bridgeport, the main Union supply base. Bragg's men covered the river, railroad, and highway connecting Bridgeport and Chattanooga. Most of the Rebel army was south of the besieged city, blocking that route. To the east, the barren country was in Confederate hands. North of Chattanooga, a rough mountain road led into the city. Supplies trickled in along this rugged route, but in no quantity, and the path was lined with splintered wagons and dead draft animals.

Rebel troops on Lookout Mountain (above) could almost peer down into empty Yankee mess tins. Corn and gruel were the rations. In the city, 11,000 horses and mules starved to death, leaving the Army of the Cumberland without animals for transport.

Washington boiled over with alarm for its trapped force, and Halleck dispatched relief forces from east and west. From the Rappahannock, Hooker took portions of the XI and XII Corps and, traveling by way of Cincinnati, Louisville, and Nashville, brought them to Bridgeport. Sherman left Mississippi with part of Grant's forces to help raise the siege of the city.

Perhaps the most important change was one in the command structure. Grant, painfully injured in a fall from his horse, was ordered to Louisville October 17, going by rail via Indianapolis. At that place, War Secretary Stanton boarded the train and produced orders creating the Military Division of the Mississippi. Grant was given charge of the new division, making him supreme commander in most of the west. In addition, Rosecrans was relieved from his command and Thomas took over the Army of the Cumberland.

Grant, still on crutches, traveled the rough northern route and arrived in Chattanooga October 23. His major task was to open a supply line into the city, and he determined

Grant Faced Bragg in Rugged Terrain Throughout the Campaign for Control of the Chattanooga Area

to crush Confederate forces guarding the approach from the west and use this route.

In a secret move by night, a detachment from Thomas embarked in pontoon boats, drifted down the Tennessee to the west, and joined up with one of Hooker's forces. Together, they beat back the Rebel outpost, bridged the twisting river, and established a supply line that ran behind protecting hills to link Bridgeport and Chattanooga.

Two problems now plagued Grant. One was to support Burnside, who held Knoxville, the other to break out of Chattanooga. Sherman arrived November 15 to help.

Bragg's defenses appeared impregnable, a concave line anchored at each end in impressive heights. Just below Chattanooga and slightly west lay Lookout Mountain, its slopes honeycombed with Rebel artillery. A little to the east was Missionary Ridge, also

heavily armed. Strong Confederate forces held the base of the ridge and the valley between. Bragg felt so secure that he dispatched Longstreet, with 15,000 men, to strike Burnside at Knoxville.

Grant planned a three-way move. Hooker would strike Lookout Mountain, the Confederate left. Sherman would make a long, semicircular curve north and east, then drop down to hit Missionary Ridge, the Rebel right, at its northernmost extremity. Thomas was to apply pressure in the center.

On November 23, enemy outposts in the center, at Orchard Knob, were carried. On the twenty-fourth, Hooker made his move up Lookout Mountain through swirling mist and rain. With a much superior force he drove the Rebels back, winning the "Battle above the Clouds," and breaking one end of the Confederate line (below).

IN ITS first stage, the Union plan went as expected. The second stage, on November 24 and 25, miscarried at the start and ended with an astonishing victory.

Hooker, with Lookout Mountain under control, was to come down into the plain and attack the lower end of five-mile-long Missionary Ridge as Sherman struck its upper end. "Fighting Joe" lost his way in the heavy woods, then ran up against an unfordable stream. For all practical purposes, he remained out of action.

To the north, Sherman hit a series of deep ravines with sharpshooters posted above. He called for more men and got them but was stopped in his tracks. From the heights, Bragg's men rolled boulders and cannon balls down on the vastly superior Union force, which could not gain any amount of ground.

Both Union flanks were halted and Grant called on the Army of the Cumberland, holding the center, to take the rifle pits at the foot of Missionary Ridge, then halt. The move was a feint to remove Confederate pressure from the flanks.

Thomas sent his men forward. They took the trenches, then looked up at the heights from which a withering fire was pouring down on them. And, without orders, they charged.

Grabbing vines and tree trunks for hand holds, the Army of the Cumberland scrambled up the sheer, steep face of the ridge. They stopped to breathe, reloaded, and pushed forward into the face of Rebel guns. Yelling, cursing, clambering, the men rushed on (right).

Grant, Thomas, and Granger watched openmouthed from Orchard Knob. The Union chief asked by whose orders these men were taking the hill. Nobody knew; the combination of courage and momentum in the soldiers themselves drove the army forward.

Bragg's mountain fastness crumbled. His troops, in full retreat, pulled back into Georgia as rear guards fought off Yankee pursuit. Grant sent an army to Knoxville to relieve Burnside. Longstreet, who had attacked the town and failed, heard of the approaching column and withdrew.

CASUALTIES

NOWHERE was the lack of preparation for war more painfully apparent than in the medical department. When the conflict began, the United States Army had 115 trained medical officers. Twenty-seven resigned, three to enter civilian practice and the remaining twenty-four to throw their lot with the Confederacy.

Shortly after Fort Sumter was fired upon, Clement A. Finley became Surgeon General of the U.S. Army, following forty-three years of service in the Medical Department. The post was a hot seat, open to fire from politicians stung into action by relatives of the men suffering from lack of attention to wounds received in early battles.

Finley lasted until early 1862, then Robert C. Wood took over in an acting capacity for a few months until the trying position was assumed by William A. Hammond. He reorganized personnel and paperwork and embarked upon a badly needed hospital building program. By autumn, 1863, Hammond had crossed swords with War Secretary Stanton and was relieved.

The new Surgeon General, Joseph K. Barnes, remained in office throughout the rest of the war and later. He saw his department burgeon until it contained 10,000 medical men.

Personnel changes did not haunt the South. Samuel P. Moore was appointed Surgeon General when war began and retained his post until the conflict ended. With limited facilities, Moore worked wonders. The statistics of his operations were destroyed in the great Richmond fire that marked evacuation of the Southern capital in 1865, and knowledge of the Confederate Medical Corps is therefore sparse.

The top medical officers started from scratch. By the conclusion of Bull Run, it was apparent large-scale medical attention had become imperative, especially if the war lasted an appreciable length of time. Adequate hospitals, trained personnel to serve in them, and assurance of a plentiful drug supply were necessities.

More important was medical attention in the field. Each of the Northern regiments had a surgeon and an assistant who traveled with the troops. Volunteer medical officers were appointed for administrative work with each division; additional surgeons became attached to brigades, corps, armies, departments, and hospitals; civilian physicians served under contract; a corps of medical cadets was appointed. Southern organization was similar to that of the North, when manpower permitted.

At the war's beginning, there was no such thing as a hospital corps. Transportation and nursing for the wounded came from enlisted men, removed from their regular jobs and placed on temporary duty. There existed a pressing need for personnel whose work would serve as a connecting link between field surgeon and hospital.

Surgeon General Hammond pleaded with Stanton and Halleck for an ambulance corps but was coldly turned down. It remained for individual units to create their own organizations in the field.

Surgeon Jonathan Letterman, Medical Director of the Army of the Potomac, convinced McClellan of the need for first aid and transportation of the wounded. With McClellan's permission, ambulances were brought together and special personnel appointed to aid the injured and do nothing else.

The system worked admirably at Antietam. By the time of Chancellorsville, ambulance men were standing by their vehicles awaiting the results of the battle (below). Grant took over the plan for the Army of the Tennessee. Congress eventually approved, and a standard ambulance system was established. In the Confederate Medical Department, a comparable plan existed.

Transport for the wounded reached a rough efficiency but it was often of little avail to the man concerned. The Civil War occurred previous to basic medical discoveries that seem commonplace in the twentieth century. Operating on the battlefield (pages 222-223), Union and Rebel surgeons employed practices and held beliefs that seem incredible today.

Antisepsis was unknown. Wounds were probed by dirty fingers or unwashed instruments, and seldom cleaned once the bullet or shell fragment had been removed. Unclean sponges or lint, which had been created by the work of unsterilized human hands, helped absorb blood. In the field, ripped flesh was bound up with dirty handkerchiefs, portions of sweat-stained uniforms, or whatever cloth was available. Under such conditions, gangrene and tetanus were common.

Army pharmacies went into the field to fill surgeons' orders (upper left). They stocked chloroform and ether, used for anesthesia, when available. Because of shortages, hundreds of operations were performed without anesthetic. Brandy or whisky sometimes substituted for the missing pain-killers.

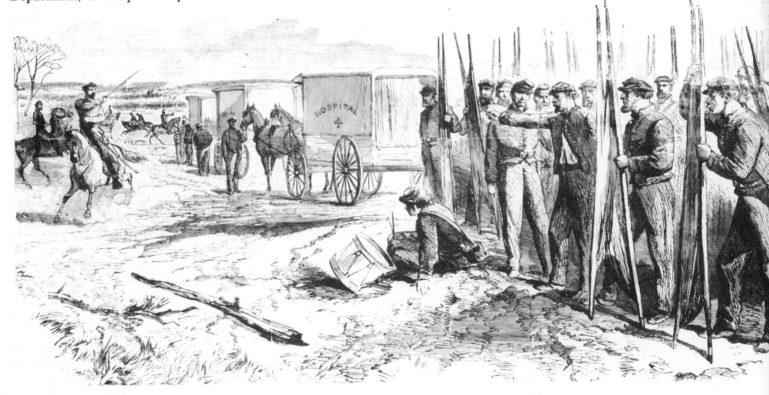

225

MOST battlefield wounds came from rifle bullets and most rifles fired the Minié ball, a conical lead slug more than a half-inch in diameter and weighing over an ounce. The heavy projectile caused fearful damage.

Mushrooming after it hit, a Minié ball smashed long bones into fragments, often making amputation necessary. Intestinal wounds, because of the tearing action of the big slug, were usually fatal.

Shell fragments caused ugly injuries, tearing as they hit. Grape and canister, small balls fired in bunches from cannon, were deadly at short range. Bayonet and sword wounds were in the minority.

When lead was flying on the field, regimental medical officers moved forward as near as possible to the front and established first-aid stations. Stretcher bearers went out under fire to pick up the wounded (above) and bring them in. They received elementary attention to halt bleeding.

As soon as possible, patients were taken from the first-aid stations and placed in ambulances for the trip to a field hospital. If fire was too heavy for the horse-drawn ambulance, stretcher bearers did the carrying. The litter used often had legs, which could be let down to create a temporary cot.

Field hospitals were selected before combat by medical personnel, on the scene of potential action. They were houses, barns, carriage shops, stores, or even bombproof shelters built into such strongholds as Fort Fisher (upper right). Efforts were made to create crude bunks in these structures, or at least to cover the floors with clean straw. As the war progressed, tents were issued for field hospital use. Compact and portable, they were widely used.

The field hospital was a receiving station in which injured men had their wounds examined in detail, when time permitted. Surgical treatment was carried out as indicated and permanent dressings replaced temporary ones.

When the wounded were ready to travel, ambulances took them from their places of temporary confinement to hospital trains (lower right). Loaded aboard, they were moved to the big general hospitals in which final recovery could take place.

Passenger cars, freight cars, or flatcars were used to carry the wounded, depending on availability. Near the Atlantic coast and major rivers like the Mississippi, the wounded sometimes traveled by water.

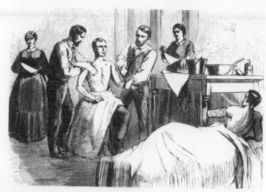

WOUNDED soldiers who survived treatment in field hospitals, and escaped infection or disease in the process, were sent to permanent general hospitals. There they received care comparable to that extended to civilians (top), and were allowed to convalesce before discharge for retirement or return to their units.

Women worked in permanent hospitals, but throughout the war there was a running battle of the sexes between top military men, officers of the medical corps, and feminine volunteers. Male nurses, either soldiers, wounded veterans, or civilians, were the order of the day. They and their superiors resented the distaff-side invasion.

Dorothea Dix became Superintendent of Women Nurses for the Union after war began, but had to fight an uphill battle to place her charges in military hospitals. Persistence, courage, and solid determination enabled her to staff such installations as the one at Georgetown, D.C., pictured above, to the unqualified approval of its patients.

The outstanding civilian welfare organization in the North, the United States Sanitary Commission, contributed male and female nurses to general hospitals. In the Confederacy, the Women's Relief Society produced volunteers to bathe, bandage, and comfort stricken soldiers.

Doctors and orderlies of North and South undoubtedly made life difficult for these patriotic women. In letters and diaries, the ladies struck back. Accusations of cruelty, drunkenness, and callous indifference among medical personnel dot these personal missives.

At the beginning of war, there was a serious shortage of permanent hospitals to handle casualties in any considerable number. Above and below the Mason-Dixon line, medical men converted churches, col-

lege buildings, warehouses, hotels, and residences into sanctuaries for the sick.

Major cities such as Philadelphia soon became thick with permanent hospitals (above). Installations at army camps, such as the hospital at Jefferson Barracks, Missouri, were expanded to meet pressing needs (right). Urban areas near battlefields saw the greatest growth in medical facilities. By late 1864, Washington and its suburbs had twenty-five general hospitals with more than 21,000 beds.

New construction was necessary. The over-all plan for general hospitals adopted in the 1860's is in use today. This called for a number of wards, constructed of wood, each to contain two rows of cots holding from forty to sixty patients. The structures were usually one story high, but sometimes had two levels. Clean, airy, easy to build, the wards could be multiplied indefinitely as the need arose.

Largest of the general hospitals was Chimborazo, at Richmond, which treated 76,000 patients. The second in size was Lincoln, in Washington, where 46,000 men were cared for.

229

MANY a Civil War soldier was lowered into the grave by his comrades (below). Some graves were crudely marked; many were not. After major battles, and in prison camps, there were mass burials in shallow trenches, the soldiers usually unidentified.

Casualty figures are uncertain. Union records, including pension data gathered by the Medical Corps, throw some light on the subject. Disappearance of Confederate documents, destroyed by fire or lost in the field, eliminated accurate statistics relating to the Southern army.

The best available statements indicate more than 360,000 Union soldiers died in the war. Of these, 110,000 lost their lives as the result of battle: 67,000 being killed in action and 43,000 perishing from wounds.

Over 224,000 Federal fighting men died of disease, and the remainder lost their lives through "other causes," which include accidental death, suicide, execution, and death in prison camps. For the Confederacy, one estimate reports 258,000 dead, 94,000 being killed in battle.

Death from injuries was brought about by (1) gunshot wounds, (2) incised wounds from sabers, swords, and bayonets, (3) miscellaneous hurts coming from blows, falls, and like causes. Treatment of such wounds by unsanitary hands and instruments brought on infection resulting in death.

Among the most shocking facts of the war was that 62 per cent of Union casualties came from disease. Many of the men who contributed to this figure never saw combat. They enlisted, went to camp or into the field, and were struck down far from enemy lines.

Epidemic diseases like typhoid fever, diphtheria, and dysentery caused havoc among men living close together. Insect-borne illness, such as malaria, took its toll. And the crude preinduction medical examinations failed to root out many disease-prone men who later succumbed to pneumonia and tuberculosis.

1864

GRANT TAKES OVER

THE early days of 1864 were dark ones for the Confederacy. Three major campaigns had brought defeat: Gettysburg in the east, Vicksburg in the west, Chattanooga in the center.

Following the abortive Pennsylvania invasion, Lee rebuilt his army and encamped it south of the Rapidan River in Virginia. Meade occupied the opposite bank. In autumn, 1863, Confederate troops crossed the stream, struck the Yankees, and pushed them back on Centerville.

Meade yielded to the pressure, then dug in and shattered the Rebel attack. A short time later, he went over to the offensive himself, but the Southern army soon halted his drive. As the new year began, both armies were in their old positions.

After Chickamauga, Jefferson Davis had visited the Army of Tennessee and found extreme discontent among Bragg's corps commanders. In the reshuffle that occurred, Polk left the command and went to Mississippi, General William J. Hardee coming in to replace him. D. H. Hill was relieved of his position and sent to North Carolina. Forrest, who refused to serve any longer under Bragg, got a recruiting task in Mississippi.

The debacle at Chattanooga lent strength to the opinions of the South's top brass about Bragg's abilities as a leader. But Davis was loyal and, although removing Bragg following the defeat, kept him on as his personal military adviser.

Joseph E. Johnston took over command of the Army of Tennessee, which was in winter quarters at Dalton, Georgia, on the railroad from Chattanooga to Atlanta. He spent his days in preparation for the major effort he knew the Union would mount in 1864.

The series of military defeats shook Southern leaders, for manpower and munitions were running out. The blockade made things worse.

Chances of foreign intervention, or even recognition, were disappearing. Southern credit was hard hit, and inflation became a menace. Paper money came from the government, the states, and even private businessmen. Its value dropped steadily.

As deprivation stalked the South, the North prospered, but the populace was sick of war. In mid-1863, ugly draft riots broke out in New York, led by hoodlums who refused to answer their country's call.

By early 1864, a major Northern need was finally filled. After a three-year search, Lincoln found the leader he had been seeking.

In February, Congress restored the former grade of lieutenant general and Grant received a commission as such March 9, being placed in command of all the armies of the United States. Halleck was made chief-of-staff, a liaison between Grant and the field commanders.

Sherman replaced Grant as head of the western armies; Major General James B. McPherson took over Sherman's command, the Army of the Tennessee. Major General Philip H. Sheridan, at Grant's request, relieved Pleasonton as commander of cavalry, Army of the Potomac.

Once in command, Grant produced a master plan that was simple, intelligent, and deadly. He proposed an all-out offensive with his entire force, the armies attacking simultaneously. Under steady pressure on all sides, the Confederacy was bound to crack.

The main effort consisted of three parts. On the left, the Army of the James, under Butler, was to move up the James River from Fort Monroe, threatening Richmond from the southeast. In the center, Meade's target was Lee and the Army of Northern Virginia. On the right, Sherman was ordered from Chattanooga to Atlanta, to destroy the heart of the South and crush Johnston's force.

There were other operations as well. Major General George Crook, in West Virginia, received orders to threaten the railroad connecting Virginia and Tennessee, forcing the Rebels to send men to protect this communication line or give it up. Major General Franz Sigel was sent south through the Shenandoah Valley to protect Washington from invasion and destroy Lee's source of food and forage. In the Deep South, Banks's men from New Orleans would move on Mobile, Alabama, one of the last Southern ports remaining open.

RED RIVER FIASCO

BEFORE the combined offensive of 1864 began to roll, the Union carried out a side-show operation that tried tempers, deflected troops from more important objectives, and failed completely. Its importance lay in the number of men employed and its part in frustrating one phase of Grant's master plan.

The scene was Louisiana and the area of the campaign the land around Red River, which crosses the state from northwest to southeast before emptying into the Mississippi a little above Port Hudson. Union plans encompassed a drive up the river and seizure of Shreveport, in the state's northwestern corner near the Texas border.

Motivations leading to the Red River Expedition were somewhat obscure. One objective appeared to be political. Union troops occupied much of Louisiana by 1864. If the expedition could sew up the remainder of the state, there was a possibility elections could be held to bring Louisiana back into the Union.

One objective was military. Control of the state would place Northern forces along the Texas border, threatening that state and Mexico, to the south, where French imperial interests were at work.

The third objective may have been economic. Louisiana was rich in cotton. Northern mills needed the fiber, and it was precious for export as it brought in gold from abroad.

Banks, based on New Orleans, was operating against the Texas coast early in January when Halleck placed him in command of the Red River Expedition. He was to have his own force, 10,000 men from Sherman and a fleet under Porter, to ascend the waterway. Additional assistance would come from Major General Frederick Steele in Arkansas, who planned to attack Shreveport from the north, diverting troops from Banks's main thrust.

Banks opposed the expedition, as did Grant who felt the troops would be better employed in capturing Mobile. But their objections came to nought and the campaign was planned for middle March when the water would be high enough to ease the passage of Porter's vessels. Defending Louisiana was General E. Kirby Smith, in charge of Confederate operations west of the Mississippi.

Porter gathered a fleet of twenty gunboats plus more than forty supply ships and transports. Sherman's force, elements of the XVI and XVII Corps under Brigadier General Andrew J. Smith, embarked and the flotilla moved up the Red River toward Fort de Russy, which covered the city of Alexandria. A. J. Smith landed at Simsport, below the fort, and marched overland to take the place by brisk assault on March 14. The fleet, meanwhile, smashed through a dam and raft blocking the river and proceeded to Alexandria where Porter and Smith joined.

Banks was detained in New Orleans on political business and sent his force overland under Major General William B. Franklin. With portions of the XIII and XIX Corps, Franklin marched northwest along the Bayou Teche, roughly parallel to the Red River, and after a 175-mile trip over ruined roads, entered Alexandria.

Banks arrived to take over his combined force. On March 27, he received orders from Grant giving him until April 25 to capture Shreveport. If the campaign's objective was not in hand by that date, the troops were to be broken up and given other tasks. The Union army pressed on up river to Natchitoches, but low water forced seven gunboats and the larger transports to stay behind.

Rebel troops in Louisiana, under Lieutenant General Richard Taylor, had been falling back before the Union advance while Kirby Smith planned how best to deal with Steele descending from the north and Banks ascending from the south. At Mansfield, only a few miles from Shreveport and covering three roads leading to the city, Taylor turned to make a stand.

Sherman's men, under A. J. Smith, blooded the Red River Expedition with the speedy capture of Fort de Russy (left) on March 14, opening the path to Alexandria. Franklin, with 20,000 men, was marching to join Smith, but bad roads and river crossings (below) slowed his progress.

BANKS'S men reached Rebel positions April 8. Taylor was concentrated while the Union force stretched more than twelve miles along a narrow country road.

After a period of skirmishing, Taylor advanced at four o'clock to open the battle known as Mansfield or Sabine Crossroads. Striking the tip of the Federal line, the Rebel attack sent the Yankee troops spinning back. Retreating troops caused panic in the teamsters of the long wagon train and mass disorder ruled the field. As night fell, elements of the XIX Corps held their ground to cover the retreat and save the army.

Banks ordered general retreat. By April 9, the army had fallen back to Pleasant Hill.

Taylor followed up his victory and struck again at Pleasant Hill with 14,000 men against the Union's 13,000. This time Union men held good ground and checked the Confederate drive, eventually turning it into a retreat (above). Banks was for following up his victory, but his associates persuaded him to continue his own withdrawal.

Porter Put Together an Impressive Fleet for the Red River Expedition, but Low Water Made It More Hindrance than Help

UNION forces fell back to Grand Écore, where they awaited the arrival of the fleet, which was having difficulties moving down river because of low water. As they waited, Banks's men entrenched in case a revived Rebel army might pursue them.

Kirby Smith had the idea in mind. But first he planned to turn and strike Steele, who threatened Shreveport from the north. Leaving Taylor's cavalry to watch Banks at Grand Écore, Kirby Smith went north to seek combat. He met Steele, drove him back to Little Rock, then sent forces down to join Taylor in attacking Banks. By the time the Confederates grouped for this effort, Banks had seen the fleet arrive safely and departed for Alexandria.

There real trouble awaited him. The river, since the fleet had ascended it, had fallen six feet, and Porter's vessels were unable to pass. Trapped just above the rapids at Alexandria, the gunboats made perfect targets.

The occasion produced a Union genius in Lieutenant Colonel Joseph Bailey of the 4th Wisconsin, then serving as chief engineer on Franklin's staff. Working with army labor, in less than two weeks he produced a series of dams that raised the water sufficiently to permit passage of the steamers, the last of which went through the rapids May 13.

With the fleet free, Banks continued his retreat; and after a final brush with the Confederates May 18, the Union army saw the campaign end. A. J. Smith's troops, because of this diversion, were too late to join in the Atlanta campaign for which they had been earmarked. Grant's plan for an offensive toward Mobile was canceled.

Bailey had to dam the river twice to assure high enough water for Porter's ships. He used felled trees, sunken coal barges, and log cribs filled with bricks, stones, and pieces of machinery from nearby sugar houses and cotton gins. The dams created chutes in which the water level rose.

COMMUNICATIONS

TRANSPORTATION during the Civil War was often a quartermaster's nightmare. Armies fought through swamp, forest, coastal marshes, mountains, and tangled, second-growth underbrush. They expended enormous quantities of food and ammunition, speedily wore out clothing, and called constantly for medical supplies. Quartermasters learned early to develop and exploit every known means of transportation.

Railroads were vital. The Confederacy had 9,000 miles of railroad but lacked steel and factory facilities to replace rolling stock and rails. The Union was fortunate. It controlled 22,000 miles of track, had a great industrial potential, and a transportation genius in Brigadier General Herman Haupt, head of the United States Military Railroad Construction Corps. Before Haupt there had been chaos. Under him, trains met schedules (upper left) while repair and new construction went on constantly.

Men of both the Railroad Corps and Engineer Corps became expert at bridge reconstruction. Lincoln, on one of his field trips, paused in open-mouthed astonishment before a rebuilt railroad bridge (pages 238-239) and reported: "I have just seen the most remarkable structure that human eyes ever rested upon. That man, Haupt, has built a bridge across Potomac Creek, about

four hundred feet long and nearly a hundred feet high, over which loaded trains are running every hour, and, upon my word . . . there is nothing in it but bean-poles and corn-stalks."

Ingenuity marked the efforts of railway men throughout the four years of conflict. To protect construction gangs repairing bridges on the Philadelphia, Wilmington, Baltimore and Ohio Railroad, Union engineers put together an armored railroad battery (above) carrying riflemen and a pivot-mounted cannon.

Western troops were no less inventive. At Vicksburg, soldiers operating under an officer of General McPherson's staff built five locomotives for the United States Military Railroad (left).

Operating on exterior lines of communication, Union soldiers traveled long distances and found military-run rail lines essential to efficient operation. In 1863, Colonel C. C. McCallum, who took over after Haupt's resignation, saw his trains move two corps, about 22,000 men, over 1,200 miles in 11½ days. General Sherman reported that a single-track railroad 473 miles long supplied his army of 100,000 men and 35,000 animals for 196 days during the drive on Atlanta, and that the campaign would have been impossible without rail facilities.

241

WATERWAYS offered great opportunities for troop movement during the Civil War. The eastern seaboard was laced with rivers running into the Atlantic. In the west, rivers such as the Ohio, Tennessee, or Cumberland were used by armies in transit. The ocean and the Gulf of Mexico also served as sea roads to battle and more than once played a part in large-scale amphibious operations.

The serious shipping shortage that plagued both sides when war began limited water transport. Ship construction was carried on at fever pitch in the South wherever possible, but, except for a few ironclads, most vessels produced were small ones. Ships purchased abroad were used as commerce raiders and blockade runners, so that Confederate soldiers seldom knew the dubious comforts of troop transports.

The two-part program of construction and purchase soon gave the North a variety of surface craft. Gingerbread-laden river boats from the Hudson and Mississippi, New York ferries, Great Lakes cargo carriers, and various tugs, barges, and trawlers were pressed into service.

Assorted armadas carried regiments, brigades, divisions, and corps up and down river and along the shelving slopes of the Atlantic coast and the Gulf. Transatlantic packets, ignominiously reduced to coastal runs, accommodated Yankee soldiers. in gilded salons. The gambling rooms of the fabulous river boats were turned into bivouac areas and hospitals for the men aboard.

Probably the greatest water-borne troop movement of the War was the one that inaugurated General McClellan's Peninsular Campaign in 1862. The forces embarked in the Washington-Alexandria area, then dropped down the Potomac and through Chesapeake Bay to land on the peninsula

formed by the York and James rivers. In the course of this operation, some 300 ships carried over 100,000 men, more than 14,000 horses and mules, 343 guns, 1,150 wagons, and tons of auxiliary equipment more than 200 miles in two to three weeks without the loss of a man.

Once McClellan reached the peninsula, he remained dependent on shipping for food, ammunition, and forage. The swarming flotilla shown above is transferring troops, livestock, and supplies to the site chosen by McClellan as a new base for offensive operations.

RIVER boats, transports, and railroad trains were comparative luxuries to the average Yankee or Rebel soldier. Most of the time, he reached his objective on foot.

The speed of marching infantry was controlled by the nature of the ground it crossed. On hard-topped Pennsylvania highways, troops could make 30 miles per day. In swamp and forest (upper left), 10 miles was good. Traveling under his own power, the infantry soldier was expected to average 16 to 20 miles per day under normal conditions, and be ready for battle when he got to his destination.

In crucial periods, troops hit the roads day after day with no protracted rest. During the Shenandoah Valley Campaign in 1862, Stonewall Jackson's "foot cavalry" marched the length of the valley five times in three months. In November, 1863, Sherman's men made 400 miles on foot and went into action the day after reaching their goal.

Completely at the mercy of weather, Southern roads were often in miserable condition. Spring rains made rivers overflow their banks, flooding the already muddy highways.

Marching troops were accompanied by wagon trains (right) carrying rations, ammunition, clothing, medical supplies, and forage for the draft animals. The usual Army wagon was about 120 inches long inside, 43 wide, and 22 high. It could carry 2,500 pounds, or 1,500 rations of bread, coffee, sugar, and salt. Under ideal conditions, it was drawn by four horses or six mules.

By rule of thumb, commanders counted on 25 wagons for each 1,000 men. Sherman, one of the Union's logistics experts, felt that 600 wagons should accompany a corps, 300 for food and 300 for ammunition, clothing, and other essentials. In mountain operations, trains of sure-footed pack mules (lower left) were occasionally employed in place of the cumbersome wagons.

A few hundred yards of open water could halt an army and its supply train. Bridging operations, of the utmost importance, were the responsibility of engineers in Northern and Southern armies.

245

LARGE-SCALE use of the telegraph for military communication began with the Civil War in America. The most spectacular employment of the new medium came as Professor Thaddeus Lowe took along telegraphic equipment on one of his balloon ascents for the Union Army.

Lowe was a civilian balloonist of fame when the war began, and volunteered his services to the North. His work was of particular value during the Peninsular Campaign. In *Intrepid, Washington,* and *Constitution* he made a series of ascensions (above) to ascertain Confederate troop dispositions and movements, direct artillery fire by means of telegraphic equipment in his basket, and chart the Rebel lines by camera, creating a mosaic map.

Generals Stoneman, Heintzelman, and Porter joined Lowe in his aerial expeditions and gained intelligence of value. Lowe discovered the evacuation of Yorktown by night observation and sent down tactical information affecting the Battle of Fair Oaks. In one of the first demonstrations of anti-aircraft fire, Rebel troops used twelve guns to try and bring Lowe down. Bursting shells sent splinters through his balloon's rigging, but did not touch the passengers or the balloon itself.

The Confederates had one balloon, a patchwork affair of many colors put together from donated silk dresses. The only gas for inflation was in Richmond, and the balloon was filled there, then attached to a locomotive that ran it down the York River Railroad to any desired point. One day, the Rebel balloon was attached to a steamer in the James River when the tide went out, leaving the ship high and dry on a bar. Yankee troops captured the balloon. General Longstreet, bemoaning the loss of the last silk dress in the Confederacy, called it the meanest trick of the war.

Transmission of information by methods less exotic than those used by Lowe was the responsibility of Signal Corps troops, who sent messages by means of flags or lights. Codes based on numerals were used. Where troops were to be in position for any length of time, high signal towers were constructed.

Far surpassing these primitive visual methods was the "electromagnetic telegraph," used from the first days of war. Alert generals were quick to seize upon this method of message transmission but operation of the telegraph system in the Union army was hindered by red tape from the start.

The telegraph service was a civilian bureau attached semiofficially to the Army. Operators, many of them young boys, remained civilians, while top officers received commissions. Telegraphers accompanied troops in the field but there was constant friction between them and army commanders. The disputes were jurisdictional ones, operators feeling they were responsible only to the War Department, and field officers attempting to keep the civilian personnel under direct control.

Despite such difficulties, telegraph men laid more than 15,000 miles of wire and sent 6,000,000 military telegrams (below). The Southern troops lacked the organization of Northern telegraphers, but used commercial lines wherever possible. Operators on both sides became adept at tapping enemy wires and taking off confidential messages (right).

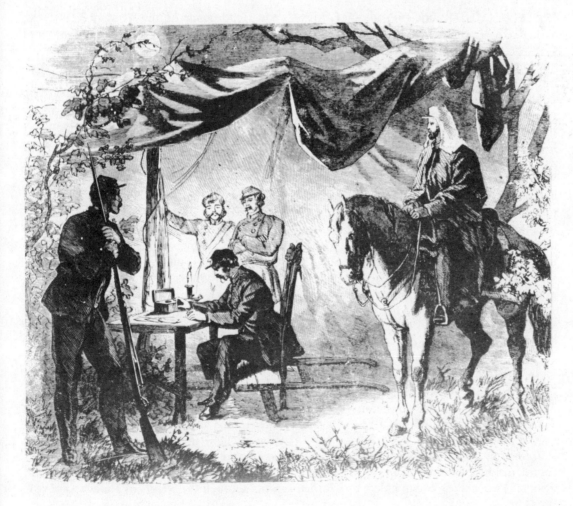

247

SHERMAN TO ATLANTA

"ON THE historic 4th day of May, 1864, the Confederate army at my front lay at Dalton, Georgia, composed, according to the best authority, of about 45,000 men, commanded by Joseph E. Johnston, who was equal in all the elements of generalship to Lee, and who was under instructions from the war powers in Richmond to assume the offensive northward as far as Nashville. But he soon discovered that he would have to conduct a defensive campaign. Coincident with the movement of the Army of the Potomac, as announced by telegraph, I advanced from our base at Chattanooga with the Army of the Ohio, 13,559 men; the Army of the Cumberland, 60,773; and the Army of the Tennessee, 24,465—grand total, 98,797 men and 254 guns."

The words are Sherman's. His part in the immense "Operation Crusher" had begun and his men moved out to smash Johnston and capture Atlanta. They were veterans, under veteran leaders, Thomas heading the Cumberland Army, McPherson that of the Tennessee, and Major General John M. Schofield the Army of the Ohio. Cavalry was in plentiful supply.

Johnston, reinforced after the campaign commenced, eventually had some 60,000 troops. Two corps, commanded by Hardee and Hood, made up the Army of Tennessee, which was joined by the Army of Mississippi under Polk.

Sherman's drive to Atlanta has been called one of the great campaigns of all time as to strategy and tactics. His course lay southeast along the Western and Atlantic Railroad, which covered the hundred and twenty miles separating Chattanooga from Atlanta. The major Union supply base was Nashville, and munitions reached the army through Chattanooga and down the single railway.

Sherman's march was a masterpiece of maneuver, with few pitched battles until the end. Johnston built up strong defenses before each successive position he occupied. The Union general then put a strong holding force against these defenses, sending flanking groups around to threaten the Rebel rear and force retirement.

To open the fighting, Sherman left Ringgold and marched to Dalton where the Rebels were entrenched on Rocky Face Ridge. McPherson flanked them to the southwest; they retired to Resaca. Sherman and Johnston brought up their forces but the latter was flanked again and pulled back. By mid-May guttering torches lighted the Union army through the streets of Resaca (above).

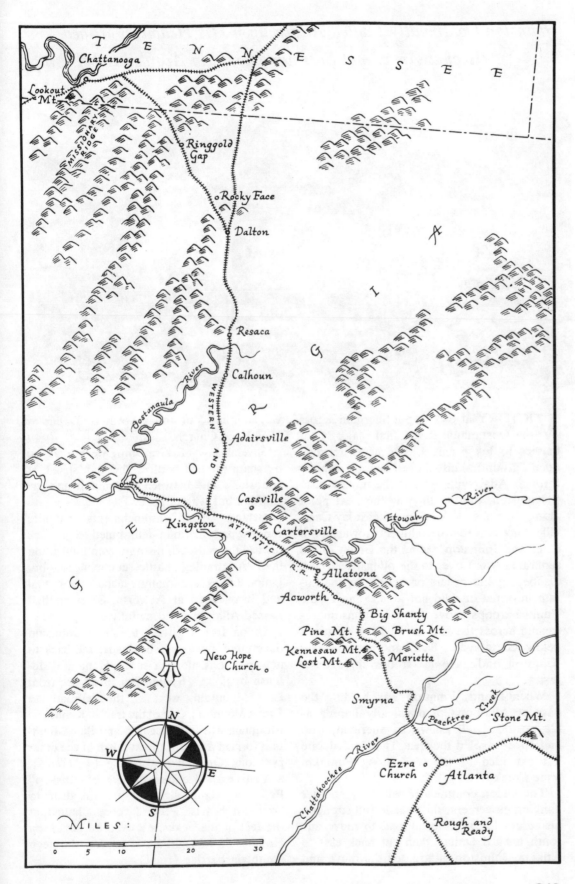

VICTORY at Resaca put Sherman across the Oostanaula River, first major water barrier to his progress. The army reached open ground and moved south rapidly through Adairsville toward the mountains.

Kingston, due south, was the next point along the railway. A few miles east lay Cassville. Sherman sent detachments toward both cities and Johnston, seeing the Union forces separated, went over to the offensive. Hood, disobeying his orders or acting on inaccurate information, did not attack and as the Yankee troops moved closer, Johnston retreated across the Etowah River to positions below Cartersville. Sherman marched into Kingston and gave his troops three days' rest.

When found, Johnston was holding the pass at Allatoona, a practically impregnable position well known to Sherman, who had once traveled the area. The Confederate left extended to the west along Pumpkin Vine Creek.

The Union commander called for another flanking movement, this time in full strength, his forces leaving the railroad to move due south toward Dallas, then cut back east to Atlanta. Johnston anticipated the move and was waiting four miles north of Dallas at New Hope Church.

Several days of skirmishing were followed by sharp pitched battles. Sherman struck at Johnston's line between the church and the railroad but was stopped.

Behind Union entrenchments, supplies ran low and Sherman determined to go back toward the railroad, his only communication line. A running battle commenced, but Union forces eventually reached their goal and bivouacked at Acworth. Sherman had passed Allatoona successfully.

Union forces girded to strike Johnston once more, but the Rebel leader fell back to new positions along a series of natural defense bastions. His line ran in an arc from Lost Mountain, west of the railroad, to Brush Mountain, east of the tracks. Kennesaw Mountain was in the center, and Pine Mountain formed a salient thrust north of the other positions. On that peak, June 14 (above), a Yankee shell ended the life of "Bishop" Polk, the staid, dignified general dear to Southern hearts. Federal forces, halted at the feet of the peaks, checked an attack by Hood as they sought a way to cross the steep mountain barrier (right).

Johnston, left, with a magnetic personality and a way of getting into trouble with his superiors, was one of the Confederacy's top tacticians. Sherman, right, a nervous, quick-thinking leader, not only understood tactics but was among the first of the Northern generals to visualize total war.

SPRING rains had opened up in May, saturating troops in the field. Wagons went up to their hubs in quagmires created from the narrow roads of clay (above). After a seventeen-day stretch of storm, one Union officer remarked the "roads were as broad as the fields." Bogged-down supply trains, failing to deliver troops and ammunition to the men, were a main reason for Sherman's return to the railway line.

Gray weather brought operations to a halt in early June. Johnston took the opportunity to concentrate his forces along Kennesaw Mountain.

Before the rains ceased, Yankee units closed up on the mountain, taking positions just below its sloping sides. Looking up, they could see well-placed timber breastworks, pierced for artillery, guarding the Southern army.

Sherman seemed stopped at last. If he tried to go around Johnston's right, he would uncover his communication line and invite attack by Southern cavalry. A move around the Rebel left would mean returning to the rain-soaked field through which his supply wagons could no longer travel. Direct assault was the only remaining approach.

Wet Weather on Red Clay Made Wagon Transportation
All but Impossible in Some Periods of the March on Atlanta

ON JUNE 27, Sherman ordered a straightforward drive on Kennesaw Mountain. Heavy cannonading preceded the attack, which was made at two points, by Thomas and McPherson, as Schofield's men demonstrated to divert enemy fire.

The push began at nine o'clock. By eleven-thirty, the Union had been bloodily repulsed and the effort was over.

The North lost 2,000 of the 16,000 men engaged. Some 18,000 defended the Rebel redoubts and casualties ran over 400.

The rain ceased suddenly after the battle and Sherman went back to his flanking tactics. Swinging far to Johnston's left, the Union men threatened Confederate com-munications and the Rebels abandoned the mountain ring around Marietta and moved back on Smyrna.

The Chattahoochee River was the last major natural barrier shielding Atlanta and its line was defended by an impressive sys-tem of forts and guns. Thomas pressed the fortifications as McPherson went down-stream to Sandtown and set up guns to cover a crossing. One division from Scho-field silently passed upstream to Roswell, crossed in a surprise move, and built pon-toon bridges to carry succeeding troops. Flanked once again, Johnston crossed the river himself and entered the entrenchments at Peachtree Creek.

"Kennesaw Mountain," in the words of a contemporary reporter, "a second Lookout among its fellows, is about four miles in length and some 400 feet high . . . presenting a most dignified ap-pearance." Tough Rebel riflemen along its steep sides had no trouble repelling Sherman's men.

253

SHERMAN'S agile maneuvering placed him at the gates of Atlanta and the Confederacy crackled with fear. Johnston, to the mind of Jefferson Davis, had handled himself badly. On July 17, he was replaced by Hood.

Sherman approved of the change. He knew Johnston for a wily, subtle opponent, quick to capitalize on any Union mistake. Hood, lacking an arm and a leg lost in battle, was fiery and pugnacious. He might be trapped by a rash error of his own making. At any rate, he was sure to take the offensive.

A main reason for the Federal drive on Atlanta was the city's importance as a railway hub. The Western and Atlantic, coming down from Chattanooga, was in Union hands, but other roads were still open. These included the Georgia, running east to Augusta; the Atlanta and West Point, leading southwest to Montgomery; and the Macon and Western, running south and southeast to Macon and Savannah.

Union interest in these lines gave Hood a chance for his first offensive move. Sherman had no intention of going against Atlanta's fortifications, especially after his repulse at Kennesaw Mountain. Instead, he planned to encircle the city slowly, cutting all its railways to leave the population without food and Hood without ammunition. Siege would get him the city.

The Georgia Railroad was the first target. It fitted into Sherman's over-all plan and had military significance as well, for Hood and Lee could exchange troops over this route.

McPherson and Schofield, on July 18, were swinging wide to cut the Georgia, then approach Atlanta from northeast. Thomas was approaching Peachtree Creek from the north. The gap between these army groups tempted Hood.

He sent a main drive against Thomas, leaving a screening force to protect his right. A portion of the main attack was delivered savagely, another portion held back. Thomas fought back stoutly and held his own, bringing up his artillery reserve. Hearing the firing, Schofield and McPherson pressed in, slamming back the screening force. Hood had to bring his men tumbling back into the city defenses. The action of July 20, known as Peachtree Creek, cost the Rebels 2,500 men they could ill afford to lose.

Hood lived up to his reputation as a battler. Two days later he sent Hardee on a long march around the Union left and rear to fall upon unsuspecting Federal troops from behind. The Yankees climbed from their trenches and fought across them in reverse. Hardee's men pressed stoutly but McPherson threw in a corps he had in reserve and momentarily checked the Rebels.

Hood planned a frontal attack concurrent with Hardee's move, but it was late and possibility of coordinated pressure on the Union front collapsed. Sherman took the field himself and rallied his men, who drove the attackers off. Hood's second failure cost him 8,000 casualties. On the Yankee side, McPherson, among the most brilliant of Northern generals, met death.

Following the action of the twenty-second, known as the Battle of Atlanta, Sherman began a move south and west of the city to slash the Atlanta and West Point Railroad. Once more Hood came out, July 28, to fight the Battle of Ezra Church west of the city. Once more he was turned back, and the Yankees proceeded to cut the line to Alabama.

Union troops settled down to besiege Atlanta. Artillery could reach any point in the city and the population took up life in caves and cellars. Federal cavalry spent a month probing for the the Macon and Western Railroad, south of the town, but with little success.

In desperation, Sherman planned another major drive, this one by almost his entire force, to cut the rail line at Jonesboro, twenty-two miles below Atlanta. Hood sent troops down the railroad to meet him and was overwhelmed on August 31 and September 1. He evacuated the city, retreated south to Lovejoy's Station, and Sherman entered Atlanta September 2.

Like a Funeral Pyre against the Night Sky When He Departed

In early July, Sherman's men saw Atlanta "glittering in the sunlight before us" from heights above the Chattahoochee River, but they were not to throng the city's streets for two more months. A major transportation nexus, Atlanta was also second to Richmond in manufacturing capacity and of utmost importance to the Confederate war effort. Upon Yankee occupation, formal surrender was offered by Atlanta's mayor September 2. Sherman immediately informed authorities that he looked upon the city as a military depot subject to the rules of military law.

Sherman treated the captured city harshly, ordering the civilian population to leave and go north or south as they wished. Noncombatants who chose to remain on Southern soil were escorted to Rough and Ready, the first station on the railway running south from the city. There they were met by guards from Hood's army who saw them across a 15-mile gap in the railroad and into Southern lines. Sherman then ordered the city's military installations destroyed. Engineers put the torch to depots, train sheds, and shops. Flames spread to stores, mills, and even private homes.

255

THOMAS HITS HOOD

UPON capturing Atlanta, and before ordering its destruction, Sherman paused to make new plans. In the northwest, Forrest, king of the Southern cavalry raiders, was slashing at Union communications. Hood's army lay below Atlanta. He decided that he too could hamper Sherman by striking at the long life line leading down from Chattanooga to Atlanta.

In early October, Hood (upper left) moved north to operate against the Western and Atlantic Railroad. Sherman had strung out garrisons along this line to ward off Confederate cavalry but none was in great strength. Hood had captured Acworth by October 5, and turned toward Allatoona.

In the face of the threat, Sherman left the XX Corps to hold Atlanta and took his remaining force north for the pursuit of Hood. There was a brisk engagement at Allatoona before the Rebels were driven off.

Hood's raiders did their work well, and Sherman found rails bent and every tie burned for an eight-mile stretch. New rails and spikes were sent from Chattanooga and 10,000 men went to work. In one week, the break was repaired.

Discouraged by the futility of permanently injuring the Yankee supply line, Hood and Jefferson Davis created a more grandiose

plan. The general was to cross the Tennessee River, wreck communications well in Sherman's rear, move into Kentucky and gather recruits, then head for Virginia to take pressure off Lee.

Sherman was making a plan of his own. Guarding the long railway line from Nashville and Chattanooga drew off his strength and weakened the army. He suggested abandoning the railway and moving his force to the Atlantic coast.

Grant looked upon Sherman's plan with a jaundiced eye at the beginning. Thomas (upper right) had been sent to Nashville, to guard against Hood's movements, but the Union commander-in-chief worried about his ability to stop a major Confederate attack. Sherman reinforced Thomas, promised additional troops, and was permitted to plan his march to the sea.

Hood left Georgia and moved into Alabama for the start of his campaign. Sherman broke off pursuit and returned to Atlanta. Thomas began to concentrate his widely scattered army.

On October 22, Hood left Gadsden and marched down the Tennessee River to cross at Florence, where he was to rendezvous with Forrest. A series of delays held up the Southern army. It didn't complete the river

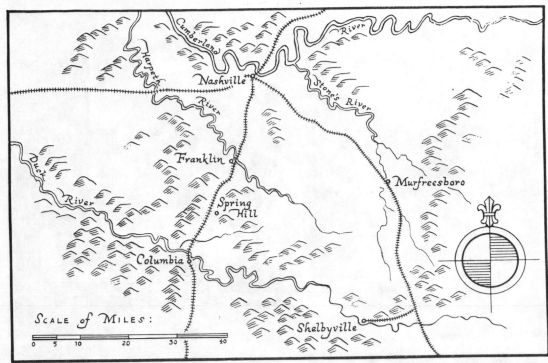

Scale of Miles:
0 5 10   20   30   40

crossing until November 16. By the nineteenth, in a flurry of snow and hail, Hood was moving on Nashville.

The Rebel delay gave Thomas time to pull together his forces. They would eventually consist of the IV and XXIII Corps, under Schofield; a detachment from the Army of the Tennessee under A. J. Smith; a provisional detachment commanded by Major General James B. Steedman; and an excellent Cavalry Corps led by Brigadier General James H. Wilson. To oppose the Federals, Hood had three corps under Lieutenant Generals Stephen D. Lee, Alexander P. Stewart, and Benjamin F. Cheatham.

Schofield, with 22,000 men, was at Columbia, Tennessee, just south of the Duck River. Hood hit him there, forced him back to Spring Hill and, through the procrastination of Cheatham, lost an opportunity to crush the Yankees. Schofield checked the Rebel advance, then fled north to Franklin, on the Harpeth River, eighteen miles below Nashville. He entrenched his men well to await the Rebel advance.

Hood, furious at his missed opportunity, ordered direct frontal assault on November 30. Stewart and Cheatham hurled their men at the Yankees, were repulsed, and came on again in repeated waves. The entrenchments held, slaughter mounted, and Hood continued to urge his troops forward. Six Southern generals were killed in the shock of battle, and the day ended a Northern victory as Hood counted his losses of more than 6,000.

Schofield pulled back into Nashville and the shaken Rebel army marched up to take positions outside the city. Thomas was consolidating his army and seeking mounts for Wilson's cavalry. Two weeks passed, as Grant and Halleck bombarded him with orders to strike the inferior Southern army before his door. Imperturbable, he bided his time until all was ready. An ice storm delayed him further, and orders to relieve him because of inaction were on their way when he struck in the Battle of Nashville, December 15 and 16.

Infantry crashed through the weak Confederate line and cavalry turned the flank. Hood fell back to a line of hills, battling gallantly. The next day was the same: savage drives by Yankee horsemen and a tornado of accurate rifle fire. Hood was routed and his army fled in complete defeat.

Thomas had created the perfect tactical maneuver and crushed an entire army. It was the end of war in Tennessee.

257

MARCH TO THE SEA

DURING Sherman's march to the sea, 60,000 men covered 250 miles in one month, living off the land as they traveled. It was one of the most discussed exploits in the Civil War, bringing jubilation to the North and leaving, in the South, scars that have never healed.

The move was planned as an awesome demonstration of Union power to move wherever it wished in enemy territory. The sum total of its effect on Southern morale was considered as the march was being planned.

Immediate results sought included bisection of the South, capture of one or more enemy seaports, opening up a new supply line via Atlantic coastal waters, and reinforcement for Grant in his massive struggle against Lee.

Unorthodox military procedure made the movement remarkable. Sherman deliberately cut himself off from the long supply line, which was hard to protect, and ordered his men to find food for themselves and forage for their beasts as they penetrated the heart of Dixie. This was not a complete innovation: Grant had done the same thing be-fore capturing Vicksburg. Because there was no supply line, Sherman was released from worry about his communications.

Infinite pains went into planning the operation. Only first-class troops were used, the sick, wounded, and infirm being sent back to Chattanooga and Nashville. Veteran soldiers making the march were inured to life in the open, skilled in supplying their wants from whatever was available.

Individual soldiers, like the army itself, were stripped down to the bone and useless luxuries disappeared. Each man carried 40 rounds of ammunition and could call for 160 more from supply wagons. Knapsacks were discarded in most cases, personal equipment being packed in the blanket roll slung over one shoulder. A tin cup for coffee and a mess plate took care of eating utensils. On his person, the fighting man had coffee, salt, and sugar, and an emergency supply of hardtack.

The stripped-down army was ready for combat if necessary. It carried 65 guns, in batteries of fours, and 200 rounds of ammunition for each piece. Some 2,500 wagons hauled staple provisions, ammunition, and medical supplies. Six hundred ambulances accompanied the army. For food at the beginning of the march, beef cattle were driven behind the troops. Oats and corn, for horses and mules, made up a five days' supply; after that the animals would be fed from the countryside.

The army was paid off (left) and departed from Atlanta for the momentous march on November 15. Sherman remained in town to supervise destruction of the city, and departed the following day. He wrote:

"About 7 A.M. of November 16 we rode out of Atlanta by the Decatur Road, filled by the marching troops and wagons of the Fourteenth Corps; and reaching the hill, just outside of the old rebel works, we naturally paused to look back upon the scene of our past battles. We stood upon the very ground whereon was fought the bloody battle of July 22nd, and could see the copse of wood where McPherson fell. Behind us lay Atlanta, smouldering and in ruins, the black smoke rising high in air, and hanging like a pall over the ruined city. Away off in the distance . . . was the rear of Howard's column, the gun-barrels glistening in the sun, the white-topped wagons stretching away to the south; and right before us the Fourteenth Corps, marching steadily and rapidly, with a cheery look and a swinging pace, that made light of the thousand miles that lay between us and Richmond."

The army was split into four corps, the XV and XVII under General Oliver O. Howard, the XIV and XX led by General Henry W. Slocum. They traveled in four broad columns, slicing through the heart of Georgia toward the sea, although the marching men did not know their destination, some of them supposing it to be Richmond. A cavalry division, under Brigadier General Judson Kilpatrick, covered the Union flanks.

Slocum, accompanied by Sherman, started along the Georgia Railroad toward Augusta. Howard, with Kilpatrick's cavalry, paralleled the Macon and Western, running to Macon and Savannah.

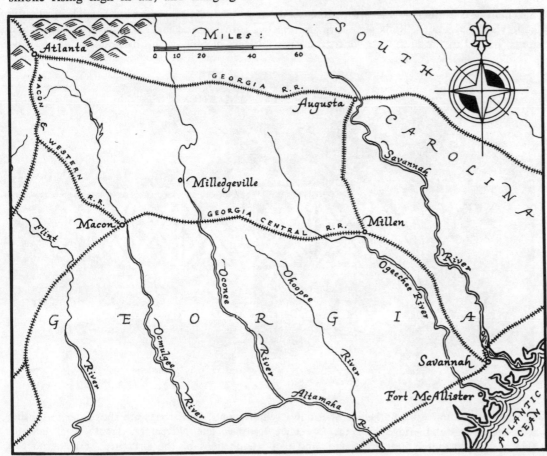

Sherman's Men Cut a Sixty-mile Swath of Destruction across Georgia, Which Crippled the State's Power to Feed the Confederacy

Sherman was explicit in his instructions to destroy railroad lines wherever possible, and often supervised operations. Rails were torn up, the ties gathered and made into bonfires. Track sections, heated in the fires, were locked into pegs driven into the earth, then pulled out of shape.

Bridge destruction was another of Sherman's requirements, and troops are shown above as they wrecked a railroad bridge over the Ogeechee River in late November. Tracks went into the river or received the heat treatment, and wooden portions of the structure were set on fire.

SHERMAN moved through rich, fertile farm areas piled high with fruits of the harvest. Winy autumn air heightened the soldiers' spirits and appetites. The army was fat and sassy. It devastated the countryside.

Ordered to "forage liberally," troops took the command at full value. Each day, brigade commanders detailed a party of about fifty men with one or two officers to bring in provisions. Foragers left their units in the morning and returned at night laden with plunder.

Raiding farms and plantations, the group emptied smokehouses of ham and bacon; wrung the necks of geese, chickens, ducks, and turkeys; emptied bins of corn meal and sweet potatoes; found the storage place of sorghum jugs.

Soldiers were ordered not to enter private houses, but to devote their time and energy to gathering food. Destruction of homes, mills, and cotton gins was entrusted to corps commanders alone, given wide latitude in use of their powers:

"In districts and neighborhoods where the army is unmolested, no destruction of . . . property should be permitted; but should guerillas or bushwackers molest our march, or should the inhabitants burn bridges, obstruct roads or otherwise manifest local hostility, then army commanders should order and enforce a devastation more or less relentless, according to the measure of such hostility."

It was easy to make a case for "local hostility," and men often plundered and destroyed as they saw fit. As the mighty force marched to Savannah and on through the Carolinas, Sherman's "bummers" ransacked houses in their path (below). Plug hats, fancy costumes, and old uniforms were favored prizes.

Looting was one thing; burning cotton baling equipment, barns, and homes was infinitely more serious. Sherman deplored the destruction but neither he nor his officers could control the atavistic conduct of 60,000 hardened soldiers.

261

Georgia's Capital at Milledgeville Was the First Objective of the March, and There Sherman Halted Briefly to Consolidate His Forces

BEAUREGARD was hastily summoned from Mississippi to fight off the Yankee invasion. The general was unable to cope with the speed of Sherman's advance. Rebel cavalry picked at the Yankee wings but did little damage and whatever forces opposed the march were quickly brushed aside.

Howard ran into opposition at Griswoldville from a group of Georgia militia but defeated them easily. Sherman, who had remained with Slocum and the left wing, marched into Milledgeville, the Georgia capital, meeting no resistance, November 23.

From there he rode over to establish contact with Howard's right wing and, finding all in order, returned to read the Southern newspapers collected at the capital. With one voice, they proclaimed that Sherman was trapped, beaten, and fleeing for his life toward the coast. This word filtered north, and was all the public knew of the Northern general and his men who had vanished into central Georgia in mid-November.

By December 3, Sherman reached Millen with the XVII Corps. Howard was south of the Ogeechee River opposite Scarboro with the XV. Slocum had the XX four miles north of Millen; the XIV was a few miles farther north at Lumpkin's Station on the Augusta Road.

The army appeared to be in good order and position. Forage wagons were full. The bounty was useful as the army was approaching rice country and food getting progressively more scarce. Two-thirds of the distance to the sea had been traversed and Sherman resolved to make Savannah his goal.

On December 9 and 10, Federal troops took up positions outside the city. Savannah was well fortified, its garrison commanded by General Hardee.

Sherman planned to make contact with the Federal blockading fleet on Ossabaw Sound, below the city, before any further move. Fort McAllister guarded the sound. A division of the XV Corps stormed the fort December 13, and Sherman was able to board *Dandelion,* a tender of the gunboat *Flag* guarding the mouth of the Ogeechee.

Slocum's men occupied Milledgeville in late November and burned the penitentiary as a building the Rebels might use for defensive purposes. Troops entered government buildings on the heels of fleeing lawmakers, set up a mock legislature, and held a burlesque debate on secessionism.

Rebel soldiers planted 8-inch shells with friction fuses, similar to modern land mines, on the approaches to Fort McAllister, and Sherman used Confederate prisoners to dig them up (above). Upon reaching the sea, he embarked to meet Foster, Union commander in the area (below).

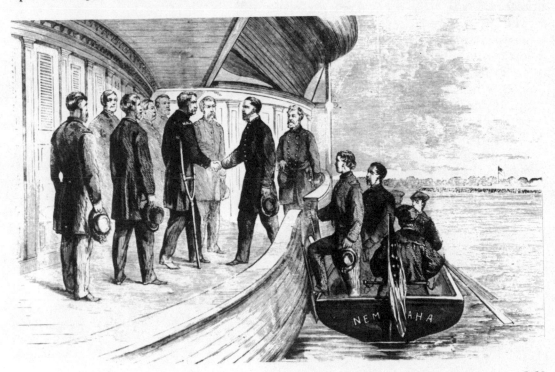

UPON contact with the fleet, Sherman met Admiral Dahlgren and Major General John G. Foster, commanding the Department of the South, and made plans to reduce the city of Savannah. Foster offered guns and ammunition from Port Royal.

Savannah lay well inland on the south bank of the Savannah River, which marked the Georgia-South Carolina border. Hardee's troops within the city numbered more than 10,000. Rail communication with the outside was cut off.

In the meantime, Grant wrote Sherman ordering him to establish and garrison a seacoast base, then come north personally with the bulk of his command, by water, to join in assaulting Lee. Sherman, desperately anxious to take the city before him, wrote back that he would send 60,000 men as soon as sufficient transports could be brought up. In the interval, he stated, he hoped to capture Savannah.

A surrender demand was sent to Hardee and promptly refused on December 17. Sherman, before beginning his siege, traveled to Hilton Head by boat to ask the use of certain troops in Foster's command. The general assented. On his return, Sherman's boat ran aground December 20. As it was refloated to continue the journey, a tug approached with news that Hardee had evacuated Savannah by means of a pontoon bridge and crossed his troops to the South Carolina shore. Yankee skirmishers, feeling for Hardee's troops December 21, discovered the evacuation and entered the city.

Hardee succeeded in partial destruction of the navy yard, and Sherman found the wreck of the Confederate ironclad ram *Savannah* smoldering in its stocks as he looked over the city from the customhouse roof. The river was mined and filled with wood-and-stone obstructions.

Filled with Cotton That Could Not Move Because of the Blockade

SHERMAN entered Savannah on December 22 and established headquarters. Hardee blew up his ironclads and fired the navy yard before escaping but left behind heavy guns, cotton, railroad cars, and steamboats. Noting the booty, the Yankee leader sent Lincoln a wire: "I beg to present you as a Christmas-gift the city of Savannah, with one hundred and fifty heavy guns and plenty of ammunition, also about twenty-five thousand bales of cotton."

Union troops settled down to spend a month in Savannah (below), an old, graceful city with a tropical air. Palmettos, moss-hung live oaks, winter-blooming flowers, and the leisure of camp life softened the hardy "bummers."

The spirit of amnesty reached Sherman himself, who announced that Savannah's 20,000 inhabitants could join their friends in Charleston or Augusta, or remain in their homes. Most chose to stay, and life in the city slowly resumed its normal pace.

Grant wrote Sherman, canceling the plan to bring troops up from Savannah by water and assenting to the victorious general's suggestion that he march north, disrupting the Carolinas. The commander-in-chief may have been influenced by Sherman's letters in which he reported destroying 200 miles of railway, capturing 5,000 cattle over and above those consumed by the army, taking 15,000 mules, and bringing in horses in such quantities that many could not be used and were consequently shot.

Sherman considered the march to the sea as "a means to an end, and not as an essential act of war." In actual fact, the move eliminated Georgia and helped number the days of Robert E. Lee.

CIVILIANS

AS MEN bled and died at Chancellorsville and Chickamauga, civilians at home supported the war effort in varying degrees. Few were apathetic. Bulletins from the front, displayed at newspaper offices, caught the eye and touched off heated street debates (upper left). The mighty struggle between union and secession left its mark on farm, factory, home, and financial district.

Money was a prime requisite for victory. Monster rallies brought the public together for hours of oratory and exhortation (right) in behalf of the war effort. After successful meetings, when returning heroes and long-winded politicians had harangued the crowd, it was hoped the populace would rush to sign up for war bonds (lower left).

Treasury Secretary Salmon P. Chase, in charge of war financing for the North, created a highly successful program despite temporary setbacks. The cost of the war to the federal government was about $3 billion.

At the outset, Chase was authorized to borrow $250 million, increase tariffs, levy a direct tax on the states, and establish an income tax of 3 per cent on those who earned $800 or more per year. But war costs skyrocketed and the government, queasy about increasing taxation, took the easy way out and issued a flood of paper money, which led to inflation.

By 1863, when the war was costing more than $2 million per day, Chase put the North on a sound financial basis by establishing a national banking system. In essence, it allowed groups of men to establish banking businesses by purchasing government bonds and depositing them in Washington. They were then allowed to issue "bank notes" backed by the bonds. The notes became solid national currency, with the government promising to redeem them should the banks fail. Bankers loaned their notes, at profitable interest rates, and credit flowed freely. With their profits, the bankers bought U.S. bonds, thus supporting the war effort.

Christopher G. Memminger, in charge of Southern finance, was not as successful as Chase. There was little actual money in the

South as war began (and that was soon exhausted), for potential profits were tied up in the huge cotton crop.

Lack of ready cash made loans and taxation almost useless as sources of revenue. The alternative was the issuance of paper money, and the government printed it in huge quantities, using it to pay for materials of war. Ruinous inflation resulted. Prices soared, coffee reaching $40 per pound, flour $1,000 per barrel. After the Yankee victories of 1863, the Confederate dollar was worth only 10 cents in gold. By the end of 1864, Southern credit was dead.

269

THE tools of war were made by civilian hands. Arsenals and machine shops mushroomed North and South, opening up new jobs to men and women. Purchasing agents sent abroad contracted for arms to fill the gaps, until home manufacturing could turn out sufficient guns and ammunition.

Colonel James W. Ripley became ordnance chief in the North and carried the military through its critical period of arms shortage. He expanded manufacturing facilities then in existence and balanced the output of government arsenals, private concerns, and European producers.

Standardization of arms became a desirable goal early in the war. State-armed troops, and those who drew from U.S. establishments, carried a wide variety of rifles. Gifts, such as the 20,000 Enfield rifles from England, presented by the state of New York, further complicated the picture.

Efforts were made to adopt a standard .58 caliber rifle, such as the serviceable weapon turned out by the Springfield Armory. Only in this way could the ammunition problem be solved.

Standardization was gradually achieved in the Union army, but all arms available were used in the beginning. As a stopgap, rifles of smaller caliber were reamed out so their bores measured .58 and they could accommodate what was to become standard ammunition.

The vast industrial resources of the North showed to best advantage in the manufacture of guns and ammunition. In early 1862, there were only 10,000 .58 caliber rifles in the government arsenals. Eighteen months later, the nation was independent of foreign sources and the Springfield Armory alone could turn out 250,000 rifles per year. By the middle of 1864, the North had in hand 2,000,000 small arms.

Manufacture of ammunition for rifle, pistol, and carbine called for deft hands, and female workers found employment at arsenals and armories. Girls, such as those at the Watertown Arsenal in Massachusetts (left), helped make almost 170,000,000 rounds of small-arms ammunition in 1864.

Artillery manufacturers turning out field and siege guns (left) ran into trouble with poor iron and purchased much metal abroad. Despite difficulties, casting proceeded and guns flowed into the field. At the conclusion of the Battle of Bull Run, Union troops were left with 30 cannon; in less than eight months, the number had grown to 520.

Immense natural resources, enormous manufacturing capacity, and control of the seas (for purchase of materials abroad) gave the North superiority in ordnance supply. The South lacked such essentials but buckled down to make the best of what it had. Colonel Josiah Gorgas became Chief of the Confederate Ordnance Department and labored mightily at a seemingly hopeless task.

Capture of state arsenals gave the Confederates a variety of antiquated arms and a handful of modern rifles. The coastal forts produced heavy guns but there were few field pieces. Gunpowder, lead, iron, and copper for percussion caps were in short supply.

Civilian hands labored night and day to create munitions. The big Tredegar Works at Richmond, with some 2,500 men employed, turned out more than 1,000 cannon. From the Richmond Arsenal came over 360,000 small arms and 72,500,000 rounds of small-arms ammunition.

A powder mill was created at Augusta, fed by Louisiana sulphur, saltpeter leached from ground beneath smokehouses, and charcoal from the abundant forests. Turpentine and brandy stills contributed copper; pipes and sash weights were melted into lead for bullets.

Despite earnest civilian efforts, the Confederacy was forced to make large purchases abroad to provide weapons for its fighting men. Northern civilians indirectly helped bring an end to this policy as the war progressed. Working in government and private shipyards (below), they put together the vessels that blockaded the stricken South and cut off the flow of war materials from overseas.

HARPER'S WEEKLY.

A JOURNAL OF CIVILIZATION.

VOL. V.—No. 235. NEW-YORK, SATURDAY, JUNE 29, 1861. [SINGLE COPIES SIX CENTS. $2 50 PER YEAR IN ADVANCE.

Entered according to Act of Congress, in the Year 1861, by Harper & Brothers, in the Clerk's Office of the District Court for the Southern District of New York.

WOMAN'S part in the Civil War stretched from hearth to hospital. Sewing bees (left) kept soldiers supplied with havelocks, which they didn't use, and socks, which they did.

Many women served the United States Sanitary Commission, an all-purpose welfare agency created in the North. In June, 1861, the body came into being with the Reverend Henry W. Bellows as president.

As its name implied, the Commission originally investigated sanitation in army camps. Doctors, enlisted at the start, were soon joined by men and women who sent food to the troops, cared for their dependents, assisted in hospitals, and raised funds.

Among the fund-raising projects were immense "sanitary fairs," held in cities such as Brooklyn (pages 266-267). Farmers and merchants donated produce and goods to be auctioned at these gatherings, the proceeds going to soldier relief.

Urban ladies who belonged to the Commission signed up for cash gifts, visited soldiers in general hospitals, and arranged for theatrical benefit performances (right). Some of their hardier sisters went into the field with the army, running hospital ships and trains and nursing men near the line of battle.

The Sanitary Commission was eulogized as "the product of divine seed that took root in the heart of woman, and by her was chiefly nourished." Begun in sentiment, the organization raised $5,000,000 in hard cash and distributed goods to the value of $15,000,000 among the grateful troops.

Southern women had a harder row to hoe than their Northern counterparts. Blockade-created shortages called for immense ingenuity on their parts to keep life on its normal course. They loomed fabrics to clothe themselves and their slaves, picked wild berries to make dyes, roasted sweet potatoes for synthetic coffee, molded candles from beeswax, and, through all their trials, managed to volunteer for hospital duty.

Although money had little value in the later days of the war, such Southern associations as the Women's Relief Society collected funds and spent them as well as they could for the benefit of ailing soldiers.

THE war caused little dislocation in the North. Life flowed on as usual, with occasional interruptions for worthy military charities.

Business boomed. There were fortunes to be made overnight. Beef and blankets, ships and shoes, coal and cartridges could be traded for government dollars. Army and Navy purchasing agents spent lavishly.

Careless inspection systems let the federal government in for large quantities of shoddy goods. Venal contractors fobbed off worthless rifles, inferior wool, and simulated leather at handsome prices. There were honest patriots in the market place who gave good value for the money received, but the cynical and grasping darted in and out to seize quick profits.

The enormous demand for goods and services combined with the free flow of money created a new crop of millionaires, lampooned in contemporary publications. Capitalists created monopolies and kept prices high.

These signs of dynamic prosperity never existed in the South. Some cotton speculators, contractors, and syndicates owning blockade runners made killings but their opportunities diminished as war went on. Much of the money the Southern government could scrape together was sent abroad to pay for munitions.

As the Confederate economy tottered, the government faced a serious disruption of its labor force. Negroes were most affected.

Liberated slaves followed Northern troops in such large numbers that they became a serious problem. They eventually fought for the North although the number of colored soldiers was never large.

Many colored people joined the Yankees as teamsters, cooks, and launderers (upper left). They were willing workers, somewhat dazzled by their freedom.

Some slaves remained with their masters. The solid defenses of Vicksburg, Richmond, Petersburg, Savannah, and Charleston (left) were built by Negro efforts.

White families, too, were dislocated as war rolled over the South. In border states, such as Missouri, refugees roamed the roads after their homes were destroyed (lower left). In Virginia and Georgia, it was often the fate of Southern wives and mothers to sit amongst their possessions to watch the burning of their homes (below).

275

LINCOLN ONCE AGAIN

SHERMAN'S capture of Atlanta, a military triumph, had political overtones. The year 1864 was bringing a presidential election and the North needed victories if the Republicans were to remain in power.

The terrible conflict between the states had raged for more than three years and there was no end in sight. War weariness invaded Northern homes. Union casualties in the summer were frightful.

Bitterness and discouragement in the North were fuel for the Democrats. Meeting in Chicago during August, they planned a campaign based on the important plank that ". . . after four years of failure to restore the Union by the experiment of war . . . justice, humanity, liberty and the public welfare demand that immediate efforts be made for a cessation of hostilities." The Democratic candidate was one-time military hero McClellan, who had won his soldiers' hearts and lost their campaigns.

The Republicans settled for Lincoln again, over opposition from Horace Greeley and others who desired a "hard war" man to grind the South into its own red soil. From the temper of the times, and lack of major Union victories, Lincoln felt he had little chance of re-election and said so.

A sudden string of Union successes in the field changed the picture completely. Farragut took Mobile Bay; Sherman captured Atlanta; Sheridan drove Confederate troops from the Shenandoah Valley. Optimism replaced pessimism. McClellan, in a patriotic statement, repudiated his party's platform, declaring it would be unfair to his former comrades to abandon the idea of re-establishing union.

On November 8, Lincoln won handily by an electoral count of 212 to 21, and was inaugurated the following Spring (right).

BUTLER IS HALTED

GRANT'S over-all offensive was precisely timed. Its success depended to a large extent on simultaneous advances in several areas. If every army moved as directed and on time, the Confederacy would be subjected to pressure on all sides.

Lee and the Army of Northern Virginia were the main objective. Johnston and the Army of Tennessee ranked second in importance. Union offensives against these mighty forces were primary; all other troops were to be used in support of these two movements.

Leading one of the supporting actions was General Benjamin F. Butler, commanding the Army of the James. His troops numbered approximately 35,000 and included the X Corps under Quincy A. Gillmore, the XVIII under William F. Smith, and a cavalry division. The army was based at Fort Monroe on the tip of the peninsula that had been the scene of McClellan's defeat in 1862. The York River bordered the peninsula on the north, the James on the south.

As Meade moved south toward Lee, Butler was ordered up the James River. He was to secure a beachhead, land his troops, en-trench, then threaten Richmond and its communications from below. Should Lee retire within the Richmond defenses, Meade and Butler would link up.

The Army of the James embarked, moved up Chesapeake Bay and the York River to fool the enemy, then turned back and steamed up the James on May 5. The fleet, which included everything from monitors to ferryboats, landed troops at the bluffs of City Point (above) and a nearby point named Bermuda Hundred.

Butler entrenched immediately, running his line from north to south between two rivers. His northern flank lay on the James, his southern was anchored in the Appomattox River. The defensive line was three and a half miles long, across a bottleneck of land, and admirably suited for defense. From the Yankee breastworks, Richmond was to the right and Petersburg to the left. The latter city, a communications nexus below Richmond, lay twenty-one miles from the Confederate capital.

Butler's position had been well-chosen for resisting the enemy. Grant, however, had called for offensive operations and the Union

general made the attempt, but failed.

Opposing him was Beauregard, in command of the Department of North Carolina and Southern Virginia. Gathering what troops he could, he prepared to contest the Yankee advance.

Butler sent a force toward Petersburg that made no progress and quickly retired. The major advance, on May 12, pointed northwest toward Drewry's Bluff, four miles from the Union lines. The bluff was strongly fortified as one of the outer shields protecting Richmond.

On the sixteenth, as Federal troops were probing the enemy fortifications, Beauregard attacked through a swirling fog, threw the Union force into confusion, and sent it back to its defenses with casualties of more than 4,000.

Beauregard established a strong line opposite Butler's, like a cork in a bottleneck, sealing the Union leader into his position and eliminating the threat to Petersburg and Richmond.

During summer and autumn, Butler busied himself by digging the Dutch Gap Canal across a narrow neck of land, but Rebel fire on the ditch (above) made it useless. Grant transferred some of Butler's men to the Army of the Potomac; the remainder settled down behind their defenses into winter quarters (below).

GRANT'S OFFENSIV

THE massive blow in the great spring campaign of 1864 was left to the Army of the Potomac. Once again its veterans went forth to slog through Virginia mud (right) and bring Robert E. Lee to account.

Numbering more than 100,000, the army had grown into an organic entity with customs, foibles, attitudes, and a steadily growing tradition. It was a spit-and-polish army, boasting better discipline, cleaner uniforms, and more respect for officers than any other Union force. McClellan's stamp was on the men. Victory eluded him, but he forged a mighty fighting unit.

Defeat after defeat had been this army's lot under a variety of leaders. Morale often dropped, but a vein of toughness ran through the troops. Hurled back time and time again in the shock of battle, they were never completely vanquished.

In the west, victories were flashy ones and Sherman's march was to become a military classic. Still, the eyes of the nation were on Meade's men. They were the shield of Washington. Someday, they might become the juggernaut that would roll over Richmond.

In coming battles, the Army of the Potomac was to dig in its teeth and hold on. Its primary function lay in grappling with the Army of Northern Virginia so Lee could send no troops to Georgia, the Shenandoah Valley, or the Peninsula. Meade's mission was holding the enemy center while other Union forces attacked the flanks.

It was no mean task. Lee's army was a slippery one, adept at maneuver, swift and terrible in combat. But it had passed the peak of its power. Jackson, the master tactician, no longer rode with Lee. Manpower shortages plagued the Rebel leader. And Gettysburg stained his memory.

INTO THE WILDERNESS

FOR the big offensive, Grant took the field with the Army of the Potomac. Meade remained in nominal command, but the commander-in-chief ran the show. The two generals (left) worked well together.

The Union Army contained three large infantry corps, the II led by Winfield S. Hancock, the V under Gouverneur K. Warren, the VI led by John Sedgwick; and a cavalry corps under Sheridan. Burnside, with the IX Corps, did not make the initial movement south but soon joined the army in combat.

Lee counted on his I Corps, under Longstreet; his II, with Ewell in command; his III, under A. P. Hill; and the corps of cavalry led by Stuart.

Grant lay north of the Rapidan River, Lee south of the stream. "The two armies had been confronting each other so long, without any decisive result," said Grant, "that they hardly knew which would whip."

Just after midnight, in the early hours of May 4, Grant began his move across the river. Lee's scouts picked up the advance almost immediately and flashed back the word. On the following day, the Battle of the Wilderness began and the long train of ambulances to the Union rear (lower left) indicated the combat's intensity.

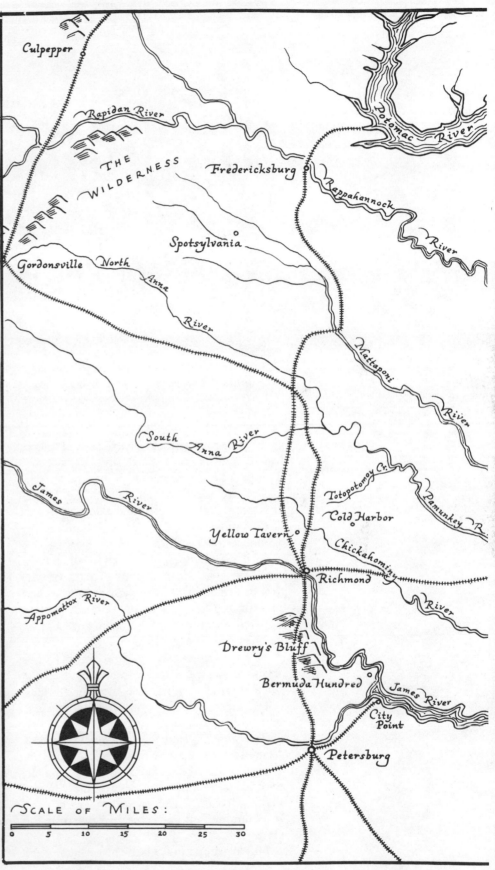

Wreaths of smoke hanging low over the battleground and heavy forest, choking out light, gave fighting in the Wilderness a macabre air. Thickets of pine, scrub oak, and cedar hid riflemen well but limited their vision, and opposing forces 50 yards apart sometimes could not see each other. Officers often found their troops had almost disappeared, swallowed up by wood and ravine.

GRANT'S crossing of the Rapidan was made at two widely separated places called Germanna's Ford and Ely's Ford. Union columns swung south into the Wilderness, just west of Chancellorsville. It was this area that sheltered Jackson's troops as they moved to strike Hooker's flank at the Chancellorsville battle.

The Wilderness, an abandoned mining area, was a dank, gloomy forest, heavily wooded and with few roads. Scrubby second growth and heavy underbrush held back the light. Streams crossed the patch and shallow ravines split the ground.

Grant planned to plunge through this forest at night and force Lee to fight on the open ground beyond. Lee, who had anticipated Grant's movements, had other ideas and ordered his forces up.

Two roads sliced through the Wilderness from east to west. Northernmost was the Orange Turnpike. Running roughly parallel, two to three miles south, lay the Orange Plank Road. Leading down from the Rapidan, and cutting across the two, was the Germanna Plank Road.

Union troops moved down the latter. Lee sent Ewell east along Orange Turnpike to make contact with the Yankee column, and Hill along Orange Plank Road with the same objective. Longstreet was not yet up; when he appeared, he was to follow Hill. Grant, having crossed his troops safely over the river, telegraphed Burnside to bring the IX Corps and join the moving army.

Ewell had been instructed not to bring on an engagement until Longstreet reached the field. But on May 5, units of Warren's V Corps spotted Ewell's men and attacked vigorously to open the two-day battle. Hancock, with the II Corps, was ahead of Warren; Sedgwick, with the VI, behind him.

Warren smashed Ewell back along the Orange Turnpike but the Rebel general rallied, sent his men around Warren's flanks, and forced him back in disorder. By afternoon, Sedgwick joined the battle and checked another flanking movement, then a thrust by Ewell at the center.

Fighting spread south and Hancock's march was reversed. He struck A. P. Hill on the Orange Plank Road, pushing him back steadily until night fell.

Both armies were reinforced during the

Grant's Main Worry in Early May Was Crossing the Rapidan, but Lee Did Not Attack until Union Troops Had Entered the Wilderness

night, Longstreet joining Lee and Burnside reaching Union positions. Early on the morning of the sixth, Hancock struck Hill a powerful hammer blow and sent him staggering back down the Orange Plank Road. As the II Corps pressed their advantage, Longstreet roared in south of the road to crack the Union left flank, roll it up and send the Federals flying in confusion. Hancock steadied his men, Grant sent troops to reinforce the threatened sector, and the Rebel charge was contained.

Fighting in the Wilderness became a nightmare. The enemy was often invisible and troops moved by compass, directing their shots toward the sound of gunfire or the sight of muzzle flashes. Trees and breastworks caught fire, spreading a pall of smoke over the field. The wounded burned or suffocated where they lay, hidden from stretcher bearers groping through the forest.

Burnside attacked in the middle, between the turnpike and the road, but achieved no great success. By afternoon, there was a slugging match along the entire line and action seesawed back and forth with no advantage to either force.

Lee, late in the day, sent Early to attack the Union extreme right, which was held by Sedgwick. The position, marking the northern limits of the fighting, had been weakened by forces drawn off to stem Longstreet's charge against Hancock. Early's men took several hundred prisoners and panicked the Yankee defenders for a time, but night fell to end the attempt at a breakthrough and the Battle of the Wilderness was over.

Neither side made any strategic gain. The fighting was brutal, bloody, and constant. Casualties were almost incredible. In two days, the Union lost more than 17,000 men. Grant had 102,000 men in the battle. Lee, whose casualties were never known, had a strength of 61,000.

As the first day's battle ended, men of the II Corps, temporarily secure behind their breastworks of earth and logs, paused to eat and draw breath before resuming action the following day. During the pause, soldiers cleared the heavy woods in front of artillery pieces to give the gunners open fields of fire, although the thick growth of trees made cannon almost useless in some sectors.

SPEAKING of the Wilderness, Grant said, "More desperate fighting has not been witnessed on this continent than that of the 5th and 6th of May." The Union commander counted the struggle a victory in that his army had successfully crossed a formidable stream, almost in the face of the enemy, and come together again as a unit.

Lee fought his heart out and temporarily checked the enemy advance. In the process, one of his great commanders was taken from him. Riding to press his advantage over Hancock, Longstreet was fired on by his own men (below) and seriously wounded. He recovered, but could not rejoin Lee for months. Major General Richard H. Anderson took over Longstreet's corps.

Put the Army of the Potomac between the Rebels and Richmond

FOLLOWING a blood bath such as that in the Wilderness, it was the custom of the Army of the Potomac to fall back and bivouac while sewing up its wounds. Grant violated the custom. On the night of May 7, he ordered his men to move southeast to a point called Spotsylvania Court House, ten miles away. There was to be no checking the massive offensive, and the men cheered as they realized this new leader was going all out to win.

The Union chief raced Lee to Spotsylvania, attempting to place his force between the Confederate army and Richmond, but Lee won out. By the time Grant brought up his troops, the Rebels were behind strong entrenchments, in a rough V, pointing northeast. Anderson held the left, Ewell the point of the V, and Early (temporarily commanding for Hill) the right.

The breastworks were impressive, built of earth and logs and topped with a large "head log" that left a small space between it and the works below through which rifles could be pointed. For almost two weeks, Grant's men battered at these solid positions in fighting every bit as vicious as that in the Wilderness.

During skirmishing on the ninth, as the battle got under way, Sedgwick fell dead from a sniper's bullet, depriving Grant of a top commanding officer. Major General Horatio G. Wright took over the VI Corps.

Federal troops waiting in reserve saw the smoke of battle beyond the trees (below). Exhausted men brought back descriptions of terrible musketry: "Trees eighteen inches in thickness were cut down by it, and bodies of men and horses lying between the two lines were reduced to shapeless masses."

On May 12, Grant sent Hancock in a pounding attack at the tip of the V-shaped line, and it cracked under pressure. Four thousand prisoners were taken, and the Federals rejoiced as Ewell fell back.

Lee took field command personally. Ewell's men rallied and held the Yankees in hand-to-hand combat over and through the breastworks. Surging back and forth for days, the battle became a bloody stalemate and Grant resolved to continue his move south, flanking Lee if possible.

YELLOW TAVERN

AS GRANT moved from the Wilderness to Spotsylvania, he ordered Sheridan to detach his cavalry from the Army of the Potomac, ride around the left of Lee's entire army, and move to the James River, where he could draw supplies from Butler.

The commander-in-chief explained his reasons:

"The object of this move was three-fold. First, if successfully executed . . . he would annoy the enemy by cutting his line of supplies and telegraphic communications, and destroy or get for his own use supplies in store in the rear and coming up. Second, he would draw the enemy's cavalry after him, and thus better protect our flanks, rear and trains than remaining with the army. Third, his absence would save the trains from drawing his forage and other supplies from Fredericksburg, which had now become our base."

Stuart, scouting Sheridan's move, hurried to place his Southern horsemen between the Union troops and Richmond. He chose Yellow Tavern, six miles north of the city, for battle.

Sheridan attacked May 11 (right). In the course of the fight, Stuart received a mortal wound and died the next day, lamented by Yankee and Rebel alike as a gallant soldier.

Sheridan won the day at Yellow Tavern, then pressed on to penetrate the outer defenses of Richmond. With no supporting force, he could not remain, but the city shivered with fear.

Leaving Richmond, the Union leader fought his way through a Rebel trap, built a bridge across the Chickahominy in the face of enemy fire, and made his way to Butler's camp on the James.

288

Grant's Drive South Became a Series of Flanking Operations
That the Confederates Referred to as the "Sidling Movement"

FOLLOWING Spotsylvania, Grant continued south, moving in a series of loops. Each attempted to put the Union army around Lee's right flank, wedging it between the Army of Northern Virginia and Richmond. Lee, agile as always, moved along the shorter inner line and held Grant off from point to point.

At staff meetings such as the one at Massaponax Church May 21 (below) there was one command: press the enemy and keep moving south. Ten days before, Grant had written Halleck that he proposed "to fight it out on this line if it takes all summer."

Day after day, the fighting went on. Skirmishing, cavalry thrusts, and pitched battles for an acre of land all became commonplace. Neither side could claim victories, but Lee was steadily losing ground in the face of Northern power.

The Union army approached the North Anna River, made a partial crossing, and was checked by Lee. Grant withdrew, swung south and east once more, and crossed the Pamunkey River (into which the North Anna flows). Turning west again to drive for Richmond after his river crossing, the Union chief found Lee ready for him. The strong positions at Totopotomoy Creek indicated another turning movement might be necessary.

In the meantime, Grant changed his supply base to White House, on the Pamunkey River. W. F. Smith and the XVIII Corps, from the Army of the James, were ordered to the new base to join the Army of the Potomac and arrived on schedule.

Heavy rains slowed troop movements in Virginia, and the Union army was forced to corduroy clay roads with logs (above) so artillery and supply wagons would not sink up to their hubs. Along such roads, Grant's infantry reached Hawe's Shop on May 29, scene of a cavalry action the previous day, and immediately began construction of temporary wooden breastworks (below).

COLD Harbor lies eight miles east of Richmond. If Grant could penetrate the six-mile-long Confederate defense line there and cross the Chickahominy behind it, he would be on the doorstep of the Rebel capital.

The Southern line was rock-solid and bristled with artillery. Sheridan's scouting cavalry had driven the enemy into their trenches May 31, and they awaited the expected Yankee onslaught. Federal infantry arrived to replace Sheridan's men and an attack was planned for June 1.

The VI and XVIII Corps struck that day, carrying the outer line and taking some prisoners (above). Enemy fire was severe from front and flank, and assaulting troops soon withdrew.

On the second, each side strengthened its lines. They were about three hundred yards apart. Grant faced a momentous decision. Should he outflank the enemy once more (which would mean a carefully planned operation under Rebel noses) or try direct assault? He determined on the latter.

The Rebel line formed a concave arc. Facing it were Hancock on the Union left, Wright in the center, and Smith on the right. Warren and Burnside lay farther north, not in contact with the enemy. Grant ordered a frontal attack on Rebel lines by Hancock, Wright, and Smith for the morning of June 3.

Promptly at 4:30 A.M. Union troops climbed from their rifle pits and advanced. A sheet of fire from Rebel guns hurled grape, canister, and Minié balls into the densely massed men.

Destruction was almost unbelievable. In ten minutes, enemy guns cut down several thousand men and brought the drive to a jarring halt. Infantrymen hit the ground and dug in as best they could among the dead and wounded. Two more attacks were ordered. The men fired from cover and took no ground. By noon, Grant called the whole operation off. It was his most expensive failure and probably the most crushing single defeat of the war.

Some 12,000 Northern men fell at Cold Harbor. For his one-month march, Grant's casualties topped 50,000. His last direct attack had been a sanguine failure and the Union leader became "Butcher Grant" to the newspapers.

The series of flanking movements that

had carried the Army of the Potomac south appeared to be at an end, for Grant was now opposite Richmond. He had no desire to attack Lee there. The capital was well fortified, and one Rebel in the earthwork and masonry defenses could be worth five attacking Yankees.

The commander-in-chief pondered the problem and decided on one more flanking movement. This would by-pass Richmond; its objective was Petersburg, south of the capital.

Petersburg formed the concentration point for all but one of the railroads that fed Richmond as well as Lee's army. The South Side Railroad came in from the west, the Weldon from due south, and the Norfolk and Petersburg from the southeast. If Grant could take Petersburg and choke off these three rail lines, Richmond would eventually wither like a flower cut off from its stem.

Moving the Army of the Potomac to Petersburg became a major task, to be carried out in secrecy if possible so Lee would not shuttle his troops south to block the move. Grant sent his men east from Cold Harbor, then swung them south to cross the half-mile-wide James River.

The maneuver was brilliantly executed. Smith and Hancock moved their corps across the James by ferry on June 14 as Meade's engineers labored on a mighty pontoon bridge. Over 2,000 feet long, with 101 pontoons, it came into being in less than eight hours. By June 16, the crossing of the James had been completed.

Beauregard held Petersburg, on June 15, with a little more than 2,000, and was desperately telegraphing Lee for reinforcement. On that day, Smith attacked, using almost 40,000 troops, including his own and Hancock's men. Union troops made some progress, then stopped unexplainably.

The same situation obtained on the following day; Grant's 50,000 found themselves unable to take the weak Rebel position. Reinforcements poured in to both sides hour by hour. Yankee attacks were continuous but lacked punch. Beauregard shortened his lines and held his own. By June 20, the Union offensive died out and Lee had garrisoned Petersburg.

Following the bitter morning battle of June 3, Lee moved against Union lines in the afternoon, but Hancock's artillery halted the push. Confederate and Union wounded lay between the opposing lines for days while Grant and Lee argued over a truce so stretcher bearers could go forward.

Union Troops Lost a Golden Opportunity When They Failed
To Exploit the Explosion of a Mine beneath the Enemy Line

BOTH armies settled down around Petersburg, the Union to carry on an active siege that would last more than nine months. Grant established trenches east of the city and ran his line to the south, then extended it west. For every new trench dug by the Union, Lee dug a countertrench. By February, 1865, Lee occupied a line of works that ran more than fifty miles, from north of Richmond to southwest of Petersburg.

Grant took the Norfolk and Petersburg Railroad early in the siege. Operations were carried out against the Weldon road, running south of Petersburg, throughout the summer, and Union lines finally extended across that artery. For supplies, Lee was left the South Side railway and the Richmond and Danville, which came from the west.

Grant established a railroad running from City Point, on the James River, to his own lines. Munitions for Union forces thereafter traveled south by water and were reshipped on the military rail line. The Federal army knew no shortages of food, clothing, or ammunition.

The most spectacular incident of the siege was the Battle of the Crater at the end of July. It came about because the Rebel troops occupied a salient that projected into Union lines east of Petersburg. Behind the salient, well within Confederate positions, was an eminence called Cemetery Hill, a height that looked down on the Petersburg defenses. Opposite the salient lay Burnside's IX Corps.

In that organization was the 48th Pennsylvania, a regiment made up largely of coal miners from Schuylkill County, commanded by Lieutenant Colonel Henry Pleasants, a one-time mining engineer. He suggested digging a tunnel beneath the area separating the lines, running it under the enemy salient,

filling it with powder, and exploding it to create a hole in the Rebel line through which Union troops could advance to take Cemetery Hill.

Grant and Meade were cool to the plan. Army engineers said it was unthinkable. Burnside had faith in it and eventually received permission for an attempt.

Pleasants' men, back again at their civilian trade, worked from June 25 to July 23 (center). Bringing out earth in cracker barrels, concealing their operations from the enemy by camouflage, they burrowed more than 500 feet into the earth and removed 18,000 cubic feet of dirt. Eight magazines ran from the main shaft and each was charged with 1,000 pounds of powder, four tons in all.

Successful completion of the project aroused the interest of the high command. It was decided the attack, which might crack Lee's defenses at a crucial point, should be made in strength. Burnside's IX Corps would lead the assault; if it was successful, the V and XVIII would follow through the gap.

Colored troops were chosen to make up the first attack wave but Meade canceled the order, fearing public opinion would feel the men were being sent in as sacrifices. They took part eventually, behind the leading elements, but their arrival was badly timed and their efforts wasted.

The explosion was set for 3:30 A.M. and attacking officers waited, watches in hand, to send in their troops. As minutes dragged on, the fuse broke and two intrepid men went into the tunnel and relighted it.

A little before five, an immense explosion shook the earth (upper right). Men, guns, timbers, and earth rose in a vast mushroom of fire and smoke. When the fumes cleared,

there was a gaping crater 170 feet long, 60 feet wide, and 30 feet deep.

The mine functioned perfectly. The Union attack was a fiasco. A heavy artillery barrage followed the explosion, then the leading elements went in (right). Instead of skirting the crater they entered it. More troops, on their heels, did the same. Unit commanders were nowhere in sight. The Confederates rallied, poured down fire on the trapped men, and by midday, sent them back to their lines in ignoble rout.

Grant was furious: "The effort was a stupendous failure. It cost us about four thousand men . . . and all due to inefficiency on the part of the corps commander and the incompetency of the division commander who was sent to lead the assault."

RAVAGING THE VALLEY

GRANT'S spring offensive in 1864 called for operations in the Shenandoah Valley and the mountainous regions just to the west. The valley was of prime importance to the Confederacy and a constant source of irritation to the Union.

Grant envisioned Union occupation of the valley, to cut off supplies to the Rebels and prevent the North from a threat of invasion. General Franz Sigel commanded the Union troops that were to effect this occupation.

The Valley Campaign began in early May. Sigel's force moved in two columns. The one under his immediate command was to drive south through the valley toward Staunton.

The other column had two parts. One, under Major General George Crook, was to come down from West Virginia to operate against the East Tennessee and Virginia Railroad. The second, under Major General William W. Averell, also from West Virginia, had lead mines and salt works in southwestern Virginia as its objectives.

Crook reached his objective, destroyed supplies and railroad track, burned a bridge, and retired to West Virginia. Averell ran into Morgan, the Confederate raider who had broken out of a Yankee prison. On May 10, Morgan fought Averell and beat him and the Union force followed Crook into West Virginia.

Sigel, leading the major Union advance through the valley, stumbled into sheer disaster. With some 6,000 men, he moved south, opposed only by Brigadier General John D. Imboden and a force of 1,500. The Rebel leader fell back slowly, harrying Sigel.

Breckinridge, commanding the area for the Confederates, gathered troops and eventually joined Imboden. The combined Southern force, numbering 5,000, attacked Sigel at New Market on May 15, won a decisive victory, and sent the Union force fleeing back along its path.

Three days later, Grant called for Sigel's relief and Major General David Hunter took over the Union force. On May 25, Grant ordered Hunter to move south, cross over the Blue Ridge east to Charlottesville, then drop south again to Lynchburg, living upon the country and cutting railroads and canals as he went.

Hunter reached Staunton, and Grant dispatched Sheridan to move toward him, breaking up the Virginia Central Railroad and James River Canal as he went (both carried supplies to Richmond and the Army of Northern Virginia). When Hunter and Sheridan had joined and completed their destruction they were authorized to join the Army of the Potomac.

Crook and Averell joined Hunter at Staunton, giving him a force of 18,000 men. Lee, hearing of this advance along with Sheridan's move, sent Breckinridge (whom he had recalled after New Market) and two additional divisions of cavalry, to protect his communications.

Sheridan tackled the Rebel cavalry, beat them off, ripped up railroad around Trevilian Station in mid-June, and returned to his base. News had reached him that Hunter was at Lynchburg and Sheridan felt the juncture between him and Hunter was no longer necessary.

In his march south, Hunter was achieving the success that had evaded Sigel. Lee could not permit continued Union victories in the Valley. He detached Jubal A. Early, with a portion of the II Corps, to halt Hunter.

As Hunter approached Lynchburg, Early moved out of the lines at Cold Harbor and reached the city ahead of the Federal troops. Skirmishing followed on June 17 and 18. Hunter, reporting he was out of ammunition, refused attack and retreated.

The retreat was a long one, taking him all the way back through the valley to West Virginia. Early pursued him. In the end, Union troops left the valley completely. Early, with some 30,000 men, was in complete command of the rich countryside. The gateway to Washington was open.

Early, his men in need of food and shoes, lost no time in exploiting his opportunities. By July 4, he was at the Potomac and he crossed the next day above Harper's Ferry. In Maryland, the Rebels garnered their essential supplies and more from the towns they passed through (left).

Early cut the Baltimore and Ohio Railroad, sent his cavalry to Hagerstown to demand a ransom of $20,000 under threat of burning the city, and passed through South Mountain passes to Frederick. Just below him lay Washington.

Horses, cattle, sheep, grain and the wagons to haul it, made up the plunder collected by Early's men on their march into Maryland during 1864. At this period of the war, Rebel soldiers were often hard pressed for food, and expeditions into Northern farming country meant feasting.

TERROR seized the Union capital as Early approached. The governors of New York, Pennsylvania, and Massachusetts were called upon for hundred-day men to repel the invasion. Militia fell out inside the city and Lincoln telegraphed Grant for help.

Major General Lew Wallace, with headquarters at Baltimore, was the only Union commander within reach. He put together a scratch army of raw troops, semi-invalid soldiers, and clerks, stiffened by one division of the VI Corps, which Meade had sent to Baltimore to aid the Washington defenses, and went forth to fight Early. The valiant little army met Early's veterans July 9, at the Monocacy River, east of Frederick, were soundly beaten, and fell back within the city.

By the eleventh, the Confederates were in the capital's suburbs, coming down the Seventh Street pike past Silver Springs. Grant, fully alerted, had sent the remainder of the VI Corps north by water, and men of this crack outfit streamed into the Washington defenses just as Early approached. The XIX Corps, just arrived by sea from Louisiana, was also diverted to the capital's forts.

Early demonstrated on the night of July 11, and Lincoln rode out to Fort Stevens (above) to watch the action. On the twelfth, the Southern general saw the well-manned

defenses were too much for him and fell back. Union troops pursued but he evaded them, and the VI Corps went back to Petersburg.

Early retired to the Shenandoah Valley. On July 24, he fought Crook and Averell at Kernstown, defeated them, and followed up as they withdrew. Rebel cavalry, under Brigadier General John McCausland, crossed the Potomac once more and rode all the way to Chambersburg, Pennsylvania. There, they demanded $500,000 from the mayor. The money could not be raised; Confederates drove the inhabitants from their homes and burned the city.

Early's threat to Washington and the burning of Chambersburg crystallized Northern anger. Lincoln and Grant, in consultation, decided on a new force under a leader who, once and for all, would smash Confederate power in the Shenandoah Valley and ravage the area so it could never again feed Rebel armies.

Sheridan got the job, and the Army of the Shenandoah was created for him. Made up of about 30,000 men at the start, it consisted of the VI Corps under Horatio Wright, the XIX Corps under Brigadier General William H. Emory, the Army of West Virginia under George Crook, and three divisions of cavalry headed by Brigadier General Alfred T. A. Torbet.

Lee, hearing of the Army of the Shenandoah, reinforced Early. Saving the valley had important priority on the Confederate schedule. The Southern troops had been pushed back as Sheridan brought his new force against them; reinforcements from Lee enabled them to push the Yankees back in turn. By mid-August, Early's men were operating against the Baltimore and Ohio Railroad and lay encamped in the vicinity of Winchester.

Sheridan moved cautiously during August, evoking some criticism, but Lincoln and Grant had faith in him. To aid the new general, Grant ordered a demonstration against Petersburg, which forced Lee to withdraw some of the troops he had sent into the valley.

On September 15, Grant visited Sheridan with a battle plan, but pocketed it when he heard Sheridan's ideas for attack. The time for caution was past. On September 19, the Union army struck Early in front of Winchester.

Sheridan planned a fast attack, led by cavalry, to smash Early before the Rebel leader could gather his army, which was spread over a wide area. The cavalry moved as planned, but Sheridan's VI Corps stalled on the road, held up the XIX, and by the time the infantry was untangled, Early had concentrated his army.

The two forces came together with a stunning shock about noon, both sides fighting without cover. Early drove in the Union center, but the attack was contained and action slowed for a time.

When it began again, Union cavalry pounded both Rebel flanks in a series of whirlwind charges, bending them back. Early was forced to withdraw slightly and, as he did, Wright, Emory, and Crook sent their infantry crashing through his center. The Confederates, smashed by Union power, fell back in near rout and Federal troops carried the day, at a cost of 5,000 casualties.

Transportation troubles made Union troops somewhat slow getting into action in the battle of September 19, but once committed, Crook's men (upper picture) and those of Emory (lower picture) charged the Confederate right and center, sending the Rebels "whirling through Winchester."

VICTORY bells rang through the North following Sheridan's success at Winchester. The legend of Rebel superiority in the Shenandoah Valley was broken at last and the nation worshiped its newest hero. Congress voted Sheridan a gold sword; Lincoln wired his personal thanks.

Sheridan followed up his enemy with all possible speed. Early fell back to Strasburg, where the valley narrows, and took up an ideal defense position. Both flanks were anchored on steep ground and the Rebel line ran along high, rocky terrain thick with trees.

Sheridan came up on the twentieth and spent the following day examining the solid Confederate position. Seeing his horsemen would be wasted in trying to attack, he sent them on a wide sweep in an attempt to gain the enemy rear.

The Union leader saw his best chance lay in a flanking move, and on the morning of the twenty-second, Crook's troops took up concealed positions on high ground to Early's extreme left. A little before sun-down, they swept down on the Confederate left and rear in a sudden surprise attack. The remainder of Sheridan's men joined in, the rout was complete, and the broken Rebel line collapsed as Early's men fled.

Sheridan, tenaciously after his enemy, followed that night, reaching Woodstock, fifteen miles away. The day after the Battle of Strasburg, or Fisher's Hill, Early reorganized his men and attempted to hold a river line at Mt. Jackson. There, Sheridan struck again (above) and once more sent the Rebels reeling.

Early gave up battle for the time being and fell back through New Market, then turned east to a camping ground at the foot of the Blue Ridge. Sheridan had uncontested possession of the valley.

The Confederates had left the Shenandoah, but one task remained: devastation of the valley. The Union army moved south to Staunton, then back north to Winchester, burning and destroying as it went. Food and livestock were taken for Yankee troops when they could be used, the rest made unusable.

Barns, granaries, agricultural implements all met the same fate. Never in the future could Rebel armies turn to the valley farmers for produce.

There was one more battle in Early, who had been reinforced. As Sheridan moved north, Early followed. On October 6, at Fisher's Hill, the Union cavalry turned on Early and pushed him back twenty-five miles. But as Yankee horsemen withdrew, Early returned to dog Sheridan's tracks.

The Union leader was summoned to Washington on October 15. He left Wright in command of the army, which lay at Cedar Creek, twenty miles south of Winchester. An intercepted message warned of possible Confederate reinforcement and attack. Careful watch was kept. Union scouts noticed nothing out of the ordinary.

In the meantime, Early closed in. One of his brigade commanders, looking down on the Union position, felt the Federal left flank could be carried. He was given three divisions for the attempt. Two more Rebel divisions would strike the Union front at the same time. On the night of October 18, the flanking force silently moved into position over the mountains.

The following dawn, Early's men struck in a wild, surprise blow that caught Sheridan's army asleep in its tents. Brought awake by the Rebel yells and crashing musketry, Union troops grabbed their equipment and fled in panic. Division after division melted away to the rear and only the cavalry managed to hold a ragged line.

Sheridan, at Winchester, heard the firing and spurred his horse. Passing stragglers, he rallied them and ordered them back. By his heroic efforts, and those of his corps commanders, the army was brought together in fighting formations.

Early's men had stopped to devour Yankee food. By the time they came forward, Sheridan had stopped their attack. He then counterattacked viciously along the entire Rebel line, breaking it for good. For the last time, the Confederates retreated. Cedar Creek marked the end of the Shenandoah Valley campaigns.

Confederate Forces Had Their Own Way in the Valley
From the War's Beginning until Sheridan Appeared in 1864

Rules against foraging were suspended as Union troops marched through the Shenandoah Valley under Sheridan, and farm wives wept to see the slaughter among their livestock (above). The smoke of burning buildings and granaries often rose against the mountain backdrop (below).

DAMN THE TORPEDOES

NAVAL news of 1864 revolved around two Confederate ironclads. *Tennessee* played a major part in the great battle that followed Farragut's brave entrance into Mobile Bay (above). *Albemarle* wrote her own small saga in Atlantic coastal waters.

There, Rebel leaders plotted to clear the sound country of eastern North Carolina as the year began, to open ports for blockade runners. In February, and again in May, ineffectual attempts to capture New Berne were made.

As the first try got under way, *Albemarle* was being constructed in a field well up the Roanoke River. An ironclad ram, mounting two guns, she was built to engage wooden blockade ships patrolling the sound waters.

In mid-April, she came downstream to battle. Rebel land forces surrounded the little town of Plymouth, on the Roanoke River (eight miles above the head of Albemarle Sound), as the ram engaged Federal ships on the river side. She sank *Southfield* and drove *Miami* out of the river, then went back upstream for repair.

By early May, *Albemarle* was ready for battle again, and steamed into Albemarle Sound, escorting two small transports. Four Union craft, each mounting six guns, were waiting, with an escort of smaller craft. The Rebel ram engaged the fleet and was holding her own when rammed by *Sassacus*. The Union vessel, severely injured, veered off, but *Albemarle* was also hurt and forced to retire to Plymouth.

Her death came in October. In a daring raid, Lieutenant William B. Cushing, U.S.N., took a tiny ship up the Roanoke and drove a torpedo at the end of a spar into the ram, sinking the threat to Yankee shipping.

303

The Alabama Port of Mobile, on the Gulf Coast, Offered a Major Harbor to Blockade Runners up to Midsummer of 1864

FARRAGUT remained in the Gulf of Mexico after his victories on the Mississippi. As blockading ships tossed on the Gulf swells, the admiral planned ways to crack the entrance to Mobile Bay and take the huge port.

Mobile Bay is an impressive roadstead in the shape of a triangle, its base along the Gulf. The distance from tip to base is thirty miles; the base stretches more than twenty.

The bay was well defended. Its eastern approaches were cut off by a long sand spit, its western ones by Dauphine Island and a series of sandy shoals. Between the spit and the island was a three-mile stretch of water. The entrance to the bay lay through this area, passing close to the tip of the spit.

On that barren point loomed Fort Morgan, a strong, old brick structure reinforced with sandbags. Three tiers of heavy guns frowned from the fort. Seven cannon were emplaced on the beach, at water's edge. Ships entering the channel came within point-blank range of the Rebel guns.

In addition, the channel was mined with the explosives called "torpedoes" in 1864. These were beer kegs, jugs, or tin cones filled with gunpowder. Various priming devices made them explode on contact with passing ships.

Across the channel, on the eastern tip of Dauphine Island, was Fort Gaines. This small structure mounted a few heavy guns but appeared to be too far away to do much damage to any fleet seeking entrance to Mobile Bay.

Farragut's squadron in the Gulf contained only wooden ships and the admiral dared not risk them in attempting to pass the forts, as he had done at New Orleans. He was doubtful of the ships' ability to run the forts without suffering mortal damage, and also worried about what might happen even if the defending structures could be passed safely. Once one of his vessels lost mobility in the inner harbor, Farragut knew she would be pounded to pieces by the lurking monster *Tennessee.*

It was the bay's value as a naval base that intrigued the Union chief. The city of Mobile was almost impregnable. It lay up a river, the channel securely blocked by driven piles which were hung about with mines. If he could capture the bay, Farragut reasoned, the city would eventually be starved out.

The admiral called for assistance in the form of ironclads and troops. Armored vessels could slug it out with the forts and take on *Tennessee.* Troops, once inside the harbor, would lay siege to the forts and reduce them so the bay could open to Federal ships.

For months, Washington turned a deaf ear to the admiral's pleas. Suddenly, there was a change of heart. Troops were dispatched to Farragut along with four ironclad monitors. The admiral lost no time in preparing for the attack and picked August 5 as the day.

The Confederates saw Yankee preparations, alerted the forts, and readied their small fleet, the gunboats *Morgan, Gaines, Selma,* and the giant ram *Tennessee.* The latter vessel was the pride of the Confederate Navy and one of the most powerful fighting ships in the world. More than two hundred feet long, she mounted six heavy guns and was shielded by 6-inch armor plate.

Farragut had fourteen wooden ships, including his flagship *Hartford,* the single-turret monitors *Tecumseh* and *Manhattan,* the double-turret monitors *Winnebago* and *Chickasaw.* His battle line was in two columns: monitors on the right, headed by *Tecumseh;* wooden ships to the left, headed by *Brooklyn,* with *Hartford* second. Each of the seven largest wooden vessels had a smaller ship tied alongside; if the larger craft's engines were disabled, the smaller one would keep her going.

The fleet was in motion at 5:45 A.M. and the first gun spoke an hour later. As the Yankee battle line reached Fort Morgan, broadsides blasted the structure. It hurled back a rain of shot, holing the wooden vessels and bouncing from the monitors' sides. *Tennessee* and her escorts lay across the front of the advancing ships and poured on shot and shell.

Volley after volley crashed out as the fight became bitter and bloody. Fort Morgan's heavy guns did fearful damage. To climax the action, *Tecumseh* hit a torpedo, blew up, and sank with most of her crew.

Brooklyn hesitated after the explosion and the Yankee line slowed dangerously, under the fort's guns. Farragut swung *Hartford* past the stalled ship, shouted, "Damn the torpedoes! Full speed ahead!" and led the column through the channel.

Once in the harbor, Farragut rendezvoused his ships to assess the damage after

sending four of them to chase the small Rebel gunboats. *Tennessee* withdrew to the shelter of Fort Morgan.

At nine-fifteen, as Union surgeons dressed their wounded, *Tennessee* emerged to engage the entire fleet. *Monongahela* rammed her; so did *Lackawanna; Hartford* closed in, but all to no avail. The ironclad's heavy armor turned aside the blows with ease.

Then the monitors came up. Pounding fire from *Chickasaw*'s 11-inch guns and *Manhattan*'s 15-inch weapons began to tell. *Tennessee*'s smokestack went, her rudder chains were carried away, and her gunports jammed shut. At ten o'clock she surrendered. Farragut had taken Mobile Bay and achieved an eternal reputation at Annapolis.

In the final minutes of the battle within Mobile Bay, *Tennessee* and *Hartford* approached each other head on, but the ram turned at the last minute and *Hartford* struck her only a glancing blow. After the shock, *Tennessee* did not fire another gun but was slowly pounded into surrender.

CAVALRY

THE cavalryman was the epitome of the romantic soldier. Oversize boots, tinkling spurs, heavy gauntlets, and occasionally a plumed hat or yellow scarf contributed to the effect. A swaggering walk and an easy seat on his horse marked the trooper.

King of them all was J. E. B. Stuart (upper left), the Virginia cavalier who led the Army of Northern Virginia's horsemen. Gracious, cultured, courteous, and gallant, Stuart personified all that was best in the Southern gentry. He fought at First and Second Bull Run, Antietam, Fredericksburg, and temporarily took over a corps at Chancellorsville when Jackson received his death wound. Stuart's absence at a critical time during the Gettysburg campaign cost Lee dearly, but the brilliant horseman served his leader well in the Virginia fighting of 1864, in which he met death in battle.

A far different man was Nathan Bedford Forrest (upper right), who led Southern horsemen, often irregulars, in the west. Lacking formal education, a former slave dealer, Forrest was a hard-driving leader and one of the Confederacy's most dynamic officers.

The North did not produce great cavalry leaders until late in the war. George Stoneman led the Army of the Potomac's cavalry for a time, fighting in the Peninsular Campaign. He was relieved by Alfred Pleasonton (opposite page, left), who commanded Meade's cavalry at Gettysburg. A career officer, Pleasonton was competent but lacked dash, daring, and imagination.

Northern cavalry received the leadership it deserved in 1864, when Grant appointed Philip H. Sheridan (opposite page, right) to relieve Pleasonton. Peppery, vigorous, blunt, Sheridan was an all-purpose officer who later commanded the Army of the Shenandoah. During the time he led the Army of the Potomac's horsemen, he welded them into a body of troops who could meet Confederate cavalry on equal terms.

The roster of Rebel cavalry leaders is studded with illustrious names: Wade Hampton, Fitzhugh Lee, Turner Ashby, John Singleton Mosby, Joseph Wheeler, John D. Imboden. Among the able Northern horsemen were John Buford, Benjamin Grierson, David Gregg, Judson Kilpatrick, George A. Custer, and James H. Wilson.

Stuart's whirlwind dashes around the Army of the Potomac, Wheeler's slashing attacks on Union wagon trains (lower right), Grierson's thrust through the central South, Forrest's savage attacks on Federal supply lines, and Wilson's push into Alabama gave Rebel and Union horsemen a secure place in the history of the rebellion.

MOUNTING and equipping the cavalry, and maintaining it in the field, was a tremendous job. In the beginning, it was better managed in the Confederacy than in the Union.

Southern soldiers brought their own horses when they joined the cavalry. Living a country life, Dixie youths had been trained in the saddle from childhood. They understood horses, used them well, and knew how to give them the care they needed.

A fair proportion of the Northern cavalry came from farm country, but many of its members were city bred. Attracted by the glamour of the mounted arm, they joined up despite their ignorance of horseflesh. Long, careful training was necessary before such volunteers could be expected to take expert care of their mounts.

Of necessity, some of the training took place in the field at the cost of the horses concerned. Ignorance and lack of care from the green troops produced a high mortality rate among Union animals. During the first two years of war, 284,000 horses were furnished the Federal cavalry, while the maximum number of Union cavalrymen in the field never exceeded a total of 60,000.

The scale of the war, and its enormous demands, drained horseflesh from the North for officers' mounts, baggage trains, and artillery, as well as cavalry. The shortage was so severe in 1862 that only 800 mounted cavalrymen could be rounded up to chase Stuart when he raided Pennsylvania in October.

In 1863, a Cavalry Bureau was formed in the North and six depots were established. At these, recruits were trained and taught care of their mounts. Agents at the depots were charged with purchasing animals for the service. Prices paid averaged about $160 per head.

Veterinary hospitals were established at the depots. In them, sick and injured horses from the field were cared for and allowed to recuperate. About 50 per cent of them returned to action. Foot diseases were the bane of the cavalry horse, and sore backs, from overloading or constant riding, disabled many animals.

Each Union cavalry company carried its own farrier, who shod horses and pack mules (above). Farriers in the Federal serv-

ice nailed the shoes on four million horses during the war, and carried out veterinary duties as well.

Cavalry recruits were trained to keep down back injuries on their mounts by grooming them carefully after a day's ride (above). Charged with keeping their steeds well fed, horsemen often raided Rebel barns to remove their supply of oats (right).

Southern farms kept the Confederacy well supplied with horses in the early years of the war, the cavalrymen purchasing their own mounts. The Rebel government paid its horsemen an allowance for upkeep and gave a compensation for horses killed in action, but not for death through any other cause. Men who lost horses by disease or exposure often found the expense of purchasing new animals too high, and the Rebel cavalry began to have holes in its ranks. The steady attrition of war also cut down the number of Southern animals drastically. In the later years of conflict, good horses were scarce. Southern cavalrymen never lost their fighting edge, but lack of mounts and inferior weapons worked against them in the crucial years of 1864 and 1865.

WHILE cavalry was usually employed for reconnaissance and raiding operations, opposing horsemen occasionally met in the full shock of battle. After Gettysburg, a series of engagements occurred as Rebel troops commanded by Imboden, guarding Lee's retreat, clashed with pursuing Union cavalry under Buford at Boonsboro, Maryland (above).

Hand-to-hand cavalry battles were wild, whirlwind affairs, punctuated by the ring of metal on metal and the whinnying of frightened horses. They were seldom protracted. Attacking groups struck fast, cut up the enemy as much as possible, and broke off action quickly.

Horsemen were armed with sabers and revolvers. The long, straight sabers common in 1861 were later replaced by shorter weapons with curved blades for "cut and

thrust" fighting. Most of the revolvers used by both sides were Colt models. The 6th Pennsylvania Cavalry, harking back to the days of Norman knights, was armed with lances up until 1863.

Up-to-date firearms gave the Union cavalry much of its power. In the later years of the war, Federal horsemen carried carbines, small rifles ideal for use in close quarters. Single-shot Sharps weapons were standard for a time, then gradually disappeared as the government issued Spencers, Colts, and Henrys, all of which were repeaters.

Union cavalry forces, armed with magazine carbines, became power-packed fighting units that could move with the speed of the wind. General officers began to use them in emergencies, sending them speeding to troubled sectors, where the troopers dismounted and fought as infantry.

UNION cavalry was used cautiously in the first two years of the war, while Rebel horsemen rode roughshod over their opponents. The Yankee infantryman had a low opinion of his mounted brother-in-arms. "Who ever saw a dead cavalryman?" was a favorite question.

By the middle of 1863, Federal horse troops were beginning to display muscle. March 17 saw Union cavalry beat back the Rebels at Kelly's Ford, on the Rappahannock in Virginia. On June 9, at Brandy Station, Virginia, Pleasonton's men met Stuart's in a series of sharp engagements that went on for ten hours. Union cavalrymen handled themselves well, inflicted sharp losses on the enemy, and withdrew in order.

In a sense, Federal horsemen were blooded at Brandy Station. The battle gave them the confidence they had lacked in the past. By the time of Gettysburg, Yankee troopers were ready and willing. It was Buford's cavalry, fighting dismounted, that held off the Confederates as Union infantry fell back and entrenched on Cemetery Ridge.

Shortly after this, Custer struck the Rebels at Culpepper, Virginia, capturing a stand of Southern artillery in a lightning attack (below) Guns, heavy and hard to move, often fell to raiding cavalry. Artillerymen learned to keep an eye peeled for roving horse troops.

Sheridan took over the Army of the Potomac's mounted arm in April, 1864. In his hands, it became an aggressive body that sought out and struck Rebel horsemen wherever possible. Union foot soldiers began to change their opinion of the troopers.

On May 9, Sheridan started south toward Richmond with 10,000 mounted men, making a thirteen-mile-long line. His raid was aimed at threatening the Rebel capital and drawing Stuart's horsemen away from Grant and Meade. Two days later, in the midst of pitched battle, Stuart received a fatal wound and Fitzhugh Lee took over. In Stuart's death, the South lost one of its most cherished heroes.

When Sheridan took over a new army to ravage the Shenandoah Valley, well-trained cavalry paced the destructive expedition. Horsemen alone captured more than 2,500 prisoners and 71 guns.

In the west, Sherman took 15,000 cavalrymen on his drive to Atlanta, and 5,000 on the march to the sea. Under Wilson, troopers beat Forrest back in Tennessee, fought dismounted at Nashville, and carried out a fatal penetration of the Confederacy on their sweeping raid through Alabama and Georgia.

1865

FORT FISHER TAKEN

BY 1865, the Confederacy was fought out. There was to be a good deal of bristling action before the war ended, but leaders in the South foresaw a bitter future as the new year began.

Bled white by battle and defeat, the South kept on desperately. Belief in the cause was the sustaining force. Materially, the Southern states were on their last legs. They were further weakened in January, 1865, by the loss of their only remaining major seaport.

Wilmington, North Carolina, on the state's southeastern coast, was an important city to the Confederacy throughout the war. Well up the Cape Fear River, Wilmington had railroads that ran north and west to

carry foreign goods from incoming ships to soldier and civilian.

Blockade runners, evading the Union ships at night and protected to some extent by coastal artillery, slipped up the river to city docks and discharged meat, textiles, and ammunition components to be used in the Southern cause. After the fall of Mobile Bay, the North Carolina city was the last remaining port through which the riches of the outside world could come to bolster the weakening South.

Below Wilmington, bordering the Cape Fear River, ran a long, narrow peninsula, thrusting south into the Atlantic. Along the dunes of this neck of land, Fort Fisher was built. Any attempt by sea on Wilmington would have to pass Fisher's fortifications, which were stout and forbidding. Over the years, Confederates in charge of the post had strengthened it to the extent that only a powerful, sustained attack could crack the defenses.

In late 1864 and early 1865, Bragg was in charge of Wilmington and the surrounding area. Under him, Colonel William Lamb commanded at Fort Fisher. The colonel labored mightily to make his position impregnable.

Fort Fisher had two sides, a land side and a sea side. The former was a series of defenses stretched across the peninsula, from the river to the ocean, so Yankee troops could be stopped if they went ashore to the north and swept down in an overland attack. On the sea side, defenses were arranged to combat direct amphibious assault.

Fort Fisher's land side was a half-mile long. Wood, earth, and sandbags made walls twenty-five feet thick and more than twenty feet high. Twenty heavy guns peered from the fort. Magazines, bombproof shelters, and trenches honeycombed the structure.

On the sea side, defenses were of the same massive character. A series of batteries extended for more than a mile, connected by shelters for infantry. Twenty-four heavy guns covered Fort Fisher's sea approaches.

Land mines were placed underground in front of Fisher's lines on the land side; submarine torpedoes, connected with an electric battery inside the fort, protected the sea side. At the extreme southern tip of the peninsula lay Fort Buchanan, a small structure covering one of the entrances to the Cape Fear River.

The Union planned to take Fort Fisher, and eliminate Wilmington as a blockade runners' haven, in December, 1864. For amphibious assault, the biggest fleet ever assembled under one command in the Navy's history was given Rear Admiral David Porter. Under him were nearly sixty ships, including five ironclads, mounting more than six hundred guns.

Army troops were led by Ben Butler, given a chance to redeem himself after failing on the James River, and Major General Godfrey Weitzel. Warships and transports met off Fort Fisher shortly before Christmas. Butler sent in a powder-filled ship that exploded close to shore, creating a great deal of noise but causing no damage, on December 23.

The fleet then shelled the fort heavily and on Christmas Day, Butler and Weitzel landed their troops well up on the peninsula (left). Once on shore they probed enemy defenses, declared them too tough to conquer, re-embarked their men, and the expedition steamed back to its bases.

Lincoln and Grant were furious. Butler was removed, his place given to Major General Alfred H. Terry, and the force sent out again in early January. This time the army did not let the navy down.

January 13, 14, and 15 saw the fleet once more lay down a tremendous curtain of fire. It pounded Rebel defenses into rubble (below). On the fifteenth, Terry's 8,000 soldiers, assisted by 2,000 sailors and marines, landed on the peninsula and stormed Fort Fisher's land side.

Lamb's 1,500-man garrison put up a gallant, futile defense. The fort fell at eight o'clock that night. Wilmington held out another month, but Fort Fisher's capture eliminated the city's usefulness and the South had no more important seaports.

CAROLINA INVASION

SHERMAN planned one more major march, to spread destruction through the South as his men moved nearer to those of Grant.

The move involved a thrust due north from Savannah, cutting through South Carolina, then a swing east into North Carolina. "Uncle Billy's" destination was Goldsboro, in that state. Procedure on the march was to be much the same as before.

On February 1, Union troops left the Savannah area. The left wing, under Slocum, included the XIV and XX Corps and a cavalry division. Howard, with the right wing, had two corps, the XV and XVII.

The final march of Sherman's troops bore little resemblance to the expedition through Georgia. In the Carolinas, the ground was tougher and so was the temper of the army.

South Carolina was a low, flat country, inundated by water. Rice fields, bayous, acres of swampland, and infrequent roads were all flooded by heavy winter rains. Swollen rivers, such as the Edisto (above), blocked the troops until pontoon bridges could be swung into place. Building corduroy roads to sustain the weight of wagons and ambulances became normal operating procedure every day.

The all but impassable countryside led Southerners to believe Sherman would bog down, or at least take months for his drive north. Tough Yankee troops, mostly from the rugged West, gave this hopeful opinion the lie. Soldiers waded, swam, floundered, and trudged but kept their pace of ten miles per day through the wild and rugged wilderness. In addition, they tore up and burned some sixty miles of railroad track in the opening phase of the march.

Speaking of South Carolina, before the march began, Sherman wrote Halleck "I almost tremble at her fate, but feel that she deserves all that seems in store for her."

The men shared Sherman's feeling. South Carolina had been the hotbed of secession. From her soil, guns aimed at Fort Sumter started the war. As the avenging army moved into the state, which had been spared the fate of her sisters, Union troops burned, smashed, and destroyed.

Destruction was cold and methodical. Soldiers who had been quiet throughout the Savannah occupation wreaked havoc when they crossed the river. The death of several Yankees from land mines planted in their path added fuel to the flames.

Houses, barns, outbuildings, the very trees themselves were put to the torch. Smoke by day and fire by night marked the trail of Sherman's men, as did the slowly increasing procession of ex-slaves.

Colored people flocked from plantations to fall in behind Sherman's men and move with the army. They brought buggies, carriages, and wagons, or arrived riding cows, horses, and mules taken from their owners.

Lee could send no troops of his own from Petersburg, but appointed Joseph E. Johnston to organize what defense he could, with Beauregard second in command. The able Confederate generals could count on Hardee's small garrison at Charleston, Bragg's army at Wilmington, and the remnants of the Army of Tennessee, brought all the way from Mississippi by forced marches and wearying rail trips, to help stop Sherman. Lieutenant General Wade Hampton contributed his cavalry for scouting.

On leaving Savannah, Sherman's right wing threatened Charleston and his left threatened Augusta. Hardee held the former, Bragg the latter. Sherman's threatening moves were feints; he closed ranks after pinning down the Rebel forces and advanced on Columbia, South Carolina's capital, driving Hampton's cavalry before him.

On February 17, Columbia was burned. Sherman believed the fire came from cotton bales ignited by Hampton's cavalry; South-erners (and some Northerners as well) attributed the blaze to drunken Union soldiers. The city became a smoking ruin. On the same day, Charleston, cut off from the rest of the South by Sherman's advance, was evacuated and Northern troops moved in.

Sherman swept through Cheraw to Fayetteville, North Carolina, where he met Union shipping coming up the Cape Fear River from captured Wilmington on March 10. The vessels brought news that General John M. Schofield's XXIII Corps, traveling by land and sea, would soon join Sherman.

Johnston saw that his only hope lay in bringing on battle before the juncture was made. On March 19, he struck the exposed XIV Corps of the left wing and forced it back. The Union line was stiffened as the XX came up and the battle raged two more days until Sherman had his entire army in position, after which Johnston's attack collapsed. Sherman moved to Goldsboro, met the XXIII Corps, and opened supply lines by rail down to New Berne and Wilmington.

Johnston placed his men behind breastworks at Bentonville to await the Union advance, then charged the Yankee troops in a hard attack. Quick concentration of Federal forces enabled Sherman to check the Rebel drive in the last major action of the war for this Union army.

THE RING TIGHTENS

SHERMAN'S mighty sweep through the Carolinas was the harbinger of a fateful spring for the Confederacy.

In the Shenandoah Valley, Sheridan dispersed his infantry, sending much of it to Petersburg. The general retained a strong cavalry force for final operations in the area.

On February 27, with two cavalry divisions, Sheridan began his departure from the valley he had won. He moved through Staunton and, on March 2, came up with the remnants of Early's command at Waynesboro. The Southern general attempted a defiant stand but was quickly swept aside, losing men, guns, ammunition, supplies, and battle flags to the powerful Union command.

Federal troops then moved to the Virginia Central Railroad, which they thoroughly destroyed, burning bridges and tearing up track. The James River Canal was also destroyed. Having cut two major Rebel supply routes, Sheridan rode into Grant's lines.

To the west, Alabama was the scene of brisk Federal operations. In March, Major General James H. Wilson, with a fine cavalry force, occupied the extreme northwest corner of the state. Orders from Thomas directed Wilson to take several thousand horsemen on a long raid into the central and southern portion.

The command moved out March 22, driving south against slight opposition from Forrest, who came over from Mississippi to dispute the Yankee advance. On April 2, Union troops took Selma, an important munitions center, and turned east to move toward Montgomery, then Columbus and Macon in Georgia.

Farther south, Canby, with 45,000 men, laid siege to the city of Mobile. Defending the town was Major General Dabney H. Maury, who had 10,000 men and 300 guns.

Canby separated his force into two columns, one from Dauphine Island, the other from Pensacola. The Union general appeared before the city March 27 and invested two forts guarding the place. By early April, the forts were evacuated, as was the city.

Grant had long advocated taking Mobile. Its fall, in the final days of the war, did him little good. Of more immediate interest was the command of Major General George Stoneman, based on Knoxville, Tennessee.

The commander-in-chief ordered Stoneman to move east, destroying railroads in the direction of Lynchburg, Virginia, as much as possible. Leaving Knoxville on March 20, the general struck east into North Carolina, turned north to Virginia, breaking up the railroad as ordered, then dropped back into North Carolina for harassing operations.

Throughout this anxious period, as Union columns stabbed into the Confederacy in the west and south, the lines at Petersburg and Richmond held firm. Within them was the Army of Northern Virginia, the sword and shield of the Rebellion.

Over and over again, Grant had sent troops against the stubborn defenses (left) with little or no result. Although numerically inferior to the Yankees, the Southern infantry lay well defended by its miles of forts, earthworks, and trenches.

Safe behind their iron ring, Davis and the Confederate Congress sought desperately for a solution to the conflict that was slowly crushing the Southern cause.

A negotiated peace was one possible answer. The Rebel leaders made the effort.

In early February, three commissioners for the Confederate States boarded a Union steamer at Hampton Roads. They were Alexander H. Stephens, Vice President of the Confederacy; Senator R. M. T. Hunter; John A. Campbell, Assistant Secretary of War. Lincoln and Seward received them.

The peace talks foundered completely. Lincoln insisted on union. The Southern commissioners were not empowered to discuss cessation of war on such terms. The President suggested an armistice, promising to go to Congress and ask for funds to reimburse slave-owners when their chattels were freed. The suggestion proved unacceptable.

Returning to Richmond, the delegation reported on the conference. At a mass meeting, the North's proposals were damned as insulting to the Confederacy and a resolve to fight to the death was adopted.

Men to carry on that fight were essential. A still untapped source of military manpower lay in the slaves. There were those who had long advocated arming them and sending them forth to battle.

The subject brought acrimonious debate in the Southern Congress. Davis had originally vetoed the idea, but the shortage of fighting men brought him around. William Smith, governor of Virginia, gave strong support to the plan.

Asked his opinion, Robert E. Lee found the measure to be completely acceptable, provided the slaves would be promised gradual emancipation. By late March, Congress passed a law authorizing Davis to request slaves for army service, but emancipation was ignored. The measure was too late to be of any value.

Also long overdue was an act passed by Congress and approved by Davis on January 23. This made Lee General-in-Chief of all Southern armies.

PETERSBURG'S FATE

ATTRITION and desertion took a terrible toll of Lee's army in early 1865. Grant could not penetrate the defenses, but he moved west constantly, below Petersburg, reaching for the railroads that supplied the city. Each move forced Lee to stretch his already thin line even more.

Lee knew the comparative quiet of the winter would end in a massive Union offensive, once the miry roads were hard enough to support guns and wagons. He also saw that remaining within the Petersburg lines was to invite disaster.

His choices appeared to be three: (1) stay in his trenches, (2) disperse the army for guerrilla warfare, (3) break out to the west. The first choice was suicide, the second dishonorable and uncertain. In the third, there was a grain of hope.

A successful break-through would leave Lee his choice of two routes. Moving straight west, he could pass through Lynchburg and enter the Blue Ridge Mountain passes. Or, he might move southwest into North Carolina and join up with Johnston.

Lee determined to break out of the lines. Before the move, he hurled a last offensive at the Union positions east of Petersburg. The thrust he planned was to penetrate Federal defenses and threaten Grant's main supply base at City Point. Such action, Lee hoped, would force the Union commander to bring in forces to repair the break, opening the way to the west so Lee could slip his men through with a minimum of damage.

Fort Stedman, a strong Union position garrisoned by units of the IX Corps, was Lee's target. To lead the attack, the Confederate chief picked Major General John B. Gordon, who was given 10,000 to 12,000 men.

Rebel soldiers were to worm their way toward the Yankee pickets, acting as deserters, then overcome their captors. A picked group of ax-men, to chop through Yankee wooden defenses, helped spearhead the attack.

Gordon's men filed from their trenches the night of March 24 and struck during the dawn of the following day. In the beginning, all went as planned. Pickets were overwhelmed. Troops in the fort, asleep, were killed, captured, or sent fleeing.

Fort Stedman, with its neighboring batteries, fell to the Rebels and communications with City Point were cut off. But the second line of Yankee defenses confused the attackers. The thrust lost power. Federal troops rallied and got batteries into position. As fire increased, the Rebels fell back, gave up what they had gained, and retired into their defenses after losing almost 4,000 men.

Grant, aware that Lee would attempt escape to the west whenever the roads were passable, planned one final blow he hoped might end the war. A heavy force of infantry and cavalry was picked to strike Lee's extreme right, south and west of Petersburg. Such a move would roll up the Confederate army's flank, block Lee's escape, and open the way for Union cavalry to drive north, slashing the Richmond and Danville and the South Side, two railroads supplying Petersburg and Richmond.

Sheridan (upper left) commanded the striking force. On March 29, in streaming rain, the Yankee troops moved toward Five Forks, a crossroads southwest of Petersburg.

The following day, Sheridan's cavalry thrust at Five Forks, menacing Lee's right. Seeing the danger to his railroads from the move, Lee detached Pickett with five brigades to check the Yankees.

On March 31, Rebel pressure forced Sheridan slowly back toward Dinwiddie Court House. He called for reinforcement. Pickett followed Sheridan a short distance, then returned to entrench at Five Forks.

Sheridan, his force increased heavily, rolled forward April 1. By dusk he reached Pickett's lines. For a time, the savage battle hung in the balance, then the Confederate position crumbled.

Hearing of Sheridan's success, Grant ordered all-out assault on Petersburg, along the entire line, for April 2.

News of victory at Five Forks triggered Grant's decision for an all-out attack on Petersburg. Union batteries fired all night preceding the assault. Fort Sedgwick, popularly known as Fort Hell from the severity of its fire, is shown below hurling hot metal at Confederate Fort Mahone.

A CAPITAL IN FLAMES

IMPATIENT for the final drive on enemy lines, Union troops had to be held in leash the night of April 1. Gunners laid down heavy artillery fire all night long, and at 4:45 A.M. infantry assaults began.

With numerical superiority of more than three to one, Grant sent the bulk of his army against the entire Petersburg defense system. One by one, the outer forts fell and prisoners came into Federal lines in constant procession.

By noon, the Rebel first line had fallen except for two strong redoubts, Forts Gregg and Whitworth. One was stormed; Rebel troops abandoned the other. Lee made frantic efforts to retake lost positions. In the course of counterattacking, he caused more than 4,000 Union casualties. Confederate losses were never known, but the brilliant A. P. Hill met death in the struggle.

At 4:40 P.M., Union troops had achieved such success that Grant telegraphed Lincoln, who was at nearby City Point, inviting him to come out the following day for a visit.

As Federal victories mounted, top-ranking officers advised Grant to break down the inner defenses and capture the city. The commander-in-chief refused to risk any more men, declaring Petersburg would be evacuated during the night.

He proved correct. Lee had departed by 3 A.M. on the third and Union scouts entered the city an hour later. Grant came in with Meade.

Petersburg's fall laid Richmond open to invasion. In that city, on April 2, Jefferson Davis was at church when handed a message from Lee. The general advised of his situation, announced he was evacuating Petersburg, and suggested Davis leave Richmond at once. Leaving the Sabbath services, Davis assembled his department heads and gave instructions for fleeing the city that night. He departed for Danville, which he understood to be Lee's destination.

No official notification of evacuation was published but the air grew electric with rumors by Sunday noon. Destruction of government records, the rush to the railway station, and Ewell's marching troops, brought through the city to strike west and join Lee, told an unmistakable story.

The city exploded into pandemonium. Warehouses and storage bins had been set afire to deny supplies to the Yankees and the entire city blazed up, the flames spreading in every direction.

Walls of fire blocked passage through the streets as government buildings burned fiercely. The old, crippled, and helpless young died, seared and suffocated, in their beds. Eddies of flame and smoke whirled upward in the wind and sparks carried the conflagration from block to block.

Richmond was the great arsenal of the Confederacy, and ammunition exploded all night long in staccato bursts. More than 750,000 shells sent fragments flying through the streets, cutting down passers-by and entering houses. As morning dawned on April 3, a dense pall of smoke blotted out sun and sky.

From the river, tremendous, shattering explosions told of ironclads being blown up. Concussion from the blasts swept citizens off their feet. Barrels of oil-soaked waste were ignited to burn the bridges.

Screaming, rioting mobs thronged the streets, robbing, plundering, and setting new fires. Half-starved men, women, and children, numbering thousands, smashed down the doors of government commissaries and fled with hams, sides of bacon, barrels of coffee, sugar, and flour.

Union troops of the XXV Corps, under Godfrey Weitzel, entered the fallen city April 3 to fight the fires and bring the raging populace under control. Military force gradually eliminated looting and brought Richmond out of its nightmare.

Arrival of Federal troops did much to save Richmond from complete destruction (left), and the flames were well under control by the time Lincoln arrived on the heels of his conquering army (below). The colored population, welcoming the Yankees with unrestrained joy, pressed close to see the victorious President, who had become a legend throughout the slave quarters.

END AT APPOMATTOX

UPON evacuation of Richmond and Petersburg, the Army of Northern Virginia moved west swiftly with Union troops in pursuit. Sheridan, with the cavalry and V Corps, followed by Meade with the II and VI, dogged the heels of the retreating enemy.

The Southern army was a starving army. Soldiers robbed their horses of corn, parched it, and chewed the hard kernels for nourishment. To feed his men, Lee ordered a supply train to Amelia Court House on the Richmond and Danville Railroad, some 30 miles southwest of Richmond.

On April 4, troops from Petersburg and Richmond assembled at the courthouse to find the supply train had been rerouted before dropping off rations. Facing famine, Lee halted the army for twenty-four hours as soldiers foraged through the countryside collecting food for man and beast.

The delay was costly. Pursuing Union columns were fanning out to get in Lee's rear and cut off any turning movement. As the Southern army resumed its march, Union infantry and cavalry blocked its course at Jetersville, seven miles southwest of Amelia.

Lee swung west. With his southern flank

threatened, he gave up hope of joining Johnston and set his course for Lynchburg and the mountains. The march would bring Rebel troops to Farmville, on the South Side Railroad, where rations awaited them.

Ten miles short of Farmville, the Confederate rear guard of Ewell and Gordon was hit hard by Sheridan. In the Battle of Sailor's Creek, on April 6, Union troops captured six generals, including Ewell, and 7,000 men.

Gordon escaped from the Sailor's Creek debacle. With Longstreet and Lee, he brought his men into Farmville, where they drew rations and took to the road again.

By April 8, Sheridan had moved ahead of Lee and cut back into the path of the Confederate army in the vicinity of Appomattox Court House. The Union leader sent back a call for infantry to back up his horsemen, and Grant pressed his foot soldiers forward.

That night, by the light of a bivouac fire, Lee brought his leaders together for the final council. There was to be an attempt to break through the Union cordon on the morrow if it was found to be made up of cavalry only, or if supporting infantry units were small in number.

With the old Rebel dash, Lee struck on the morning of April 9. Fitzhugh Lee's cavalry circled the Union left flank, infantry pounded the center and took two guns, and the ragged battle flags moved ahead.

As Sheridan's cavalry fell back, masses of blue-coated infantry appeared, their cannon sparkling in the sunlight. Longstreet was pinned down, Gordon hard pressed. The Army of Northern Virginia, surrounded, could do no more.

Gordon sent a message: "Tell General Lee that my command has been fought to a frazzle and I cannot long go forward." There were no more reinforcements. Lee spoke: "There is nothing left me but to go and see General Grant, and I would rather die a thousand deaths."

Since April 7, Grant and Lee had been in communication with each other. On that day, the Union general called for Lee's surrender. Lee refused the request and asked for peace terms. Grant replied he had no authority to treat the subject of peace but that event would be hastened if the South laid down its arms and ceased resistance.

On April 9, Lee, his army fought out, requested an interview with Grant to discuss surrender. The Federal commander assented immediately and prepared for a meeting. Truce flags went up on both sides and men rested by their guns.

Lee, with his military secretary, Colonel Charles Marshall, rode into the village of Appomattox Court House. A Confederate orderly and a member of Grant's staff accompanied him. The home of Wilmer McLean, who had moved south from the Bull Run battlefield to escape the war, was chosen for the meeting.

Grant and his generals arrived about 1:30 P.M. The Union leader wore a mud-splashed private's uniform with the stars of rank on his shoulders. He lacked sword and spurs. Lee was resplendent in a new outfit of Confederate gray, a jeweled sword at his side.

After a brief conversation, the generals agreed on these terms: rolls of Lee's army to be made in duplicate, a copy each for the Confederates and Federals; all Confederates to be paroled prisoners; all materials of war to be turned over to the Union officers appointed by Grant, except side arms, horses, and personal baggage of Confederate officers. To prevent vengeful punishment, the terms stated ". . . each officer and man will be allowed to return to his home, not to be disturbed by the United States authorities so long as they observe their paroles . . ."

Lee told Grant his artillerymen and cavalrymen owned their own mounts. The Union chief replied that each man who claimed to own a horse or mule could take the animal with him to assist in spring plowing. Lee thanked the general for his thoughtfulness, signed the documents (left), and swung into Traveller's saddle to bring the heart-breaking news to his men.

The morning of April 12 saw the Army of Northern Virginia in line for the last time, marching to stack its arms. Union troops saluted as the Rebels moved by, and saw their salute returned. Four years ago, to the day, a Confederate gun had boomed out across Charleston harbor to open hostilities.

Appomattox Sealed the Confederacy's Fate, but Union Officers In the Field Pressed for Surrender of All Far-flung Rebel Units

The home of James Bennett served as headquarters for surrender discussions between Sherman and Johnston on April 17 and 18. As the talks proceeded, Union and Confederate officers took full advantage of the temporary truce to discuss their actions in the recent campaign.

LEE'S surrender ended the Civil War in the crucial Virginia theatre. At Lee's request, the Union command supplied 25,-000 rations to feed famished Rebel soldiers and their Union prisoners.

Some 28,000 surrendered at Appomattox. Other Rebel troops were scattered throughout the South. The most sizable force was Johnston's, which Sherman faced in North Carolina.

On the day following Lee's surrender, Sherman advanced and slowly pressed Johnston back through Raleigh and toward Greensboro. When news of Lee's surrender reached Union lines, Sherman ordered destruction of railroads and other Confederate property to cease.

Grant prepared Meade, with the Armies of the Potomac and the James, to move against Johnston if necessary. He also sent a message to Sherman, describing the Grant-Lee surrender terms and authorizing him to offer similar terms to Johnston.

Leaving Raleigh, Sherman met Johnston on the seventeenth and eighteenth to talk of terms. On the second day, Confederate Secretary of War Breckinridge joined the conclave. A surrender agreement was reached. It was to be conditional until approved by Washington. In the interim, an armistice halted the fighting.

The agreement was in many ways surprising. Sherman, ruthless in war, proved most generous in discussing peace.

The general exceeded his authority, which was to arrange for a military surrender on terms that had been given him. He agreed that Rebel troops should march to their state capitals and there store their arms. He stipulated conditions under which the Southern states would be recognized by the Federal government. He guaranteed the rights of the defeated people.

The Union general erred on the side of leniency in his earnest desire to heal quickly the ruptures caused by war. When terms of the conditional agreement reached Washington, the government dissented violently.

Stanton blew up, disdainfully scrapped the proposal, and questioned Sherman's regard for his country. Smear campaigns filled the newspapers. Much of the populace who had thrilled to Sherman's victories now denounced him. Once the agreement was turned down, the possibility of renewed battle in North Carolina came alive.

After a bitter Cabinet meeting, Grant was selected to visit North Carolina and take matters into his own hands. He saw Sherman at Raleigh and advised him to notify Johnston that the conditional surrender had been vetoed by the Federal government.

The commander-in-chief then tactfully withdrew and Sherman proceeded with new negotiations. On April 26, Johnston surrendered officially, upon the same terms that governed Lee's submission to Grant.

General Richard Taylor became senior Confederate officer east of the Mississippi. On May 4, he surrendered to Edward Canby, his troops including the commands of Dabney Maury and N. B. Forrest. On the twenty-sixth, Kirby Smith gave up the Trans-Mississippi Department, leaving no other Confederate army to continue the war.

As the military surrendered in the field, the disintegrating government of the Con-federacy moved south and west by rapid stages. Leaving Richmond, Davis shifted his staff to Danville and placed the city in a state of defense.

When Lee capitulated, the government fled to Greensboro. By May 18, Davis and a part of his cabinet were en route to Charlotte, North Carolina. The flight continued from city to city. Washington, Georgia, became the scene for the final cabinet meeting of the Confederate States of America. Further resistance was declared futile and the government dispersed.

A detachment of the 4th Michigan Cavalry captured Davis near Irwinsville, Georgia, May 10. Immediately after his arrest, the Confederate president was imprisoned at Fort Monroe. During his incarceration, which lasted two years, the United States Court for the District of Virginia indicted him for treason.

In May, 1867, Davis was released on a bail-bond of $100,000, signed by Cornelius Vanderbilt, Gerrit Smith, and Horace Greeley. The following year saw the charges against Davis dropped. He lived quietly until his death in 1889.

From the Headquarters of the Trans-Mississippi Department at Shreveport, La., Kirby Smith issued a general order April 21, exhorting his Confederate soldiers to stand firm and continue the struggle. The appeal came too late. Weary of war, the men dispersed of their own accord.

LINCOLN MURDERED

GENERAL Order No. 50, from the Adjutant General's Office of the War Department, proclaimed "That, at the hour of noon, on the 14th day of April, 1865, Brevet Major-General Anderson will raise and plant upon the ruins of Fort Sumter, in Charleston Harbor, the same United States flag which floated over the battlements of that fort during the rebel assault, and which was lowered and saluted by him and the small force of his command when the works were evacuated on the 14th day of April, 1861." Several thousand persons flocked to Charleston for the ceremony and were ferried to the fort.

The guest of honor stepped forward, assisted by a sergeant, to raise the tattered ensign with its attached evergreen wreath. In a brief address, Anderson said, "I thank God I have lived to see this day." The "Star-Spangled Banner" rose from the audience, and guns that had once fired on Sumter boomed in solemn salute.

On that same April 14, Lincoln held a Cabinet meeting. Secretary of State Seward, recovering from injuries sustained in an accident, could not be present. His son Frederick, acting in his place, convoked the governmental chiefs.

Amiability was the keynote. Conversation was general until Grant entered, fresh from Appomattox, and the audience hung on his words as he described the surrender.

Early afternoon saw the end of the meeting. Lincoln invited Grant and his wife to accompany him to the theater that night. The general declined, pleading anxiety to leave the city and join his children.

The theater party met that evening. Substituting for the Grants were Major Henry R. Rathbone and his fiancée, Clara Harris. The group made its way to Ford's Theatre, where Laura Keene was starring in *Our American Cousin.*

Lincoln's party arrived late, but the band struck up "Hail to the Chief." The presidential box, decorated with flags surrounding a portrait of Washington, awaited its occu-

pants. As the guests entered, Miss Keene ad libbed a line for the President's benefit and the audience applauded. The Lincoln party sat back to pick up the thread of the English play.

About ten o'clock, actor John Wilkes Booth, a fiery and deranged Southern sympathizer, entered the theater, where he was well known. Making his way to the hall leading into the presidential box, Booth entered and secured the door so it could not be opened from outside. He quietly entered the box, carrying a derringer in his right hand and a dagger in his left. Placing the pistol five feet from Lincoln's head, he pulled the trigger.

With the crashing explosion, Lincoln slumped forward in his chair. Rathbone leaped up to grab at Booth and was savagely stabbed. The murderer reached the front of the box, vaulted the railing, and jumped to the stage. One spur caught in a draped flag. He hit the boards hard on his left leg, breaking it, but managed to stagger through the wings. In the alley back of the theater, a horse awaited to carry him into the night.

The stunned audience reacted slowly. Mrs. Lincoln clasped her husband to keep him from falling, Rathbone struggled to unbar the door, and Charles A. Leale gained entrance. A young army surgeon, Leale examined the fallen man and attempted artificial respiration as other doctors arrived.

Booth's bullet had plowed through Lincoln's brain and lodged behind the right eye. Leale held that there was no chance of recovery.

Doctors and soldiers moved the injured President across Tenth Street, to the house of William Peterson. There the slow process of dying began. Lincoln never regained consciousness.

Family, friends, and chiefs of government came together for the sorrowful vigil at Peterson's home. The President lasted the night. Cold, gray rain accompanied the cheerless dawn. At seven twenty-two, the great heart stopped.

FRANK LESLIE'S
ILLUSTRATED

NEWSPAPER

Entered according to the Act of Congress, in the year 1864, by FRANK LESLIE, in the Clerk's Office of the District Court for the Southern District of New York.

No. 500—Vol. XX.]   NEW YORK, APRIL 29, 1865.   [PRICE 10 CENTS. $4 00 YEARLY. 12 WEEKS $1 00.

ABRAHAM LINCOLN.
Assassinated Good Friday, 1865.
BY EDMUND C. STEDMAN.

"Forgive them, for they know not what they do!"
He said, and so went shriven to his fate—
Unknowing went, that generous heart and true.
Even while he spoke the slayer lay in wait,
And when the morning opened Heaven's gate
There passed the whitest soul a nation knew.
Henceforth all thoughts of pardon are too late;
They, in whose cause that arm its weapon drew,
Have murdered MERCY. Now alone shall stand
Blind JUSTICE, with the sword unsheathed she wore.
Hark, from the eastern to the western strand,
The swelling thunder of the people's roar:
What words they murmur—FETTER NOT HER HAND!
So LET IT SMITE, SUCH DEEDS SHALL BE NO MORE!

N. Y. Tribune.

The Martyr President.

On the 14th of April, 1861, the flag of the United States went down on the beleaguered walls of Fort Sumter. Its little garrison of seventy men succumbed to the thousands of traitors who had been permitted to pile up, unmolested, battery on battery around it, and the treason nursed so long in South Carolina had there its first triumph. The rebellion, then commenced in cowardice, ended on the fourth anniversary of that eventful day in assassination. Every step in its progress had been marked by some crime more heinous than the last. Persecution and murder of men and women for their adhesion to the flag of their fathers; Fort Pillow massacres; systematic starvation of Union prisoners; plots to burn crowded cities, and to dash railway trains down precipices, to say nothing of wholesale incendiarism on the high seas, have been among the common incidents of the war on the part of the South, and have passed into history as the characteristics of the rebellion. But one thing was necessary to complete the deep damnation of the monster treason of the 19th century. That hideous culmination was achieved on the night of April 14th, 1865, when ABRAHAM LINCOLN, the loved and honored head of the nation, was slain by a rebel assassin! Slain while unarmed and unsuspicious, slain from behind, with every incident that could lend a darker hue to the atrocity of the act. Almost at the same moment, maimed and wasted statesman, helpless on a couch of suffering in a dimly-lighted sick chamber, was assaulted and stabbed by another foul emissary of the monster crime! Nor was there a single accessory of cowardice and brutality wanting here. Nothing indeed was wanting in the design, scope and execution of both acts, to invest them with a character more horrid and repulsive than attaches to any similar events in the wide annals of murder! The commencement, the progress, and the close of the rebellion—treason, wanton barbarity, assassination! Unrelieved by a single trait, lightened up by no single act of generosity, it stands in history one black, hideous blotch on civilization and mankind! Posterity will regard it, even through the haze of time, with a shudder, and parallels for its atrocities will only be found in the records of the darker days of the French Revolution, or in the bloody traditions of Dahomey!

Abraham Lincoln has joined the noble army of Freedom's Martyrs. "Christ died to make men holy; he died to make men free!" When that great, kind, expansive heart ceased to beat, humanity lost not alone its first representative man, but mankind lost its truest and best friend. Even the red-handed, dismayed and skulking traitors of the South found room in his broad sympathies, and a mercy there which perhaps encroached on God's first attribute of justice. Passing strange that the two men highest in position in the nation, and most disposed to leniency and forgiveness, were these that this hell-born treason selected for its last and most distinguished victims! Did Heaven order that its ultimate act should be to shut fast and bar for ever the half-opened door of national sympathy? Did Providence frown on the possible weakness that would condone treason and betray the cause for which five hundred thousand of our brothers have died and still fester in uncoffined graves!

Far be it from us to attempt lightly to interpret the inscrutable ways of the Almighty, but

Booth.   Mr. Lincoln.   Mrs. Lincoln.   Miss Harris.   Major Rathbone.

ASSASSINATION OF PRESIDENT LINCOLN IN HIS PRIVATE BOX AT FORD'S THEATRE, WASHINGTON, APRIL 14.

ON APRIL 18, sable drapery hung in the East Room of the White House as a vast procession of weeping men, women, and children passed the mahogany coffin.

The following day, six hundred dignitaries crowded the room for funeral services. As pallbearers carried the dead leader from his mansion for the last time, church bells tolled slowly and death guns boomed from Washington forts. In mournful procession, Lincoln's body was borne to the Capitol and placed in state under the great dome.

On April 21, the coffin was placed in a seven-car funeral train that was to carry the President's remains to Springfield, Illinois, for burial. Running slowly, with a pilot engine ahead to clear the way, the train rolled through Baltimore, Harrisburg, Philadelphia, New York, Albany, Buffalo, Cleveland, Columbus, Indianapolis, and Chicago.

In big cities like New York, business ceased as the coffin was borne through mourning-draped streets (right). At way stations, tearful crowds threw flowers into the cars.

Poet Walt Whitman caught the nation's mood:

Coffin that passes through lanes and streets,
Through day and night with the great
　cloud darkening the land,
With the pomp of the inloop'd flags
　with the cities draped in black,
With the show of the states themselves as
　of crape-veil'd women standing,
With processions long and winding and
　the flambeaus of the night,
With the countless torches lit, with the si-
　lent sea of faces and the unbared heads;
With the waiting depot, the arriving cof-
　fin, and the sombre faces,
With dirges through the night, with the
　thousand voices rising strong and sol-
　emn,
With all the mournful voices of the dirges
　pour'd around the coffin,
The dim-lit churches and the shuddering
　organs—where amid these you journey,
With the tolling bells' perpetual clang,
Here, coffin that slowly passes,
I give you my sprig of lilac.

VICTORY PARADE

LINCOLN'S tragic death blunted the edge of victory in the North. The nation cried for revenge. Stanton's men went forth to seek the President's murderer.

Booth was brought to bay near Bowling Green, Virginia, April 26, as men of the 16th New York Cavalry trapped him in a barn. The building was set afire to drive the actor out. While the building blazed, Sergeant Boston Corbett fired through a crevice in the barn wall. The bullet penetrated the fugitive's neck. He died four hours later.

Booth, it was discovered, led a terrorist group with designs on the lives of Vice-President Johnson, Seward, Stanton, and Grant. The clique was a self-contained organization, connected in no way with the Confederate government or its military.

One member, calling himself Lewis Payne, gained entrance to Seward's home the night of Lincoln's murder and severely stabbed the invalid secretary before escaping. Payne was soon found, as were his alleged accomplices: David E. Herold, G. A. Atzerodt, Michael O'Laughlin, Edward Spangler, Samuel Arnold, Mary E. Surratt, and Dr. Samuel A. Mudd.

In Washington, May 9, a military commission tried the captured group on the charge of conspiracy to assassinate the President and other high government officers. Herold, Atzerodt, Payne, and Mrs. Surratt were hanged; the others were imprisoned.

Death or imprisonment could never redress the great wrong done to humanity. Still, the nation felt the scales of justice had been somewhat balanced.

By late May, the symbols of mourning had been removed from Washington buildings and citizens prepared for celebration. Meade's great army came into the capital from Virginia and Sherman moved his troops up from North Carolina bivouacs.

In War Department Special Order No. 239, a grand review of all the armies in and near Washington was ordered, to be witnessed by the President and his Cabinet. Flags broke out from capital buildings, and yards of tricolor bunting hung over the streets. Citizens donned their gala best, crowding roof tops and sidewalks to watch the impressive procession.

May 23 saw Meade bring the Army of the Potomac swinging up Pennsylvania Avenue, the street trembling under the steady tread

of veteran troops (above). This was the "paper collar army," the disciplined and well-equipped force that struck again and again at Robert E. Lee.

Taunts of "spit and polish" perfection had no power to hurt these copper-faced fighting men. They won their battles the hard way and their battle flags carried the place names to prove it.

On the twenty-fourth, Sherman's western soldiers passed in review. Grant watched them and he later wrote:

"Sherman's army was not so well-dressed as the Army of the Potomac, but their marching could not be excelled; they gave the appearance of men who had been thoroughly drilled to endure hardships, either by long and continuous marches or through exposure to any climate, without the ordinary shelter of a camp."

Triumph was in the air. Vacant chairs, pinned-up sleeves, and widows' weeds bought the victory that let drums roll and trumpets blare in this last mighty march. The dead man's iron resolve had been fulfilled.

335

BITTER AFTERMATH

THE Civil War preserved the Union. Never again were the states to separate. In achieving its major goal, the North paid dearly, and the cost to the South was even greater. With its young men dead, its economy ruined, the former Confederacy was to be further ravaged by vengeful and shabby politics.

Andrew Johnson sat in the presidential chair. There were few who envied his position. Ahead lay the tumultuous era known as Reconstruction.

The new President believed in Lincoln's doctrine of a soft peace. Unfortunately, he faced a Congress in which the Radicals, led by Thaddeus Stevens, carried a great deal of weight. These were the "hard war" men, aching to place their collective heel on the neck of the fallen Confederacy and treat it as a conquered province.

Joined with Stevens' group was Charles Sumner of Massachusetts and his followers. Actuated by humanitarian principles, these men called for complete social and political equality for the Southern Negro.

The first year of Johnson's reign saw one event that met widespread approval. This was adoption of the 13th Amendment to the Constitution, prohibiting slavery in the United States. The amendment passed through Congress, to cheering and wild applause (above), early in 1865. By the end of the year, the necessary ratification was achieved and on December 18, slavery in the U.S.A. was outlawed.

Future legislation during Johnson's term of office was to encounter rough going. But before new laws of any type could be created, the President moved to reunite the nation by executive order while Congress was not in session. On May 29, he granted amnesty to most of the former Rebels.

Provisional governors were appointed, by presidential order, in North and South Carolina, Georgia, Florida, Alabama, Mississippi, and Texas. Lincoln had earlier recognized loyal minorities in Virginia, Tennessee, Arkansas, and Louisiana as constituting the legal governments of those states.

State conventions were held, legislatures chosen, laws passed, and senators and representatives picked to go to Washington. When Congress convened in December, it refused to seat delegates of the "Johnson governments."

The Radical-dominated Congress had its reasons: (1) Johnson had moved without Congressional approval and it was time to trim executive powers; (2) the Johnson governments had passed stringent "vagrancy" and "apprentice" laws to keep down the Negro (Southerners said they were protecting themselves from four million suddenly liberated slaves); (3) prominent secessionists had been chosen as senators and representatives; (4) the Southern delegates were almost all Democrats and the Republicans, secure in Congress, would not have their supremacy threatened.

Having blasted Johnson's plan, Congress appointed a committee to explore terms under which the "erring sisters" might gain readmission to the Union. The committee recommended a new amendment to the Constitution that would guarantee citizenship rights to every person born or naturalized in the United States, reduce representation in Congress of any state that refused the vote to Negroes, disqualify leaders of the Confederacy from holding federal or state office, and affirm the Federal war debt while repudiating that of the Confederacy.

Tennessee ratified the 14th Amendment in July, 1866, and was promptly admitted to the Union. The ten other Rebel states, furious over the disqualifying clause, turned down the amendment, which failed of ratification.

The Radicals reacted savagely. By the Reconstruction Act of March 2, 1867, the ten states that rejected the 14th Amendment were split into five military districts, under Union generals. New governments, under the military, replaced those brought about by Johnson. Negroes were to participate in framing new state constitutions and running the governments. Most' of their former masters were to be disqualified, under the terms written into the 14th Amendment. When the new state governments ratified that amendment, and it became part of the Constitution, Southern states could come back into the fold.

The social pyramid was suddenly reversed. Negroes, who had not asked for political power, had it thrust upon them. The majority were illiterate, with no political education. In five Southern states they made up a majority of the voters, and in the remaining states they were important minorities. "Carpetbaggers" from the North and "scalawags" from the South rushed to join the new state governments and exploit them to the hilt.

Local governments became pathetic travesties. Southern whites, powerless to help rebuild their ravaged land, felt bitterness swell in their hearts. Ugly secret societies began their night rides, to frighten and persecute the Negro and drive carpetbaggers and scalawags across state borders.

Childlike faith in the intellectual capacity of newly free slaves, misguided humanitarianism in awarding the ballot without any prerequisites, the vicious desire to humiliate former Rebel leaders, and a venal greed for Republican majorities in Southern states brought about the "crime of Reconstruction."

By summer of 1868, Arkansas, North Carolina, South Carolina, Louisiana, Georgia, Alabama, and Florida had re-entered the Union. Admission of these states brought ratification of the 14th Amendment, which became law on the first day of 1869. Later that year, Congress approved the 15th Amendment, which forbids the United States or any state to deny the vote to citizens "on account of race, color or previous condition of servitude."

Johnson's term of office had been a disastrous one despite his good intentions. Let loose by a vengeful Congress, exponents of greed and exploitation ravaged the bleeding South. Military defeat and the nightmare decade that followed sank the iron deep into Southern souls.

Grant became President in 1868 and inherited the reconstruction problems. During his tenure, the last of the holdout Rebel states re-entered the Union. By gradual stages, competent Southerners drove graft and corruption from their statehouses and established sound government once more. But the scars remain.

INDEX